Praise for *The Intellectual World of C. S. Lewis*

"Thoughtful and thought-provoking, these essays expertly h⌐¹
intellectual world of C. S. Lewis in its broader conte
corpus in detail and casts a friendly though not unq
work which have hitherto received surprisingly little
to currents and schools of thought that have a refres.
our understanding of the man. The figure who emerg
more interesting and important theological thinker th.
previous comparable study." **Michael Ward, Oxford Un**

"Alister McGrath's *The Intellectual World of C. S. Lewis* is a very welcome addition to the growing number of scholarly studies of Lewis. Well-researched and written, this book offers fresh insights into several areas of Lewis's literary corpus, including his autobiography, *Surprised by Joy*, his intellectual development as an Oxford student, and his ideas on myth and metaphor. McGrath also offers penetrating discussions of Lewis's argument from desire, the role of reason and imagination in his apologetics, his religious identity as an Anglican, and his status as a 'theologian.' I highly recommend *The Intellectual World of C. S. Lewis* as well as McGrath's biography of Lewis, *C. S. Lewis: A Life*." **Don King, Montreat College**

"In the mass of recent writing about C. S. Lewis, this volume stands out as essential, and should be on everyone's reading list, whether that of the research scholar or general reader. The author has the same feeling for the 'great tradition' of western literature and theology as Lewis himself did, and has similar skills in exploring it, so that Lewis is for the first time properly set in his intellectual context. It is appropriate to deploy the metaphors of light and vision that the author detects in Lewis, to affirm that this is a series of brilliant essays, brightly illuminating the intellectual resources on which Lewis draws, enabling us better to see the 'big picture' which connects myth, metaphor, memory, realism, religious desire, the Anglican mind, and the dynamics of academic power. In reviewing these themes, this exceptional study combines reason and imagination as Lewis did himself. Like Lewis's own work, it is both deeply learned and accessible to a wide range of readers." **Paul Fiddes, Professor of Systematic Theology at Oxford University**

"This important new study of Lewis sets the man and his ideas in the intellectual world of his day, and so helps us to appreciate all the more fully his distinctive contribution as a scholar, an artist, and an apologist. Through a series of finely researched and characteristically well-written essays, Alister McGrath both reveals the extent to which Lewis was a product of his own age, and reminds us why he remains every bit as relevant for ours. A penetrating engagement with one of the most important Christian voices of the twentieth century." **Trevor Hart, University of St Andrews**

Alister E. McGrath is Professor of Theology, Ministry and Education and the Head of the Centre for Theology, Religion & Culture at King's College London, and Senior Research Fellow at Harris Manchester College, Oxford University, having previously been Professor of Historical Theology at Oxford University, UK. He is one of the world's leading theologians, and is in constant demand as a speaker at conferences throughout the world. McGrath is the author of some of the most widely used theology textbooks, including the bestselling *Christian Theology: An Introduction*, 5th edition (2010, Wiley-Blackwell), as well as *C. S. Lewis: A Life* (2013).

Also by Alister E. McGrath from Wiley-Blackwell

Christian History: An Introduction (2013)
Historical Theology: An Introduction to the History of Christian Thought, Second
  Edition (2012)
Reformation Thought: An Introduction, Fourth Edition (2012)
Theology: The Basic Readings, Second Edition (edited, 2012)
Theology: The Basics, Third Edition (2012)
Luther's Theology of the Cross: Martin Luther's Theological Breakthrough, Second
  Edition (2011)
Darwinism and the Divine: Evolutionary Thought and Natural Theology (2011)
The Christian Theology Reader, Fourth Edition (edited, 2011)
Christian Theology: An Introduction, Fifth Edition (2011)
Science and Religion: A New Introduction, Second Edition (2009)
The Open Secret: A New Vision for Natural Theology (2008)
The Order of Things: Explorations in Scientific Theology (2006)
Christianity: An Introduction, Second Edition (2006)
Dawkins' God: Genes, Memes, and the Meaning of Life (2004)
The Intellectual Origins of the European Reformation, Second Edition (2003)
Christian Literature: An Anthology (edited, 2003)
A Brief History of Heaven (2003)
The Blackwell Companion to Protestantism (edited with Darren C. Marks, 2003)
The Future of Christianity (2002)
Reformation Thought: An Introduction, Third Edition (2000)
Christian Spirituality: An Introduction (1999)
Historical Theology: An Introduction (1998)
The Foundations of Dialogue in Science and Religion (1998)
The Blackwell Encyclopedia of Modern Christian Thought (edited, 1995)
A Life of John Calvin (1990)

The Intellectual World of C. S. Lewis

Alister E. McGrath

WILEY-BLACKWELL

A John Wiley & Sons, Ltd., Publication

This edition first published 2014
© 2014 John Wiley & Sons, Ltd

Wiley-Blackwell is an imprint of John Wiley & Sons, formed by the merger of Wiley's global
Scientific, Technical and Medical business with Blackwell Publishing.

Registered Office
John Wiley & Sons Ltd, The Atrium, Southern Gate, Chichester, West Sussex, PO19 8SQ, UK

Editorial Offices
350 Main Street, Malden, MA 02148-5020, USA
9600 Garsington Road, Oxford, OX4 2DQ, UK
The Atrium, Southern Gate, Chichester, West Sussex, PO19 8SQ, UK

For details of our global editorial offices, for customer services, and for information about how to
apply for permission to reuse the copyright material in this book please see our website at www.wiley.
com/wiley-blackwell.

The right of Alister E. McGrath to be identified as the author of this work has been asserted in
accordance with the UK Copyright, Designs and Patents Act 1988.

Library of Congress Cataloging-in-Publication Data

McGrath, Alister E., 1953-
  The intellectual world of C. S. Lewis / Alister E. McGrath.
      pages cm
  Includes index.
  "Works by Lewis cited": pages.
  ISBN 978-0-470-67280-8 (cloth) – ISBN 978-0-470-67279-2 (pbk.)   1. Lewis, C. S. (Clive Staples),
1898-1963–Philosophy.   2. Lewis, C. S. (Clive Staples), 1898-1963–Criticism and interpretation.
3. Christian literature, English–History and criticism.   I. Title.
  PR6023.E926Z7948 2013
  230.092–dc23
                  2012043029

A catalogue record for this book is available from the British Library.

Cover image: C. S. Lewis outside Magdalen College, Oxford University, 1946. (Photo by Hans Wild/
Time & Life Pictures/Getty Images)
Cover design by Design Deluxe

Set in 10/12.5 pt Meridien by Toppan Best-set Premedia Limited
Printed in Malaysia by Ho Printing (M) Sdn Bhd

1   2014

Contents

Acknowledgments vii

A Brief Biography of C. S. Lewis ix

Introduction 1

1. The Enigma of Autobiography: Critical Reflections on
   Surprised by Joy 7
2. The "New Look": Lewis's Philosophical Context at Oxford
   in the 1920s 31
3. A Gleam of Divine Truth: The Concept of Myth in Lewis's
   Thought 55
4. The Privileging of Vision: Lewis's Metaphors of Light, Sun,
   and Sight 83
5. Arrows of Joy: Lewis's Argument from Desire 105
6. Reason, Experience, and Imagination: Lewis's Apologetic
   Method 129
7. A "Mere Christian": Anglicanism and Lewis's Religious
   Identity 147
8. Outside the "Inner Ring": Lewis as a Theologian 163

Works by Lewis Cited 185

Index 187

Acknowledgments

The research underlying this work was carried out mainly at the Bodleian Library, Oxford, in parallel with the detailed archival and textual study underlying *C. S. Lewis – A Life*, details of which are provided in that work. I gratefully acknowledge the award of a Clyde S. Kilby Research Grant for 2011 at the Marion E. Wade Center, Wheaton College, Wheaton, Illinois. I also wish to acknowledge helpful and perceptive conversations relevant to this material with leading Lewis authorities Don King, Alan Jacobs, and Michael Ward.

A Brief Biography of C. S. Lewis

Many reading this work will need no introduction to Lewis. Others, however, might appreciate a sketch of his intellectual and spiritual development, to help set his ideas in their proper context.[1]

Clive Staples Lewis was born in the Irish city of Belfast on November 29, 1898, entering into a turbulent political world increasingly shaped by the growing influence of Irish nationalism, and demands for "Home Rule." Lewis was the second son of Albert and Flora Lewis, who were pillars of the Protestant establishment of the day. After learning his trade in the Irish capital city, Dublin, Albert Lewis had established a successful solicitor's practice in Belfast's prestigious Royal Avenue. Flora came from the heart of the now-fading "Protestant Ascendancy." Her grandfather had been a bishop, and her father a clergyman, of the Church of Ireland.

A close relationship developed between Clive and his elder brother, Warren. At an early stage, for reasons that remain unclear, Lewis insisted on being called "Jack." In 1905, the family moved to Leeborough (or "Little Lea"), a large, newly built house in the Strandtown area of Belfast. Lewis's earliest memories of this house involved the presence of substantial quantities of books, scattered throughout the vast house. Both his father and mother read widely, and Lewis was free to roam and read as he pleased. When his brother Warren (usually referred to as "Warnie") left home to go to school in England, Lewis found solace in reading, developing a vivid sense of imagination and longing.

Lewis's mother died of cancer in August 1908, ending the security of his childhood. "It was sea and islands now; the great continent had sunk like Atlantis."[2] Unwisely, Albert Lewis decided to send his younger son away from home, to be educated at boarding schools in England. As Lewis's autobiographical narrative in *Surprised by Joy* makes clear, he found life at these schools – Wyvern School, Watford; Cherbourg School, Malvern;

and Malvern College – somewhat difficult. In the end Albert Lewis decided that his only option was to have his son privately tutored. Lewis was sent to study with William Kirkpatrick, Albert Lewis's former headmaster, now retired to the southern English county of Surrey.

It was the right move, and Lewis flourished in this new environment. In effect, Kirkpatrick introduced Lewis to the Oxford tutorial model, forcing him to develop and defend his views. Lewis's experience with Kirkpatrick was educationally and spiritually formative. Thanks to Kirkpatrick's astute mentoring, Lewis won a scholarship to University College, Oxford, to study classics in December 1916. By this time, Lewis had become a trenchant, even strident, atheist. Lewis's letters of this period make it clear that this was not an adolescent reaction against the faith of his parents, but a considered rejection of belief in God based on arguments that he believed to be unanswerable.

By now, the First World War was in its third year, and Lewis realized that he faced a threat of conscription. Lewis took the decision to volunteer to enlist. He went up to Oxford in April 1917, combining a somewhat desultory study of the classics with military training – initially, in the Oxford University Officers' Training Corps, and then in an Officer Training Unit based at Keble College. In November 1917, Lewis was commissioned as a second lieutenant in the Somerset Light Infantry, and deployed to the front line near Arras, in northern France.

His wartime experiences reinforced his atheism. His poetry of the period rails against silent, uncaring heaven. Lewis's "Ode for New Year's Day," written when under fire in January 1918, proclaimed the final rejection of a God who was in any case an unpersuasive human invention. Several months later, Lewis received a shrapnel wound during a British assault on the village of Riez du Vinage, and was sent home to England to recover. He was demobilized in December 1918, and resumed his studies at University College, Oxford, in January 1919. It was at this point that Lewis can be said to have really begun his academic studies at Oxford.

Lewis proved to be an outstanding student. Kirkpatrick's mentoring ensured he could hold his own in tutorials, and had given him a deep grasp of both Latin and Greek, allowing him to study the history, literature, and philosophy of the ancient world from the original texts. He was awarded first-class honors in classical moderations in 1920, and first-class honors in *Literae Humaniores* in 1922. On realizing that he needed to widen his academic competency in order to secure a teaching position, he gained first-class honors in English language and literature in 1923, cramming two years of studies into a single year. At this time, Lewis's outlook was shaped by intellectual currents prevalent at Oxford, which he adapted into his own "New Look."

Lewis was appointed to a temporary lectureship in philosophy at University College for the academic year 1923–4, before being appointed to a tutorial fellowship in English language and literature at Magdalen College, Oxford, in 1925. Lewis became a member of the Oxford University Faculty of English Language and Literature, where he developed a growing friendship with J. R. R. Tolkien, playing a key role in encouraging Tolkien to complete and publish the "romantic trilogy" now known as *The Lord of the Rings*.[3]

Although Lewis was still an atheist when he took up his fellowship at Magdalen College, he was clearly experiencing doubts about the intellectual coherence and spiritual adequacy of this position. There are signs that he was prepared to consent (though with considerable reluctance) to the possible existence of some abstract notion of God by around 1920; nevertheless, his conversion to theism was characterized by a more developed belief that God was an active agent, not simply an explanatory principle. Although this transition is traditionally dated to the summer of 1929, I have argued that the evidence clearly indicates that this change of belief dates from the following year, 1930.[4]

This was followed by a further development, partly catalyzed by a 1931 conversation with Tolkien over the nature of myth, which led Lewis to embrace Christianity. While the timescale of this second phase of Lewis's conversion remains frustratingly unclear at points, his process of intellectual realignment was essentially complete by the summer of 1932, when he penned *The Pilgrim's Regress*, an allegorical account of his own journey to faith and its implications.

Lewis's conversion to Christianity – which he later described in *Surprised by Joy* (1955) – initially had little impact on his academic career. His *Allegory of Love* (1936) was well received, winning the Sir Israel Gollancz Memorial Prize in 1937. The publication of this work marked the beginning of his inexorable rise to academic fame, sealed with his magisterial *English Literature in the Sixteenth Century* (1954) and his election as a Fellow of the British Academy. Other academic landmarks along the way included the 1941 Ballard Matthews Lectures at University College, Bangor (published as *A Preface to Paradise Lost*); the 1943 Riddell Memorial Lectures (published as *The Abolition of Man*); and his election as a Fellow of the Royal Society of Literature in 1948.

Yet Lewis's academic standing was damaged to no small extent by his decision to write popular works, dealing with issues relating to Christian apologetics. Lewis's first work of popular apologetics, *The Problem of Pain* (1940), probably did Lewis's academic reputation little harm. *The Screwtape Letters* (1942), however, alarmed many of his Oxford colleagues. How could such a trivializing tale of satanic incompetence have been written by an Oxford don? It was probably the immense popular success of this work, as much as its populist tone, that irritated many of his colleagues. A question mark now hung over Lewis's academic credentials in Oxford, leading to him being passed over for at least two significant preferments during the late 1940s.

Yet many admired Lewis's more accessible writings, and encouraged him to write more. Lewis was not so much a popularizer as a *translator* of theology – an apologist who was able to give a good account of the rationality of the Christian faith, and state its core themes in a language that was accessible outside academic circles. The British Broadcasting Corporation invited him to give a series of wartime talks in 1942 which proved so successful that they led to three further series of addresses. Lewis eventually published these, with some minor changes, in *Mere Christianity* (1952), now generally considered to be his most influential non-fiction work.

Lewis achieved celebrity status in the United Kingdom during the Second World War, and in the United States shortly afterwards. This fame might have faded away, had Lewis not developed a quite unexpected line of writing, which took most of his close friends and family by surprise. In October 1950, the first of the seven "Chronicles of Narnia" appeared. *The Lion, the Witch, and the Wardrobe* became a children's classic, showing Lewis's remarkable facility to engage the imagination, and use it as a gateway for theological exploration – most notably, in relation to the notion of incarnation. Aslan, the great and noble lion of Narnia, became one of the most firmly established literary characters of the twentieth century.

Yet by the time the final novel in the series – *The Last Battle* – was published in 1956, Lewis had moved on from Oxford University. Now a married man, Lewis had been elected as the first holder of the University of Cambridge's newly established Chair in Medieval and Renaissance English. After his move to Cambridge, Lewis wrote rarely in an explicitly apologetic mode, preferring to supplement his academic writings with more popular works exploring aspects of the Christian faith for the benefit of believers – such as *Reflections on the Psalms* (1958) and *The Four Loves* (1960). The death of Lewis's wife, Joy Davidman, from cancer in 1960 prompted Lewis to write, under a pseudonym, *A Grief Observed*, now often cited as one of the finest accounts of the grieving process.

By June 1963, it was clear that Lewis himself was very unwell. Long-standing problems with his prostate gland had become more serious, with renal complications developing which placed his heart under strain. Lewis accepted the inevitable, resigning from his Cambridge chair, and discussing his death openly with his correspondents. He died at his Oxford home in the early evening of November 22, 1963, shortly before

President John F. Kennedy died from gunshot wounds in Dallas, Texas. Lewis is buried in the churchyard of Holy Trinity Church, Headington Quarry, Oxford.

Notes

1 See further Alister McGrath, *C. S. Lewis – A Life: Eccentric Genius, Reluctant Prophet*. Carol Spring, IL: Tyndale House, 2013. British and Commonwealth edition: London: Hodder & Stoughton, 2013. All references are to the American edition of this work.
2 *Surprised by Joy*, 22.
3 Lewis used this description of the work in his recently discovered nomination of Tolkien for the 1961 Nobel Prize in literature: see McGrath, *C. S. Lewis – A Life*, 351–2.
4 For analysis, see McGrath, *C. S. Lewis – A Life*, 131–51.

Introduction

By the time of his death in November 1963, C. S. Lewis (1898–1963) was widely recognized as one of the most significant and successful writers of the twentieth century. He had achieved a high profile both as a Christian apologist (particularly during the Second World War), and as a highly acclaimed writer of fiction. He was elected a Fellow of the Royal Society of Literature in 1948, some years before the publication of the Narnia series of novels, regarded by most as his most influential and innovative novels.

Yet alongside his apologetic and fictional writings, Lewis had achieved international distinction in the field of English language and literature. He was appointed as Cambridge University's first Professor of Medieval and Renaissance English in 1954, and elected a Fellow of the British Academy in 1955. This deep immersion in the western tradition underlies Lewis's creative synthesis of theological reflection and literary imagination, widely regarded as one of his most significant achievements.

Following Lewis's death in 1963, his popularity and influence declined, partly reflecting the rapid changes in western culture during the 1960s, which relegated many of Lewis's approaches and attitudes to the margins of culture. Many believed that religion was declining in the face of a rising tide of secularism, especially in the United States. The rise of "logical positivism" at Oxford and elsewhere threatened to make any discussion of God meaningless, as the seemingly irresistible intellectual virtues of radical empiricism captured hearts, minds, and faculties of philosophy. Lewis himself had taken the view that his writings would fade into obscurity

The Intellectual World of C. S. Lewis, First Edition. Alister E. McGrath.
© 2014 John Wiley & Sons, Ltd. Published 2014 by John Wiley & Sons, Ltd.

within five years of his death, and had no expectations of remaining a long-term presence on the literary or religious scene.

Yet by 1980, Lewis had bounced back. Logical positivism failed to deliver its promised intellectual virtues. Questions of meaning resurfaced as important in western culture. Religion, dismissed as an outmoded irrelevance by the angry young prophets of the 1960s, began to become an increasingly significant force in private piety and public life in the United States. Lewis enjoyed a resurgence. For many, his renewed appeal lay in his imaginatively winsome "Chronicles of Narnia," especially *The Lion, the Witch, and the Wardrobe*, now regularly cited as one of the best children's books of the twentieth century.

Others locate the reason for this resurgence in Lewis's religious appeal, his emphasis on Christian basics, and his eschewing of denominational politics. Some suggest his new popularity reflects his remarkable ability to communicate orthodox theological ideas in culturally accessible forms. Others point out that his appeal to the imagination secured a new lease of life for religious ideas and values in a post-rationalist western culture. Yet whatever the explanations for this unexpected development might be, it is an inescapable fact that, more than a generation after his death, Lewis's works are now more popular and widely read than at any point during his lifetime.

Fifty years after Lewis's death, it is clearly appropriate to reflect further on his intellectual achievements and heritage. To mark this occasion, I wrote a substantial new biography of Lewis, expanding and correcting earlier accounts in the light of intensive archival work and the substantial secondary literature that has now accumulated concerning Lewis.[1] During the course of that rigorous research, it became clear that many aspects of Lewis's thought needed detailed and careful reconsideration, especially in the light of their intellectual context. A biography, however, is not well adapted to the demands of such sustained intellectual engagement, which would inevitably disrupt its narrative flow.

While the substance of this research was woven into the biographical narrative, it seemed appropriate to publish an additional collection of academic essays, providing a full analysis of these questions, and document the grounds for reaching certain conclusions. This collection of essays opens up new questions for critical examination (such as the development of Lewis's "New Look" and his privileging of a "metaphoric of vision"), as well as revisiting some more familiar questions which merit further discussion (most notably, Lewis's "argument from desire," and his status as a theologian).

These eight substantial pieces of research, none of which have been published before, aim to set Lewis in the greater context of the western literary and theological tradition, exploring how he appropriated and modified its narratives, ideas, and images. Lewis himself was nourished by this great tradition,[2] which he described as "the clean sea breeze of the centuries,"[3] refreshing and reanimating our ideas and blowing away what is stale and ephemeral. Lewis's work is not embedded within a Christian sub-culture (though he has clearly found a substantial base of support here), but within the western intellectual tradition as a whole, which enriched and deepened his personal scholarly vision, as he in turn enriched and extended it.

These essays both position Lewis against an informing context, while at the same time encouraging Lewis scholarship to see itself in a deeper and broader intellectual perspective, from which it has much to learn, and to which it has much to contribute. Thus Lewis's discussion of the nature and significance of "myth" (55–81), and his extensive and creative use of metaphors based on sight (83–104) locate him within both classic and contemporary discussions of these themes, most notably recent debates about the role of myth in contemporary culture, and the "hegemony of vision" in the western philosophical and literary tradition.

The collection of essays opens with a consideration of the difficulties and questions attending Lewis's celebrated autobiography, *Surprised by Joy* (1955). This work is widely used as an historical source for Lewis's early reflections on the notion of "Joy," and his complex intellectual transition from atheism to Christianity. Yet it is clear that this work needs to be used with caution in this respect, partly because of issues attending the correlation of Lewis's inner and outer worlds, partly because of Lewis's difficulty in recalling dates, and perhaps most fundamentally because of Lewis's covert agendas in writing the book in the first place.

The second essay deals with what Lewis styles his "New Look" – Lewis's personal appropriation of the philosophical and cultural ideas and values that so influenced Oxford University in the early 1920s, and which helped shape Lewis's outlook as an undergraduate in the aftermath of the Great War. The movement known as "Oxford Realism" has only just begun to receive its due attention from historians of philosophy; this recent research helps clarify Lewis's shifting views on realism and idealism in the 1920s. Apart from illuminating some aspects of Lewis's complex transition to theism, this analysis helps highlight the fact that many of the views that Lewis would later critique in his apologetic and literary works were those which he himself had held as a younger man.

The third essay focuses on Lewis's changing understanding of the nature of "myth," and especially its implications for his conversion from theism to Christianity. Lewis's later works of fiction, particularly the "Chronicles of Narnia," make extensive – though generally implicit – use of this literary form. The essay explores the discussions of "myth" which were prevalent at Oxford University in the early twentieth century and notes how Lewis fits in to a wider academic and literary discussion of the nature of myth at this time. The implications of Lewis's approach for the celebrated "demythologization" controversy associated with Rudolf Bultmann during the 1940s and 1950s are considered. Lewis's contribution to this debate has not been properly recognized, and remains of importance for contemporary discussion.

The fourth essay considers one of the most distinctive features of Lewis's fictional and apologetic writings, which has been overlooked by Lewis scholarship – his extensive use of ocular imagery as a metaphor for truth and knowledge. Lewis's works make frequent reference to the images of illumination, light, sun, and shadows, all of which have a rich history of deployment within the western literary canon. This essay sets Lewis's imagery in its intellectual context, and examines how he develops it for his own purposes.

One of the most distinctive features of Lewis's apologetic writings is his restatement of the "argument from desire." Although Lewis clearly draws on earlier writers in developing this approach, he adapts it for his own ends, leading to a rich and complex way of exploring and affirming the rationality and existential appeal of the Christian faith. Previous analyses have tended to assimilate Lewis's approach to existing philosophical defenses of theism; the fifth essay in this work establishes the distinct logic of Lewis's own, more imaginative, approach, and sets it in the broader context of his apologetic method.

This naturally leads into the sixth essay, which examines Lewis's general approach to apologetics, looking at the historical emergence of Lewis's apologetic enterprise, considering in particular his formulation of an imaginative apologetics that transcended the limits of the rationalist approaches more characteristic of his time. Lewis is now widely considered as a role model in popular Christian apologetics; this essay will be an important resource for those wishing to model their approach on Lewis.

The seventh essay considers Lewis's relationship with Anglicanism, the specific form of Christianity that he knew as a child in Belfast, and chose to adopt in Oxford after his reconversion to theism in 1930. Lewis regarded the Church of England as a localized embodiment and enactment of a deeper vision of Christianity, which he came to designate "mere Christianity." This essay reflects both on Lewis's views on the relation of "mere Christianity" to its specific denominational enactments, and more specifically on whether Lewis can be described as an "Anglican" in the confessional sense of the term.

Finally, the eighth essay explores the controversial question of whether Lewis can be regarded as a theologian. It moves beyond the traditional debate over this issue, which has tended to focus on how Lewis developed and handled religious ideas, and explores the more fundamentally sociological issues that underlie this debate – most notably, the role of intellectuals in creating and maintaining group identity, and the dynamics of power and exclusion within such groups. In defending the propriety of referring to Lewis as a theologian, the essay offers some unsettling reflections concerning the anxieties and agendas of those wishing to deny Lewis this status.

It is hoped that these more detailed engagements with aspects of Lewis's thought may help encourage a deeper exploration of his ideas and methods, especially by situating them within a broader historical narrative. Lewis was deeply conscious of standing within a tradition of literary, philosophical, and theological reflection, which he extended and deepened in his own distinctive manner. There is more that remains to be discovered about Lewis's rich intellectual vision, and even more that remains to be properly understood. Half a century after his death, the process of receiving and interpreting Lewis has still only begun.

Alister E. McGrath
King's College London
September 2012

Notes

1   Alister McGrath, *C. S. Lewis – A Life.*
2   Lewis, of course, had a somewhat greater vision of this tradition than the rather sparse account set out in F. R. Leavis, *The Great Tradition.* London: Chatto & Windus, 1948.
3   "On the Reading of Old Books"; *Essay Collection*, 440. Works by Lewis are referred to simply by their short titles; the editions used are detailed in the final section of this work, entitled "Works by Lewis Cited."

1
The Enigma of Autobiography: Critical Reflections on *Surprised by Joy*

In 1955, Lewis published *Surprised by Joy*, subtitled "The Shape of My Early Life." It is one of Lewis's most cited works, and contains some of his finest prose and most intimate reflections. No study of Lewis can fail to engage with (and, at certain critical points, depend upon) Lewis's personal narrative of conversion. Lewis had no hesitation in referring to this "story of my conversion" as his "autobiography."[1] But what did he mean by this? What are we, his readers, to understand by this term?

The Ambivalence of Autobiography in Lewis's Literary Outlook

The teasing title of Lewis's autobiography draws on the opening words of the Miltonic sonnet of the same name by the English Romantic writer William Wordsworth (1770–1850).[2]

Surprised by joy – impatient as the wind.

Wordsworth wrote this sonnet in the aftermath of the death of his three-year-old daughter, Catherine. On experiencing a rare moment of joy following Catherine's death in 1812, Wordsworth found this precipitated a series of emotional traumas. His fleeting experience of delight gave way to a somber realization that the one person with whom he longed to share that joy – Catherine – was gone, followed immediately by a pang of guilt over his ability to forget her even for that brief moment.

The Intellectual World of C. S. Lewis, First Edition. Alister E. McGrath.
© 2014 John Wiley & Sons, Ltd. Published 2014 by John Wiley & Sons, Ltd.

Lewis chose to appropriate the title, rather than the substance of Wordsworth's poem, and develops the idea of "Joy" in his own distinct way (see chapter 5). *Surprised by Joy* is a narrative of a human collision with divine reality, in which old ways of thinking were shattered and disrupted, and new ways of seeing opened up. Picking up on the "visionary gleam" of joy[3] that so briefly intruded into Wordsworth's grief, Lewis offers his reflections on the source of a deeper vision of Joy, rooted at one level in the yearnings of the human heart, and at another in the nature of God. For Lewis, it is God who shoots such "arrows of Joy" as a means of heightening his sense of longing, stimulating his reflection, initiating his questing, and ultimately achieving his transformation.

Surprised by Joy remains something of an enigma among Lewis's works, not least because at first sight it seems to subvert Lewis's own views on the significance of texts. Especially during his "Personal Heresy" controversy of the late 1930s with E. M. W. Tillyard, Lewis made his reputation by insisting that the historical and experiential worlds of an author were not of great importance; what really mattered was their writings. Writers were not themselves a spectacle; their texts were rather a set of spectacles through which the world might be viewed.[4]

> The poet is not a man who asks me to look at him; he is a man who says "look at that" and points; the more I follow the pointing of his finger the less I can possibly see of him.

Yet, by definition, an autobiography invites its readers to look at its author. In writing *Surprised by Joy*, Lewis would seem to be pointing his finger *at himself*, choosing to make himself into a spectacle.

Perhaps this helps us understand why Lewis is almost apologetic about the whole enterprise of writing the story of his conversion. It is not something he *wants* to do; it is something he has *been asked* to do. The rhetoric of self-deprecation with which the work opens is not to be seen as a false humility on Lewis's part. It is something rather more interesting – a belief that this kind of work is, in the first place not of importance *as history*; and in the second, is not something he feels sits easily with his views on literature. It is possible that this helps to make sense of its otherwise puzzling tendencies to mis-remember things in their proper context.

If Lewis is true to himself, we must see this work not as something we are meant to look *at*, but something we are meant to look *through*. The poet is "not a spectacle but a pair of spectacles;" a window through which we attend to the landscape.[5] If we follow the "pointing of his finger," we find Lewis inviting us to attend to the "arrows of Joy" that rain down upon us, and reflect on their deeper significance. Memory, joy, and longing then become gateways to God. Perhaps we should read *Surprised by Joy*, not primarily as a book about the life of C. S. Lewis, but a book about life itself. Lewis's autobiography is then to be seen as much as a reflection on the meaning of human life in general as it is on the meaning of his *own* life.

Perhaps the most obvious influence on Lewis at this point is G. K. Chesterton's *Orthodoxy: The Romance of Faith* (1908). Although Chesterton himself dismissed this as a "slovenly autobiography," most critics have regarded it as one of Chesterton's finest works.[6] Probably modeled on John Henry Newman's *Apologia pro vita sua* (1864), Chesterton's autobiography is a powerful intellectual defense of the rationality of the Christian faith, and especially its capacity to make sense of things. Christian doctrine is not something that was forcibly imposed upon reality, but is rather the key that unlocks "life's real meaning." The Christian faith, he argued, was to be considered as a hypothesis which, once tested, can become a means of perception, making sense of what was previously obscure. While still an atheist, Lewis had been deeply impressed by Chesterton's *Everlasting Man*;[7] his subsequent career could be seen as a gradual assumption of Chesterton's mantle as an apologist.

Might reading Chesterton have helped Lewis to grasp the apologetic potential of a spiritual autobiography? And alert him to how a potentially self-aggrandizing literary genre might be subverted for more noble ends? Or are we to see *Surprised by Joy* in a more literary and cultural context, understanding it, at least in part, as Lewis's attempt to make sense of his own identity and agency, discerning or constructing a coherent narrative within his life?[8]

Surprised by Joy is not Lewis's only autobiographical work. Lewis's first attempt at autobiography is found in *The Pilgrim's Regress* (1933), where Lewis represents his understanding of his own intellectual journey to faith through a proxy – the "pilgrim," named John. Lewis's difficult and at times perplexing work, written in two intense weeks during August 1932, surveys and assesses the intellectual byways that he explored – and occasionally inhabited – as he sought the true goal of the longings he experienced within himself.[9] This work of allegory, modeled only very loosely on John Bunyan's seventeenth-century classic *Pilgrim's Progress*,[10] remains an important source for any understanding of Lewis's struggle to reconcile reason and imagination, yet makes little reference to identifiable events in the external world. In many ways, it shows a preoccupation with internal mental struggles and reflections, even if this is presented in the form of an historical journey.

The third autobiographical work is *A Grief Observed*, written in the aftermath of the death from cancer of Lewis's wife, Joy Davidman, in July 1960. This work, initially published in 1961 under the pseudonym "N. W. Clerk," offers a raw account of Lewis's emotions and doubts following his bereavement. Once more, the focus is on Lewis's internal thoughts, documented without any attempt to blunt its force or soften its tone.[11] Lewis allowed himself to express his grief "in all its rawness and sinful reactions and follies." Although *A Grief Observed* "ends with faith," it nevertheless "raises all the blackest doubts *en route*."[12] The work remains a classic account of the bereavement process, and is an important source for understanding the difficulties and pressures of Lewis's final years.

Surprised by Joy is different. Written at a time when Lewis's reputation as a scholar and popular Christian writer was at its height, this autobiography mingles personal historical information and theological reflection. The publication of the "Chronicles of Narnia" had generated huge interest in Lewis, both as a writer of fiction and as a Christian apologist. How, many wondered, did Lewis come to discover Christianity? Lewis presents *Surprised by Joy* as his response to that question.

In fact, Lewis had already begun to draft such a work much earlier. Lewis's brother Warren noted in his diary entry for March 25, 1948, that Lewis was working on his "autobiography," which by that stage was focusing on their Belfast childhood. Lewis's surge in creative genius during the late 1940s and early 1950s led to the writing of the Narnia series, which both delayed the production of his autobiography on the one hand, while creating a sustained public interest in it on the other.

Lewis presents *Surprised by Joy* as unproblematic.[13] Its goals are quite simple: it "aims at telling the story of my conversion and is not a general autobiography, still less 'Confessions' like those of St. Augustine or Rousseau."[14] It is Lewis's own account of how he "passed from Atheism to Christianity." Yet while this illuminates the topic of the book, it discloses little concerning its literary form, style, or approach to its topic. Lewis clearly presents himself as narrating the *histoire d'une âme*. But how should one tell such a story? What narrative vehicle is to be adopted? What models shaped this narration?

Augustine of Hippo: A Model for Lewis?

Although Lewis eschews any suggestion of similarity between his own *Surprised by Joy* and Augustine's *Confessions*, written during the years 397–8, the close reader of both works is left wondering quite what

Lewis meant by this statement. The parallels between the two works sometimes appear more striking than their divergences. Lewis's writings from the mid-1930s show that he clearly had a high regard for Augustine's *Confessions*,[15] and it would be surprising if its ideas, themes, and narrative structure were not directly or indirectly echoed in *Surprised by Joy*.

Both the *Confessions* and *Surprised by Joy* concern what Augustine vividly describes as the "fields and vast mansions of memory."[16] For Augustine, memory is a means of discernment of meaning and identity, storing treasures as a resource for the construction of narratives and preservation of continuities with other worlds: "The huge repository of the memory, with its secret and unimaginable caverns, receives and stores all these things, to be retrieved and brought out for use when needed."[17]

Like Augustine before him, Lewis uses an autobiographical format to weave together into a complex (and occasionally confusing) narrative factual recollections of the external world, "suffocatingly subjective"[18] memories of his own emotional states, and theological interpretation of the course of his life which is subtle in its intentions, though perhaps not in its execution.

Perhaps the most significant aspect of Augustine's *Confessions* is the implicit recognition that "autobiography" is closely related to – indeed, entails – "conversion," in that any attempt to narrate one's own life constantly demands *two* authorial voices: the protagonist and the narrator. With Augustine, the voice of the narrator dominates – a narrator who is somehow outside the narrative and who can look back at the protagonist's life and discern its fundamental patterns. The narrator knows more than the protagonist, who is unable to stand above and beyond the flow of his life, and discern its patterns.

The gift of retrospection often allows an incident, perhaps seen as somewhat peripheral or tangential at the time, to be seen against a broader backdrop, and its place in the overall trajectory of events to be discerned. Augustine thus notes five incidents in his life which he comes to realize stood out from the continuum of his experience: his youthful stealing of pears,[19] the death of an unnamed friend, his escape from his mother through an act of deception, his conversion experience in a garden, and the mystical vision he and his mother shared shortly before her death. The point which Augustine appreciated is that the significance of these events was not always obvious at the time. Similarly, Lewis singles out his reading of George MacDonald's *Phantastes* and a visit to Whipsnade Zoo as marking turning points in his life, on the basis of his later discernment of what proved significant to bringing him to the "vita nuova" of the Christian faith.

Yet perhaps the most important parallel between the two autobiographies is the manner of their depiction of God.[20] God is not represented or understood as a passive object, a concept hidden in the interstices of the cosmos, awaiting discovery by the active, questing agent – whether Augustine or Lewis. Even the human experiences of longing and desire, which lead to the apprehension of God, are to be seen as "arrows of Joy" (Lewis), originating from God, with the objective of leading the soul back to God.[21] Both Augustine and Lewis portray God as an active questing subject, who masters, overwhelms, and seduces the narrator. The autonomy of the narrator is thus *subverted*, in that God becomes both a voice and presence – however subtle and understated – in the narrative process.

There is, however, another point at which Augustine can be seen to offer an appropriate point of comparison with Lewis. Lewis's "re-conversion"[22] involved two stages; an initial conversion to theism, and a subsequent conversion to Christianity. It is clear that Lewis himself regarded these as two quite distinct outlooks, with the latter having a richer "mythopoeic" dimension absent from his more philosophical theism. Some scholars have also discerned two phases in the development of Augustine's thought. Older studies spoke of Augustine's earlier "neo-Platonic" phase following his conversion in 386, characterized by a generally philosophical disposition, followed by a later transition to Christianity proper.[23] Some would suggest that Lewis's conversion was initially philosophical in character, arising from his developing commitment to Idealism, which only later developed into an explicitly Christian commitment, particularly through his realization of the theological implications of the notion of "myth."

Yet it is important to be cautious here. Like Lewis, Augustine offered a later retrospective on his intellectual and religious development, which tends to emphasize the continuity of his development, rather than point to fundamental breaks or discontinuities.[24] Similarly, although Lewis's correspondence points to a moment of spiritual breakthrough as a result of his conversations with Hugo Dyson and J. R. R. Tolkien about the nature of myth in September 1931, *Surprised by Joy* offers a subtly modulated narrative, which makes only a veiled reference to this event. Dyson and Tolkien, Lewis recalls, gave him "much help" in "getting over the last stile."[25] What his correspondence of the time suggests to have been either a discontinuity or a dramatic leap forward is accommodated in *Surprised by Joy* within an essentially continuous narrative of development, conceived as a series of distinct yet interconnected moves in a chess game.

Autobiography and the Medieval *Ars Memorativa*

Lewis scholarship has generally failed to engage with the issues of literary genre arising from *Surprised by Joy*. We should not be surprised that Lewis, who established his reputation as one of the finest scholars of medieval literature of his day, should draw on the classics of this age in searching for literary models for his own narrative of retrieval of memory and self-disclosure.[26] Who can miss the parallels with Dante's *Vita Nuova*, which its author described as *il libro della mia memoria*?[27] Dante there relates his journey *per librum experientiae* (to borrow a phrase from Alan of Lille), offering a model of autobiography which is clearly based on Augustine's *Confessions*, while developing the approach in new directions.

Dante's masterpiece is a luminous example of the "high art of a singular human memory discovering meaning in history."[28] It concerns the retrieval and transformation of memory, offering a means by which the retrieval of the past acts as a key to unlock the meaning of the pilgrimage of life. Medieval writers were intrigued by Aristotle's argument that the human gift of memory distinguishes humanity from the animals.[29] Although Aristotle concedes that animals can remember certain things, they cannot preserve, polish, and return to their memories of the past. Human beings alone are able to use and develop this power of memory, using this *ars memorativa* to find continuity, integrity, and purpose in life.[30] The *ars memorativa* was not understood in terms of a wooden rote learning, but was conceived and practiced as a tool of invention and discovery, through the retrieval and selective combination of memories.

The medieval concern with memory was not, however, limited to the retrieval, interpretation, and colligation of memories; it also engaged the question of how certain memories might be forgotten or suppressed, purged from the individual's recollection of the past. This deliberate and selective act of forgetting was itself seen as an activity of memory. Some late medieval treatises on the *ars memorativa* specifically engage what might be called the *ars oblivionalis*.[31] How can painful and inconvenient memories – such as that which evoked Wordsworth's "Surprised by Joy" or Lewis's traumatic memories of the Great War – be deliberately erased or systematically suppressed? How can one tell one's story *selectively*, omitting what is thought to be embarrassing to one's reputation, leading to contempt and ridicule; or disruptive to the pattern of meaning that is to be discerned within one's life, leading to anxiety and melancholy? The art of forgetting was seen as important to two audiences, one external (concerned with the writer's reputation), the other internal (concerned with the writer's mental and spiritual wellbeing). Lewis's important unilateral "treaty with reality," to be discussed in the next essay (39–42), can be seen as reflecting this latter concern.

Writing *Surprised by Joy* clearly allowed Lewis to heal some of the wounds from his past through the cultivation of the *ars oblivionalis*. In his narrative, Lewis passes over certain moments of his own past, clearly considering these to be ambivalent or disturbing.[32] It is as if he has "vetoed" incidents that are too painful to discuss in public.[33] By the time he moved to Cambridge in January 1955, Lewis seems to have come to terms with his past, and purged himself of both the pain and guilt of such memories. Perhaps the writing of *Surprised by Joy* contributed to this process of healing.

Yet while these medieval influences have clearly affected Lewis's approach in *Surprised by Joy*, we also find other means of recalling the past woven into his narrative. One of the most remarkable of these concerns the ability of a fragrance to evoke memories, seemingly without any intermediate active process of recollection. Perhaps the most famous literary example of this found in Marcel Proust's vast autobiographical *À la récherche du temps perdu* (1913–27), when he recalls how an emotional and vivid recollection of a childhood experience was evoked by the aroma of a "piece of madeleine."[34] Lewis's memory of a childhood event was similarly triggered by an odor – the fragrance of "a flowering currant bush on a summer day." Lewis describes how this evoked his "memory of a memory" in a strikingly realistic and dramatic manner.[35]

So what principles appear to have guided Lewis as he wove together his memories and reflections? In order to reflect on this, we need to locate Lewis's work on a conceptual map, which is best done by considering more about the literary genre of autobiography itself.

The Nature of Autobiography: Critical Reflections

What is an autobiography? What conventions govern or inform this literary genre? Some scholars hold to a straightforward literary understanding of autobiography as a personal memoir, an account of an individual's life written from the standpoint of the subject rather than of external observers.[36] Yet this is to overlook the role of literary conventions and forms in shaping the text,[37] and the author's intentions and agendas in writing.[38]

Lewis wrote *Surprised by Joy* before literary theorists began to take an interest in the literary genre of autobiography. In one of the first scholarly works to take this genre seriously, Roy Pascal declared that "autobiography proper" was essentially a retrospective account of things that was ultimately a "search for the true self."[39] Writing an autobiography was about self-discovery. Yet Pascal was perhaps too willing to overlook the fact that some writers seem to have been concerned to construct – rather than discern – their selves. Autobiography is thus about the person we had hoped we would be, or the person that we would wish others to discern – with appropriate adjustments being made to the narrative in order to achieve the desired outcome.[40] For this reason, autobiography could rightly be described as "simultaneously historical record and literary artefact, psychological case history and spiritual confession, didactic essay and ideological testament."[41]

This point is reinforced by research into the reliability of personal recollections by individuals, concerning the past in their own lifetime, which suggest that memories of the past are sometimes actively constructed in response to certain needs. In recent years, some scholars have begun to use the somewhat clumsy (yet potentially illuminating) term "mnemohistory" to emphasize that history is an active process of the construction of meaning over time, giving identity to communities or individuals – an "ongoing work of reconstructive imagination." Mnemohistory is not concerned with "the past as such, but with the past *as it is remembered*."[42]

Approaching *Surprised by Joy* with such a framework in mind alerts us to its complexities, and prepares us for some of the difficulties that the text raises for us. One of the most obvious of these difficulties concerns Lewis's curiously extended account of his schooldays at Malvern College ("Wyvern"), which seriously slows the pace of his narrative, and overwhelms his readers with detail of his trials and tribulations.[43] Lewis seems bent on securing revenge on those who he believed to have tormented him as a schoolboy by ridiculing them. "If I had never seen the spectacle which these coarse, brainless English schoolboys present, there might be a danger of my sometimes becoming like that myself."[44] There seems to be an overall stylistic dissonance between these chapters and their neighbors, suggesting that they may represent earlier autobiographical fragments that were redacted – not entirely successfully – into a work with a somewhat different focus.

While the provenance of these passages requires further consideration, their accuracy has long been disputed. One of the significant sources of tension between Lewis and his brother in the late 1950s was Warren Lewis's belief that Lewis had significantly misrepresented his time at Malvern College in *Surprised by Joy*. Lewis himself later conceded that he had not been entirely honest in his account of this period of his life. George Sayer (1914–2005), a close friend who penned one of the most revealing and perceptive biographies of Lewis, recalls Lewis admitting later in life that his account of his time at Malvern was "lies," reflecting the complex interaction of two strands of his identity at that time.[45] Humphrey Havard, a member of the Inklings, mischievously – but seriously – suggested that *Surprised by Joy* should be entitled *Suppressed by Jack*.

Sayer's recollection of the difficulties in penetrating the "smoke screen" Lewis created around himself leaves readers of *Surprised by Joy* wondering about both the extent and motivation of Lewis's reconstruction of his past.[46] Northrop Frye is one of many to observe that an autobiographical narrative ultimately leads to reality being *constructed*, as much as reported.[47] Frye notes how most autobiographies have certain covert teleological goals which influence the choice of material to be included, its position within the narrative, and the manner in which it is interpreted. Sayer's misgivings about *Surprised by Joy* reflect this ambivalence toward history, which Frye regards as intrinsic to the genre of autobiography.

Yet there is no doubt that the autobiographical genre permits precisely this reconstruction of the past. As medieval authors made clear, the *ars memorativa* was a tool for the forging of personal identity. The genre of the autobiography allows a reaffirmation and reassertion of the identity and importance of the self,[48] especially at a time when an individual's personal or cultural identity is seen as being under threat.[49]

Autobiography thus becomes a manner in which the identity and purpose of the self is constructed, allowing a pattern to be seen in what might otherwise be simply a parade of historical happenstance.[50] This theme can be discerned in Lewis's reflections. In a letter written to Dom Bede Griffith in 1956, shortly after the publication of *Surprised by Joy*, Lewis reflected on the importance of being able to discern patterns within one's life. This was something that writing his autobiography had made possible; he could now discern a pattern to things. "The gradual *reading* of one's life, seeing the pattern emerge, is a great illumination at our age."[51] For Lewis, the narration of his own story is about the identification of a pattern of meaning within his life, which enabled events to be seen in their proper context, and assume their true and deeper meaning.

This point is clearly anticipated in Augustine's *Confessions*. One of Augustine's most significant insights is that the full significance of events does not become clear until later. A seemingly inconsequential happening may turn out to be laden with significance, in the light of later developments. It is only at the end of one's life that one can discern its patterns of meaning, and fully understand the significance of its constituent events. A mere narrative of happenings fails to disclose their significance; an interpretative standpoint is necessary to identify their meaning. For Augustine, conversion to Christianity provided him with a standpoint from which he could deploy a critical detachment, enabling him to look at his past and decipher what was hitherto opaque, shrouded in mist, or out of focus. To borrow Plato's famous term,[52] Christianity provided Augustine with a *synoptikon* – a way of seeing things (whether the cosmos or his own personal existence) in their totality, allowing their inner coherence to be perceived.

The Historical Reliability of Lewis's Autobiography

One of the more troubling questions raised by a close reading of *Surprised by Joy* concerns the reliability of Lewis's memory. Although there is no reason to doubt Lewis's recollection of his own inner experiences and feelings, as described in this book, there are significant questions about the accuracy of Lewis's correlation of these subjective recollections with the objective world of places and dates. Does he get his dates wrong? This is not necessarily a question of *inventing* the past to serve certain agendas, but may simply be a matter of a failure to recall when certain things actually took place.

Lewis himself remarked on this failing in 1957, shortly after the publication of *Surprised by Joy*: he could now, he confessed, "never remember dates."[53] His brother did not consider this to be a development dating from Lewis's later career. Lewis, he declared, had a "life-long inability to keep track of dates."[54] When Lewis became Vice-President of Magdalen College, Oxford in 1941 – a fixed-term appointment with essentially administrative responsibilities, which rotated around the fellowship – he was soon found to be incapable of carrying out one of the chief responsibilities of this role: arranging for the booking of rooms for college meetings or private engagements. Lewis simply could not remember dates. Rooms were double-booked, if they were booked at all. In the end, his brother Warnie was enlisted to carry out this role, and the problem receded.

This issue of the correlation of Lewis's vivid and subjective memories with the objective realities of historical calendars becomes acutely difficult in relation to what is perhaps the central event described in Lewis's autobiography – his conversion. The passage describing this development in *Surprised by Joy* is remarkably (and uncharacteristically) precise about dates. "In the Trinity Term of 1929 I gave in, and admitted that God was God, and knelt and prayed: perhaps, that night, the most dejected and reluctant convert in all England."[55] Oxford University's official publications for the academic year 1928–9 allow us to narrow this down to some point in the eight weeks between April 28 and June 22, 1929.[56]

Lewis offers no indication of the identity of the external landmarks by which his subjective memory of submission to God can be correlated with events in the world around him. Yet while there are no reasonable grounds for doubting Lewis's vivid memory of "giving in," and "admitting that God was God," there are four very good reasons for challenging Lewis's recollection that this is to be dated to Trinity Term 1929.[57]

First, a close and continuous reading of his works – especially his correspondence – reveals no sign of a significant change in tone or mood throughout 1929, and even into the first weeks of 1930. Between September 1925 and January 1930, Lewis's writings disclose no hint of any radical change of heart or mind. If Lewis was converted in 1929, this supposedly pivotal event made no impact on his writings – including his letters to his closest friends at that time, Owen Barfield and Arthur Greeves.

Second, Lewis's father died in September 1929. If Lewis's chronology of his own conversion is accepted, Lewis had come to believe in God at the time of his father's death. Yet Lewis's correspondence makes no reference at all to any impact of a belief in God, however emergent, upon his final days spent with his father, his subsequent funeral, and its emotional aftermath. Lewis's father knew that he was dying. He had a robust belief in God, and was reconciled to his own imminent death. If Lewis did indeed come to believe in God as a living personal reality (as opposed to an abstract philosophical idea) in Trinity Term 1929, that faith seems to have made no impact on him at a time when it would be expected to have functioned as a significant consolation for him, not least in that his father had shared that faith.

Third, Lewis's account of the dynamics of his conversion in *Surprised by Joy* speaks of God closing in on him, taking the initiative, and ultimately overwhelming him. We find echoes of this language in a short letter to Owen Barfield, written hastily on February 3, 1930.[58]

> Terrible things are happening to me. The "Spirit" or "Real I" is showing an alarming tendency to become much more personal and is taking the offensive, and behaving just like God. You'd better come on Monday at the latest, or I may have entered a monastery.

Barfield was unequivocal about the significance of this letter for Lewis's spiritual development: it marked "the beginning of his conversion."[59] The letter reflects Lewis's language about the pressures he experienced immediately before his conversion, which is clearly *ahead* of him, not *behind* him.

Fourth, Lewis made it clear that his behavior changed as a result of his new belief in God. Although still not committed to Christianity, he now began to attend both his local parish church (Holy Trinity, Headington Quarry, Oxford) on Sundays, and college chapel on weekdays. Yet Lewis's correspondence makes no reference to regular attendance at any Oxford church or Magdalen College chapel in 1929, or the first half of 1930.

Yet things change decisively in October 1930. In a letter to his close friend and confidant Arthur Greeves, dated October 29, 1930, Lewis mentions that he now goes to bed earlier than he used, to, as he has now "started going to morning chapel at 8."[60] This disclosure – mentioned to no other correspondent – is presented as a *new development*, a significant change in his routine, dating from the beginning of the academic year 1930–1. If Lewis's own date for his conversion is correct, he should have begun attending college chapel in October *1929*. Yet the date of this change of habit makes sense if Lewis discovered God in the summer of *1930*.

The traditional date of Lewis's conversion, based on his own narrative in *Surprised by Joy*, and repeated in every major study of Lewis to date,[61] clearly needs review. The best explanation of things is that Lewis's subjective location of the event in his inner world is regarded as reliable, but his chronological location of the event in terms of his outer world is misplaced. If Lewis was converted during any Trinity Term, it was the Trinity Term of 1930, not 1929 – namely, at some point between April 27 and June 21, 1930.

There are also points of importance for any understanding of Lewis's *itinerarium mentis ad Deum*. Following his rediscovery of faith in God, Lewis gradually came to a more explicit acceptance of the fundamental beliefs of Christianity. A conversation of September 19, 1931, between Lewis and Hugo Dyson, a lecturer in English at Reading University, and J. R. R. Tolkien at Magdalen College led to Lewis realizing that Christianity was a "true myth," opening the way for a new and more imaginative understanding of his faith. On October 1, Lewis wrote to his confidant Arthur Greeves, telling him of his new outlook on life.[62]

> I have just passed on from believing in God to definitely believing in Christ – in Christianity. I will try to explain this another time. My long night talk with Dyson and Tolkien had a lot to do with it.

Lewis then wrote Greeves a second, more detailed letter on October 18, explaining his new understanding of things in some detail, allowing Greeves to understand the critical role that Tolkien and Dyson played in his conversion to Christianity, and above all the importance of the nature of "myth" in helping him overcome his remaining difficulties. Yet *Surprised by Joy* records merely that Tolkien and Dyson provided Lewis with "much help in getting over the last stile."[63] This short statement about Tolkien and Dyson is not fleshed out or given substance, despite

the critical importance of their intervention for Lewis's spiritual development, and subsequent reflections on the role of myth (a matter we shall
return to in a later essay: 55–81). Without those two letters of October
1930 to Greeves, we would never have understood quite what was
involved in Lewis's final conversion to Christianity, nor the role played
by Tolkien.

Lewis's account of his development in *Surprised by Joy* offers an impres-
sionistic overview of his conversion to Christianity, organized more in
terms of the ideas involved in Lewis's spiritual journey than the dates of
critical milestones along the way. We learn much about Lewis's recollections of his inner feelings and reflections, but little of any historical landmarks which might allow us to organize these themes into a coherent
narrative. Furthermore, Lewis's memory of historical landmarks is not
entirely reliable. At one critical point Lewis seems to have merged his
memories of this important period, conflating two events into one.

Lewis's narrative in *Surprised by Joy* includes an account of a visit he
made to Whipsnade Park Zoo in Bedfordshire, in which the gradually
coalescing elements of his understanding of the Christian faith finally
crystallized Christologically, leading to his mature understanding of the
identity and significance of Jesus Christ:[64]

> I know very well when, but hardly how, the final step was taken. I was
> driven to Whipsnade one sunny morning. When we set out I did not believe
> that Jesus Christ is the Son of God, and when we reached the zoo I did.
> Yet I had not exactly spent the journey in thought.

Lewis scholars agree that this development probably took place shortly
after Lewis's extended discussion of September 19, 1931, with Tolkien
and Dyson about the nature of myth. This journey is traditionally assigned
to September 28, 1931, nine days after these conversations, when Lewis's
brother Warren drove Lewis to Whipsnade in the sidecar of his motor-
bike. Warren later remarked that it was during this "outing" in September
1931 that Lewis decided to rejoin the church.[65]

Lewis's vivid account of that critical day at Whipsnade Zoo in *Surprised
by Joy* includes a poetic passage recalling "the birds singing overhead
and the bluebells underfoot," commenting that "Wallaby Wood" had been
quite ruined by subsequent development work.[66] The impact of seeing
vast expanses of bluebells in the woods of his native Shropshire inspired
one of the finest lines by the English poet and literary scholar A. E.
Houseman (1859–1936):[67]

> And like a skylit water stood
> The bluebells in the azured wood.

Yet Lewis's reference to bluebells in *Surprised by Joy* – perhaps given added significance on account of his heightened perception of the iconic significance of a "blue flower"[68] – raises certain difficult questions. The English bluebell typically blooms from late April into late May, and its leaves wither and disappear by the late summer. The simple fact is that there would have been no "bluebells underfoot" at Whipsnade in late September. Lewis's recollection of the birds and bluebells at Whipsnade Zoo recorded in *Surprised by Joy* is clearly a memory of a late spring or early summer day, not a day in early autumn.

Lewis seems to have merged his memories of two, quite different visits to Whipsnade – a first visit made in September 1931, and a *second* visit, made in the first week of June 1932, when Lewis was again driven to the zoo – but this time in a car on a "fine day" by Edward Foord-Kelcy (1859–1934). On June 14, shortly after this trip, Lewis wrote to his brother, specifically noting the "masses of bluebells" he had seen, and commenting on the state of "Wallaby Wood"[69] in terms very similar to the critical passage in *Surprised by Joy*. The sight of such expanses of bluebells at Whipsnade Zoo is often highlighted in their publicity literature, along with the significant observation that the bluebells bloom slightly later there than elsewhere, on account of the zoo's elevated and exposed conditions.[70]

While it remains possible Lewis's Christological breakthrough took place later than traditionally accepted – that is to say, in June 1932, rather than September 1931 – this seems unlikely, given the very specific Christological comments made by Lewis in his letter to Arthur Greeves of October 1, 1931, stating that he had "just passed on from believing in God to definitely believing in Christ."[71] Lewis seems to have fused his memories of two quite distinct visits to Whipsnade, mingling his memory of an observation and reflection which took place in September 1931 with an event which took place in June 1932. Once more, the historical reliability of Lewis's narrative needs to be treated with caution.

The Implied Audience of "Surprised by Joy"

Finally, we must reflect on the readership that Lewis envisaged for this work. What clues does the text of *Surprised by Joy* disclose about Lewis's hopes or expectations for his implied audience? By this time, Lewis had mastered the art of scholarly prose on the one hand, and translating his ideas into the cultural vernacular on the other. "Lewis did not set out to write at a particular stylistic level or texture; rather, he maintained that an author's style must be molded and modified to meet the needs of his particular audience."[72] Unusually, Lewis was capable of writing at a number of levels, the choice resting on his assumptions concerning a given book's likely audience. It is normally quite easy to work out (especially from his shorter pieces) who Lewis has in mind from his vocabulary, style, level of analysis, and authorial tone.

Surprised by Joy proves surprisingly resistant to such an analysis. In the first place, the intellectual demands made of its readers are unexpectedly high. Some representative examples may be noted to illustrate this point. The rich and complex German technical term *Sehnsucht* is used without explanation or contextualization.[73] Novalis's "Blue Flower" motif is mentioned without elaboration,[74] apparently on the assumption that the reader knows that it symbolizes a longing for the elusive reconciliation of reason and imagination, between the observed world outside the mind and the subjective world within.

Furthermore, Lewis punctuates his text with untranslated maxims and epigrams in French,[75] German,[76] Italian,[77] and Latin.[78] As a rare concession, Lewis at one point offers a footnote providing an English translation of an untransliterated Greek epigram he cites in his text: "Oh, I desire too much."[79] This epigram is often encountered in Renaissance art – for example, in Moretto da Brescia's "Portrait of a Young Man" (1516–18), which incorporates this slogan into a band on the subject's feather beret. Lewis seems to assume his readers are aware of its cultural significance, so that it requires no explanation or comment.

Surprised by Joy also assumes that the reader is familiar with Lewis's everyday worlds, and does not need jargon or technical terms explained. This is perhaps most obviously the case when speaking about his extended time at Oxford University, when Lewis uses Oxford jargon without explanation. For example, we learn that Cecil Harwood was a student of "The House."[80] Someone such as myself, steeped in this cultural milieu, knows immediately that this is a reference to Christ Church – Oxford's college and cathedral, re-founded in 1546 by Henry VIII as *Aedes Christi* ("The House of Christ"). Yet Lewis makes no attempt to introduce or explain such terms to outsiders.

Lewis also assumes that his readers are deeply steeped in the western literary tradition; otherwise, they would be unable to appreciate his turns of phrase and lines of thought – such as his extensive use of allusion. For example, consider the following statement, made in the simplest of styles: "No more Avalon, no more Hesperides."[81] The sentence is a mere six words long; yet its meaning and impact are determined almost entirely by the capacity of the rich imaginative literary associations of "Avalon" and "Hesperides" to evoke memories, aspirations, and yearnings. To read is not necessarily to understand, still less to be engaged at the deep level that Lewis intended – and presumably experienced for himself.

Lewis is a master of translation, having discovered that effective communication entailed the learning of the language of his audiences, and restating and explaining ideas and concepts in accessible ways (131–3). Despite Lewis's stated supposal of his likely audience, such translation is conspicuously absent from *Surprised by Joy*, which makes considerable linguistic and cultural demands of its readers. Lewis's facility for translation of complex literary and religious notions for the benefit of his readers is well known. So is Lewis here subtly indicating that his readers must rise to his level, rather than expect him to descend to theirs?

It is as if Lewis imagines himself to be conversing with someone rather like himself, who shares his own deep knowledge of the field of western literature and the curious habits and customs of Oxford dons. He clearly believes that he can share his thoughts and allusions without having to explain them. Might Lewis actually be writing for *himself*?

Perhaps. But there is another explanation. To make sense of *Surprised by Joy*, his readers need to learn Lewis's language, and realize that this inversion of Lewis's normal approach is really a compliment to his readers. When Lewis bares his soul, he does so on his own terms, obliging his readers to come to terms with his unaccommodated language and allusions. The price of being allowed access to Lewis's private world is that we must allow him to speak to us on his own terms – and in his own words.

Conclusion

In the end, *Surprised by Joy* remains something of an enigma. Fully unlocking its key would require access to whatever notes Lewis used in compiling it, successive dated revisions of the manuscript, and the deeper recesses of Lewis's creative mind – above all, his capacity to weave narratives, correlating and colligating his external and internal worlds. It is unlikely we shall ever achieve such an understanding. Yet perhaps the unanswered questions which hover over its pages help explain its abiding appeal. To cross the threshold of *Surprised by Joy* is to enter a private world, revealed only in part, with darkened recesses tantalizingly beyond our reach.

Surprised by Joy is a curious work – one that arguably seeks to conceal as much as to reveal, and which raises important and difficult questions concerning the correlation of Lewis's external and internal worlds. Oscar

Wilde (1854–1900) famously quipped that "To reveal art and conceal the artist is art's aim." So can autobiography be art? Or must it conceal its author if it is to disclose its artfulness? It is difficult not to see the wisdom of James Como's comments:[82]

> The consideration of C. S. Lewis's self is a very great challenge. He at once hid it absolutely, distorted it, and invented parts of it to parade forth; he repressed, explored, and denied it; he indulged and overcame it; certainly he would transform, and then transcend it; almost always he used it.

Perhaps Lewis intends us to see his own story, so artfully presented, as a mirror of the human soul – a mirror in which we can discern our own story reflected in part, while being seen in the light of a greater vision of reality, which – like Plato's *synoptikon* – sets everything in its proper context. Lewis's personal story is then to be recognized as an echo of the "grand narrative" of God and the universe – something worth exploring in its own right, but more fundamentally because of its ability to disclose something greater and deeper.

Notes

1 See Letter to Peter Milward, July 4, 1955; *Letters*, vol. 3, 627; Letter to Arthur Greeves, August 18, 1955; *Letters*, vol. 3, 642.
2 William Wordsworth, *Major Works*. Oxford: Oxford University Press, 1984, 334. In a letter to his publisher, Jocelyn Gibb, Lewis indicated that it did not matter "whether the title suggests Wordsworth or not," implying that a knowledge of Wordsworth's original poem was not important to an understanding of his own work: Letter to Jocelyn Gibb, June 1, 1955; *Letters*, vol. 3, 614.
3 *Surprised by Joy*, 276.
4 C. S. Lewis and E. M. W. Tillyard, *The Personal Heresy: A Controversy*. London: Oxford University Press, 1939, 11.
5 Lewis and Tillyard, *The Personal Heresy*, 12; 21.
6 See William Oddie, *Chesterton and the Romance of Orthodoxy: The Making of GKC, 1874–1908*. Oxford: Oxford University Press, 2008, 341–67.
7 *Surprised by Joy*, 260.
8 See the points made in Monika Wohlrab-Sahr, "Die Realität des Subjekts: Überlegungen zu einer Theorie biographischer Identität." In *Subjektdiskurse im gesellschaftlichen Wandel: Zur Theorie des Subjekts in der Spätmoderne*, edited by Heiner Keupp and Joachim Hohl, 75–97. Bielefeld: Transcript Verlag, 2006.

9   Andrew Wheat, "The Road before Him: Allegory, Reason, and Romanticism in C. S. Lewis' *The Pilgrim's Regress." Renascence: Essays on Values in Literature* 51, no. 1 (1998): 21–39.

10 U. Milo Kaufmann, "*The Pilgrim's Progress* and *The Pilgrim's Regress*: John Bunyan and C. S. Lewis on the Shape of the Christian Quest." In *Bunyan in Our Time*, edited by Robert G. Collmer, 186–99. Kent, OH: Kent State University Press, 1989.

11 Ann Loades, "C. S. Lewis: Grief Observed, Rationality Abandoned, Faith Regained." *Literature and Theology* 3 (1989): 107–21.

12 Letter to Sister Madelva, October 3, 1963; *Letters*, vol. 3, 1460.

13 For useful reflections on Lewis's rhetorical purposes in this work, see Michael Ward, "C. S. Lewis, 1898–1963." In *The Heart of Faith: Following Christ in the Church of England*, edited by Andrew Atherstone, 121–30. Cambridge: Lutterworth Press, 2008.

14 *Surprised by Joy*, ix.

15 Lewis explicitly refers to re-reading Augustine's *Confessions* in Lent 1936; see his letter to Dom Bede Griffiths, April 24, 1936; *Letters*, vol. 2, 190. He later debated with Griffiths – who he encouraged to read Augustine's work in the original Latin – over whether a "Berkeleyian idealism" could be discerned in this text: Letter to Dom Bede Griffiths, April 19, 1938; *Letters*, vol. 2, 225. Lewis consistently recommended Augustine's *Confessions* to those who asked to be directed toward some stimulating Christian reading: see, for example, his letter to Mrs Morland, August 19, 1942; *Letters*, vol. 2, 529; Letter to Margaret Gray, May 9, 1961; *Letters*, vol. 3, 1265.

16 Elizabeth de Mijolla, *Autobiographical Quests: Augustine, Montaigne, Rousseau, and Wordsworth*. Charlottesville, VA: University Press of Virginia, 1994, 13–45; Annemaré Kotzé, *Augustine's Confessions: Communicative Purpose and Audience*. Leiden: Brill, 2004, 18–27.

17 Augustine of Hippo, *Confessions* 10.8.13.

18 *Surprised by Joy*, x.

19 Danuta Shanzer, "Pears before Swine: Augustine, *Confessions* 2.4.9." *Revue des Études Augustiniennes* 42 (1996): 45–55.

20 Lawrence Byrne, "Writing God's Story: Self and Narrative Structure in Augustine's *Confessions." Christianity and Literature* 38 (1989): 15–31.

21 For Augustine's description of this process, see Carl G. Vaught, *Access to God in Augustine's Confessions: Books X–XIII*. Albany, NY: State University of New York Press, 2005, 36–80.

22 For Lewis's use of this term to refer to his return to Christianity, see *Surprised by Joy*, 135.

23 See the analysis in Carol Harrison, *Rethinking Augustine's Early Theology: An Argument for Continuity*. Oxford: Oxford University, 2006, 4–18. Harrison rejects the "two Augustines" notion in favor of a narrative of continuous development and reformulation.

24 Karla Pollmann, "*Alium sub meo nomine*: Augustine Between His Own Self-Fashioning and His Later Reception." *Zeitschrift für antikes Christentum* 14 (2010): 409–24.

25   *Surprised by Joy*, 252.
26   On this general theme, see Mary J. Carruthers, *The Book of Memory: A Study of Memory in Medieval Culture*, 2nd edn. Cambridge: Cambridge University Press, 2008.
27   Dante, *Vita Nuova*, 1, 1.
28   Barbara Nolan, "The 'Vita Nuova': Dante's Book of Revelation." *Dante Studies* 88 (1970): 51–71; quote at 52.
29   Aristotle, *De memoria et reminiscentia* 1.450a–b. For further comment, see David Bloch, ed., *Aristotle on Memory and Recollection: Text, Translation, Interpretation, and Reception in Western Scholasticism*. Leiden: Brill, 2007.
30   For the use of texts and images to enhance this "art" in the later Renaissance, see Lina Bolzoni, *The Gallery of Memory: Literary and Iconographic Models in the Age of the Printing Press*. Toronto: University of Toronto Press, 2001.
31   Bolzoni, *Gallery of Memory*, 139–45; Mary J. Carruthers, "*Ars oblivionalis, ars inveniendi:* The Cherub Figure and the Arts of Memory." *Gesta* 48 (2009): 1–19. For this issue in human culture as a whole, see Harald Weinrich, *Lethe: The Art and Critique of Forgetting*. Ithaca, NY: Cornell University Press, 2004, especially 19–37. As Weinrich notes, the idea was re-introduced by Umberto Eco in 1966, apparently unaware of its historical provenance: Weinrich, *Lethe*, 12. Martin Heidegger's suggestion that *aletheia* is essentially the suppression or overwhelming of *lethe* should be noted here, although the scholarly evidence for this is somewhat unimpressive: Ernst Tugendhaft, "Heideggers Idee von Wahrheit." In *Heidegger: Perspektiven zur Deutung seines Werks*, edited by Otto Pöggeler, 286–97. Weinheim: Beltz, 1994.
32   The three significance "absences" from *Surprised by Joy* are his complex relationship with Mrs Moore, his difficult relationship with his father, and the trauma of the Great War. See McGrath, *C. S. Lewis – A Life*, 123–4.
33   Louis A. Renza, "The Veto of the Imagination: A Theory of Autobiography." *New Literary History* 9 (1977): 1–26.
34   A madeleine is a small vanilla-flavored cake. For the phenomenon of odor-evoked memories, see Rachel S. Herz and Jonathan W. Schooler, "A Naturalistic Study of Autobiographical Memories Evoked by Olfactory and Visual Cues: Testing the Proustian Hypothesis." *American Journal of Psychology* 115, no. 1 (2002): 21–32; Marieke B. J. Toffoloa, Monique A. M. Smeets, and Marcel A. van den Hout, "Proust Revisited: Odours as Triggers of Aversive Memories." *Cognition and Emotion*, 26, no. 1 (2012): 83–92.
35   *Surprised by Joy*, 16. The "flowering currant" (*Ribes sanguineum*) is a fragrant flowering bush, common in Belfast gardens around this time.
36   For example, Arthur Melville Clark, *Autobiography: Its Genesis and Phases*. Edinburgh: Oliver & Boyd, 1935, 10–21.
37   See especially Ronald Bedford, Lloyd Davis, and Philippa Kelly, eds., *Early Modern English Lives: Autobiography and Self-Representation, 1500–1660*. Aldershot: Ashgate, 2007.
38   Leigh Gilmore, "The Mark of Autobiography: Postmodernism, Autobiography, and Genre." In *Autobiography & Postmodernism*, edited by Kathleen M.

Ashley, Leigh Gilmore, and Gerald Peters, 3–18. Amherst, MA: University of Massachusetts Press, 1994.

39 Roy Pascal, *Design and Truth in Autobiography*. Cambridge, MA: Harvard University Press, 1960, 39.

40 A point made particularly by James Olney, *Metaphors of Self: The Meaning of Autobiography*. Princeton, NJ: Princeton University Press, 1972. The issue is somewhat more complex than Olney suggests: see, for example, Wolfram Fischer, "Über die allmähliche Verfertigung des Selbst beim Sprechen von Sich. Begrenzung und Entgrenzung der Erinnerung im autobiographischen Dialog." In *Psychotherapie in Zeiten der Globalisierung*, edited by Bernhard Strauß and Michael Geyer, 307–36. Göttingen: Vandenhoeck & Ruprecht, 2007.

41 Albert E. Stone, *The American Autobiography: A Collection of Critical Essays*. Englewood Cliffs, NJ: Prentice-Hall, 1981, 2.

42 Jan Assmann, *Moses the Egyptian: The Memory of Egypt in Western Monotheism*. Cambridge, MA: Harvard University Press, 1997, 9 (my emphasis).

43 *Surprised by Joy*, 95–135. Lewis's account of Malvern College takes up 18 percent of the text of the book.

44 Letter to Arthur Greeves, June 5, 1914: *Letters*, vol. 1, 59.

45 Sayer, *Jack*, 86.

46 Sayer, *Jack*, 326–7.

47 Northrop Frye, *Anatomy of Criticism: Four Essays*. Princeton, NJ: Princeton University Press, 1957, 307–8. See further Charles Berryman, "Critical Mirrors: Theories of Autobiography." *Mosaic* 32, no. 1 (1999): 71–85.

48 See the analysis in Wolfram Fischer-Rosenthal, "Melancholie der Identität und dezentrierte biographische Selbstbeschreibung. Anmerkung zu einem langen Abschied aus der selbstverschuldeten Zentriertheit des Subjekts." *Bios: Zeitschrift für Biographieforschung und Oral History* 12, no. 2 (1999): 143–68.

49 Clare Blake, "Making Sense of the Self: Cultural Identities under Pressure." In *The Uses of Autobiography*, edited by Julia Swindells, 56–63. London: Taylor & Francis, 1995; Wohlrab-Sahr, "Die Realität des Subjekts: Überlegungen zu einer Theorie biographischer Identität." See also the earlier piece by Paul de Man, "Autobiography as De-Facement." In *The Rhetoric of Romanticism*. New York: Columbia University Press, 1979, 67–82.

50 Paul John Eakin, "What Are We Reading When We Read Autobiography?" *Narrative* 12, no. 2 (2004): 121–32. See also Paul Jay, *Being in the Text: Self-Representation from Wordsworth to Roland Barthes*. Ithaca, NY: Cornell University Press, 1984; Paul John Eakin, *Fictions in Autobiography: Studies in the Art of Self Invention*. Princeton, NJ: Princeton University Press, 1985.

51 Letter to Dom Bede Griffith, February 8, 1956; *Letters*, vol. 3, 703.

52 Plato, *Republic*, 537C7.

53 Letter to Laurence Krieg, April 21, 1957; *Letters*, vol. 3, 848.

54 W. H. Lewis, *C. S. Lewis: A Biography* (1974). Unpublished typescript held in the Wade Center, Wheaton College, Illinois, and the Bodleian Library, Oxford, 43.

55   *Surprised by Joy*, 266.
56   *Oxford University Calendar 1928*. Oxford: Oxford University Press, 1928, xx–xxii; *Oxford University Calendar, 1929*. Oxford: Oxford University Press, 1929, xiii–x. Lewis is here referring to the eight-week "Full Term" during which tutorials and lectures took place.
57   I first pointed this out in McGrath, *C. S. Lewis – A Life*, 141–6.
58   Letter to Owen Barfield, February 3, 1930; *Letters*, vol. 1, 882–3.
59   Owen Barfield, in *C. S. Lewis Remembered: Collected Reflections of Students, Friends & Colleagues*, edited by Harry Lee Poe, and Rebecca Whitten Poe, 25–35. Grand Rapids, MI: Zondervan, 2006.
60   Letter to Arthur Greeves, October 29, 1930; *Letters*, vol. 1, 942.
61   For example, see David C. Downing, *The Most Reluctant Convert: C. S. Lewis's Journey to Faith*. Downers Grove, IL: InterVarsity Press, 2002.
62   Letter to Arthur Greeves, October 1, 1931; *Letters*, vol. 1, 974.
63   *Surprised by Joy*, 252.
64   *Surprised by Joy*, 275.
65   W. H. Lewis, "Memoir of C. S. Lewis." In *The Letters of C. S. Lewis*, edited by W. H. Lewis, 1–26. London: Bles, 1966. Quote at 19.
66   *Surprised by Joy*, 276. On this passage, see Michael Ward, "Escape to Wallaby Wood: Lewis's Depictions of Conversion." In *C. S. Lewis: Lightbearer in the Shadowlands*, edited by A. J. L. Menuge, 143–67. Wheaton, IL: Crossway, 1997.
67   A. E. Houseman, *A Shropshire Lad*, XLI, 17–18. This poem, written in 1896, is noted for its stylistic simplicity and its nostalgic depiction of pastoral life in rural England. See Benjamin F. Fisher, "The Critical Reception of *A Shropshire Lad*." In *A. E. Houseman: A Reassessment*, edited by Alan W. Holden and J. Roy Birch, 20–36. Basingstoke: Macmillan, 2000. Shakespeare's "azured Harebell" (*Cymbeline*, IV, 2) is actually the English bluebell.
68   *Surprised by Joy*, 6.
69   See his letter to Warnie Lewis, June 14, 1932; *Letters*, vol. 2, 84.
70   "Beautiful Bluebells"; ZSL Whipsnade Zoo Press Release, May 17, 2004.
71   Letter to Arthur Greeves, October 1, 1931; *Letters*, vol. 1, 974.
72   Gary L. Tandy, *The Rhetoric of Certitude: C. S. Lewis's Nonfiction Prose*. Kent, OH: Kent State University Press, 2009, 83.
73   *Surprised by Joy*, 6.
74   *Surprised by Joy*, 6.
75   E.g., *Surprised by Joy*, 58: "maison tolérée" (a euphemism for a brothel).
76   E.g., Goethe's phrase *"des Lebens goldnes Baum,"* which comes from Goethe's *Faust*: *Surprised by Joy*, 230. There is a misprint here: "goldnes" ought to be "goldner." Merely translating this decontextualized phrase fails to indicate its significance; it needs to be set in its full context: "Grau, theurer Freund, ist alle Theorie, und grün des Lebens goldner Baum." "All theory, dear friend, is gray; and the golden tree of life is green." Goethe's point – with which Lewis agreed totally – is that theory fails to capture the richness and vibrancy of reality. Similarly, Lewis cites the German libretto of Wagner's opera *Siegfried* at one point, but this time offering an English translation: *Surprised by*

Joy, 265. As with the Goethe quote noted above, the German is misprinted, offering the nonsensical "Spärer" in place of Wagner's original "Spürer" ("spy" or "tracker"). Both these misprints date back to the first edition: see C. S. Lewis, *Surprised by Joy*. London: Geoffrey Bles, 1955, 188; 218.

77   E.g., *Surprised by Joy*, 60: "ogni parte ad ogni parte splende," a reference to Dante, *Inferno* VII, 75.

78   E.g., *Surprised by Joy*, 221: The Latin tag "odora canum vis" comes from Vergil's *Aeneid*, IV.131 – "keen-scented dogs."

79   *Surprised by Joy*, 16. In transliterated Greek, this reads: *iou lian potho*. The Greek is incorrectly rendered in recent editions of *Surprised by Joy*, which contract these three Greek words into two, and incorrectly render the Greek letter *upsilon* by the typographically similar *nu*. The first edition presents the Greek correctly: see C. S. Lewis, *Surprised by Joy*. London: Geoffrey Bles, 1955, 22.

80   *Surprised by Joy*, 233.

81   *Surprised by Joy*, 237.

82   James Como, *Branches to Heaven: The Geniuses of C. S. Lewis*. Dallas, TX: Spence, 1998, 54.

2

The "New Look": Lewis's Philosophical Context at Oxford in the 1920s

C. S. Lewis's long relationship with Oxford University began halfway through the Great War in November 1916, when he applied for a place to study classics at New College, Oxford.[1] The reasons for his decision remain unclear. Why classics? Why New College? Neither his correspondence of the period nor his later recollections of his life cast much light on this decision. New College declined to offer Lewis a place; University College, however, recognized his talent, and offered him a scholarship to study classics with effect from October 1917. In the event, the Great War forced Lewis to change his plans. The massive casualty rates sustained in the first two years of war meant that every able-bodied male aged between 18 and 41 was expected to enlist;[2] Lewis had celebrated his eighteenth birthday in November 1916.

Realizing that it was inevitable that he would have to enlist in the British Army, Lewis arranged to go up to University College in April 1917, and spend the Trinity Term of 1917 in residence. As a student, he was entitled to join the Oxford University Officers Training Corps, which allowed him to transfer to No. 4 Officer Cadet Battalion, based at Keble College, Oxford, in May. After a period of training and leave, Lewis was commissioned as a Second Lieutenant in the Somerset Light Infantry. He was wounded in battle, and was sent back to England to recover. After he was formally demobilized in December 1918, Lewis returned to University College, Oxford, in January 1919, to resume his study of classics. Yet the Oxford that Lewis returned to bore little resemblance to the university of the pre-war years. Everything was in a state of flux – institutionally, culturally, and intellectually.

The Intellectual World of C. S. Lewis, First Edition. Alister E. McGrath.
© 2014 John Wiley & Sons, Ltd. Published 2014 by John Wiley & Sons, Ltd.

Oxford University was slowly returning to normal after the substantial reductions in student numbers and income it had suffered as a result of the wartime emergency.[3] Yet the impact of the Great War on western culture was at least as great as on the British economy and institutions. The war shook the cultural and intellectual tectonic plates of western Europe, causing many to lose their faith in civilization and the inevitability of human progress.[4] The years immediately following the Great War saw radical alterations in western European self-consciousness.[5] The trauma of the war caused many to question the settled cultural assumptions of the Edwardian age, especially its positive views on human nature and cultural progress. Oswald Spengler's *Decline of the West* (1918) and J. B. Bury's *Idea of Progress* (1920) called into question the idea of a continuous upward development of human culture and civilization.[6] In 1919, Sigmund Freud's radical ideas about hidden psychological influences on human judgment began to attract public attention, partly through the founding of the *International Journal of Psycho-Analysis*.[7]

The impact was felt also at the literary level. Many, like the Anglo-American poet T. S. Eliot, felt that the Great War marked the final collapse of the cultural heritage of the nineteenth century.[8] James Joyce's *Ulysses* appeared in 1922, its radical literary innovation signaling a complete break with the Victorian literary tradition. Theologically, the rise of Karl Barth's radical "dialectical theology" can be seen as a fundamental rejection of core themes of late nineteenth-century Liberal Protestantism.[9] Others turned away from traditional Christianity to forms of spiritualism,[10] believing that the Great War had damaged the credibility of the churches.[11] A longing for authority, particularly in a defeated Germany during the late 1920s, gave credibility to totalitarian political movements such as Nazism and Communism.[12]

Radical re-thinking was seen to be required at every level. Change was in the air. It was impossible for a young man, entering Oxford's intellectual culture, to avoid being affected by these swirling currents.[13] During his first two years at Oxford, Lewis's views began to crystallize. Some elements of his way of thinking – such as an intellectually aggressive yet somewhat sterile atheism – were already established; others came to fall into place around them, yielding what Lewis termed his "intellectual 'New Look.'"[14]

In using this phrase "New Look," Lewis was not drawing on an accepted designation for a distinct school of thought; he was simply adopting a turn of phrase from the world of fashion and applying it to the intellectual trends of his day, as he chose to appropriate them – as it turned out, in a somewhat transient and loosely connected amalgam of ideas. Lewis wove together into his personal worldview both general cultural themes that were already well established in late Edwardian culture and certain ideas which had solidified in Oxford's intellectual culture in the aftermath of the Great War. The precise manner of their colligation, however, appears to have been Lewis's own creation.

Although Lewis is now remembered primarily as an author and literary critic, it is important to realize that his first sustained period of study at Oxford brought him into contact with the philosophy of the ancient world, and some of its more recent reformulations.[15] Lewis achieved the distinction of achieving First Class Honors both in classical moderations and in the Final Honor School of *Literae Humaniores*, which demanded immersion in the world of ideas, ancient and modern.[16] While Lewis never developed a systematic philosophy of his own, he nevertheless wrote from within a broad philosophical tradition, which informed and stimulated his own thinking.

Lewis's decision to take an additional Final Honor School (English language and literature, in which he also gained First Class Honors in 1923) partly reflected his concern about finding academic positions in either classics or philosophy.[17] It is, however, clear that Lewis's first love was philosophy. His competency in this field was not in doubt. When University College's philosophy don, Edgar F. Carritt (1876–1964), arranged to spend the academic year of 1924–5 teaching in the United States, Lewis was appointed to a temporary academic position at the college to cover his teaching. Carritt clearly saw Lewis as someone who could be trusted.

So what was the intellectual "New Look" that Lewis adopted in the early 1920s?

In this essay, we shall attempt to identify what Lewis meant when he spoke of the "New Look" by weaving together themes evident in his writings over the period 1915–25 and his later memories and assessment of his earlier views (especially as found in the autobiographical *Surprised by Joy*), correlating these with what is known of the intellectual history of this period at Oxford.

Two matters must be borne in mind when trying to explore this aspect of Lewis's intellectual development. First, we must note the difficulties inherent in an appeal to the narrative of *Surprised by Joy*, some of which were noted earlier (7–29). Lewis's narrative is not so much inaccurate as potentially misleading on account of its inalienable subjectivity. Lewis's presentation of his changing way of thinking, as presented in *Surprised by Joy*, rests on his own intimate familiarity with this narrative, which occasionally leads his public presentation of that narrative to lack apparent continuity or thematic unity. It is, however, possible to correlate Lewis's statements in his autobiography with trends in Oxford philosophy in the late 1910s and early 1920s, occasionally casting light on Lewis's autobiographical narrative.

Second, it is important to appreciate that, in speaking of his "New Look," Lewis did not mean to align himself *exclusively* with one specific current of thought in early 1920s Oxford. Lewis's way of thinking involved bringing together a number of strands of thought, which were not necessarily seen by others as being connected with each other. For example, Lewis weaves together some themes derived from "Oxford Realism" and modern psychology. Yet few in "Oxford Realism" had any time for such eclectic ways of thinking. One of its leading lights, Horace William Brindley Joseph (1867–1943), was dismissive of the "new ideas" of Freud, Darwin, or Marx.[18] Yet Lewis took at least some of these seriously, incorporating their themes according to his taste into his emerging "New Look."

Nevertheless, Lewis does appear to have aligned himself with the general themes of the movement known as "Oxford Realism" in the early 1920s, before moving away from it by about 1925, in favor of a form of idealism. At this time, Oxford philosophers tended to advance their debates through conversation, rather than publication, so that it is not always possible to reconstruct Oxford's philosophical atmosphere in the early 1920s with confidence. However, a good case can be made for arguing that Lewis's account of his personal development fits in well with what is known of Oxford's philosophical culture at that time.

In what follows, we shall identify the leading themes of Lewis's "New Look," and consider their impact on the radical changes in his outlook, evident initially in his decision to return to faith in God in the late spring or early summer of 1930, and his later recommitment to Christianity in the autumn of 1931.

Lewis's Early Atheism

In turning to explore Lewis's "New Look," we may first consider the atheism that was so characteristic of his early period. This was of the most noticeable themes of Lewis's first published work – the collection of poems entitled *Spirits in Bondage*.[19] These poems were published in March 1919 under the pseudonym "Clive Hamilton" ("Hamilton" was Lewis's mother's maiden name). The most interesting parts of the cycle are its protests against a silent, uncaring heaven. The "Ode for New Year's Day," written when under fire from German artillery near the French town of Arras in January 1918, speaks of the final death of theism.

Lewis's atheist rhetoric mingles two themes. In the first place, Lewis argues that modern explanations of religion make it clear that God was simply a human fabrication, an understandable and entirely natural mistake, which could now be corrected in the light of the deeper understanding of human psychology that modern science had made possible. Lewis clearly identified himself with the classic critique of belief in the gods found in the writings of the Roman philosopher Lucretius, suggesting that the inadequacies of the world were the "strongest" argument for atheism:[20]

> Had God designed the world, it would not be
> A world so frail and faulty as we see.

Lewis here fits into a broader pattern, in that many Enlightenment writers made appreciative reference to Lucretius's naturalist philosophy, particularly his criticisms of theism.[21] Following Lucretius, Lewis came to the view that reality was a "meaningless dance of atoms," so that any suggestion of "beauty" within nature was simply a "subjective phosphorescence."[22]

In the second place, Lewis declares that the carnage of the Great War put paid to any idea that there was a God who might "lend an ear" to human cries of misery. This belief was simply indefensible in the light of the senseless slaughter Lewis saw around him. God was a disgraced "Power who slays and puts aside the beauty that has been."[23]

These views were widely held – if not always openly flaunted – in Oxford circles in the aftermath of the Great War. Although it is virtually impossible to argue that this war was caused by religion, many regarded it as marking a decisive point of religious transition.[24] On the far side lay an earlier age of tradition and credulity; on the other side lay a rationalist and realist age, unfettered by the superstitions of the past. Belief in God, if not intellectually discredited, was certainly seen as culturally unfashionable by the social *avante garde*.

Yet while Lewis seems to have regarded his atheism as rationally sound and culturally fashionable, his writings of the early 1920s suggest that he also found it imaginatively unproductive and existentially uninteresting. His reading of English literature – which began in earnest in October 1922 – seems to have raised doubts in his mind about the catastrophic imaginative failure of this way of thinking. "Nearly all that I loved I believed to be imaginary; nearly all that I believed to be real I thought grim and meaningless."[25]

Lewis's continuing commitment to atheism at this stage was grounded in his belief that it was *right*, a "wholesome severity,"[26] even though he conceded that it offered a "grim and meaningless" view of life. Atheism's intellectual rectitude trumped its emotional and existential inadequacy. Lewis did not regard atheism as liberating or exciting; he seems simply to have accepted it, without enthusiasm, as the thinking person's only intellectual option – a default position, without any particular virtues or graces.

However, there are signs that Lewis was entertaining doubts about his atheism even in the early 1920s. Late in 1920 Lewis penned a long letter to his Oxford friend Leo Baker, in which he commented that the "least objectionable theory" to explain some philosophical issues now seemed to him to be to "postulate some sort of God."[27] Lewis speaks of himself "playing at philosophy" in the years before his conversion,[28] implying that his reflections about God were somewhat abstract, having little impact on his day-to-day life. This is certainly borne out by his correspondence and diary, which give little, if any, indication that his everyday life has been altered, or even affected, by such godly musings. In *Surprised by Joy*, Lewis explains, in a somewhat condescending manner, how he never allowed his intellectual dabbling with a philosophical notion of God to degenerate into interest in the "God of popular religion."[29] Yet a diary entry of January 18, 1927, speaks of his theological views in terms of an uneasy and unresolved dialectic between "childish superstitions" and "dogmatic materialism."[30]

Yet the intellectual transition Lewis hinted at maps onto a broader context – Lewis's gradual move away in the period 1920–5 from a certain form of "realism" to an "idealism" which recognized some kind of "absolute" as the foundation or integrating principle of reality, without entailing a theistic or Trinitarian view of God. We shall consider this philosophical transition in what follows.

Oxford Realism

During the early 1920s, Lewis became involved in a philosophical debate that was, in one sense, local to Oxford, and in another, universal in its scope. When intellectual life began to resume at Oxford in early 1919, the dominant philosophy remained that of its Edwardian period: the idealism of T. H. Green (1836–82).[31] This philosophy created at least some degree of intellectual space for religious beliefs,[32] even though Green's personal religious commitments proved to be somewhat elusive.

Yet the Oxford situation was fluid and unstable, with new ideas and influences combining and conspiring to overthrow Green's influence. A new form of realism, originally associated with the Cambridge philosophers G. E. Moore (1873–1958) and Bertrand Russell (1872–1970), foreshadowed in the 1910s by writers such as G. F. Stout (1860–1944) and Thomas Percy Nunn (1870–1944),[33] began to gain influence at Oxford.[34]

This was initially championed by John Cook Wilson (1849–1915), Wykeham Professor of Logic at New College, Oxford. It went on to gain support from Edgar F. Carritt, Horace William Brindley Joseph (1867–1943), and Harold Arthur Prichard (1871–1947).[35] Lewis adopted this as his "New Look," and became an enthusiastic advocate of this form of realism, which was quite distinct from the forms that were then associated with the University of Cambridge on the one hand, and Vienna on the other.[36]

The personal influence of Edgar Carritt, Lewis's tutor at University College, appears to have been significant here. Lewis's diary for this period makes frequent reference to him, hinting that his role became that of a mentor rather than that simply of a tutor. For example, in February 1924, Lewis dined with Carritt, who gave him a copy of the announcement of an official fellowship in philosophy at Trinity College.[37] When this came to nothing, Carritt's support led to Lewis being appointed to teach philosophy at University College during his year of absence in the United States. But was Carritt's support here reflective merely of Lewis's professional competence? Or did it reflect a more fundamental approbation of Lewis's philosophical views at this time, which seem to have been close to Carritt's?

Although the roots of the form of realism that was capturing the Oxford mind in the early 1920s are traditionally traced to Moore and Russell, Lewis makes little reference to either in his correspondence of this period. Indeed, this "Oxford Realism" took a form seemingly detached from its Cambridge roots, shaped locally by the specific ideas of its Oxford advocates.[38] This movement, so important to a proper understanding of Lewis's intellectual development, has received little scholarly attention. "Oxford Realism is an important chapter of twentieth-century British philosophy that has been largely consigned to oblivion."[39] Yet one cannot quite understand sections of *Surprised by Joy* without at least a basic understanding of its themes and problems.

The fundamental assumption of realism is that objects of knowledge are independent of the act of knowing. Knowing makes no difference to what is known. This commitment was shared by the leading representatives of realism at both Oxford and Cambridge in the early 1920s. Coming to know something is about discovery, not invention. Cook Wilson made this point with characteristic confidence:[40]

> The man who first discovered that equable curvature meant equidistance from a point didn't suppose he had "produced" the truth – that absolutely contradicts the idea of truth – nor that he had changed the nature of the circle or curvature, or of the straight line, or of anything spatial.

Pritchard took a similar view, arguing against a constructivist approach to truth:[41]

> Knowledge unconditionally presupposes that the reality known exists independently of the knowledge of it, and that we know it as it exists in this independence. It is simply *impossible* to think that any reality depends on our knowledge of it. If there is to be knowledge, there must first *be* something to be known.

Lewis concurred with this: as a "realist," he and others like him "accepted as rock-bottom reality the universe revealed by the senses."[42]

Yet a few years later, Lewis had moved away from this position. Why? The answer lies not in any basic difficulties with the assumption that there is some fundamental reality that may be known, but rather in the question of how this insight is to be developed and applied in areas such as morality or aesthetics. In his 1912 paper "Does Moral Philosophy Rest on a Mistake?," Pritchard argued that people possessed an immediate, intuitive moral apprehension, which tells them how to act in a given situation.[43] This "moral knowledge" was not a matter of argument, but was essentially a form of self-evident knowledge or intuition.

This view was taken up within "Oxford Realism" in the period immediately following the Great War, leading to the evolution of "Intuitionism."[44] Carritt's aesthetics, which draw on the ideas of the Italian philosopher Benedetto Croce (1866–1952), similarly regard beauty as essentially intuitive and expressive. "Art is vision or intuition."[45] It is this line of thought that Lewis appears to have accepted around this time, without reflecting fully on its implications. As he puts it in *Surprised by Joy*: "We maintained . . . that our moral judgement was 'valid,' and our aesthetic experience not merely pleasing but 'valuable.'"[46]

But could these intuitions be trusted? In conversation with Owen Barfield (1898–1997), Lewis began to experience doubts – not about the idea of some fundamental reality, but about the validity of the thought processes that lead to some things being judged as ugly and others as beautiful, some actions as good and as others evil. "Oxford Realism," Lewis came to realize, affirmed the validity of certain aesthetic and moral intuitions without any informing theory of knowledge which prevented these from lapsing into some kind of radical subjectivism.[47]

By about 1923, Lewis was in the process of moving away from "Oxford Realism" to embrace a form of "Absolute Idealism." He retained his belief in a universe revealed by the senses. However, he came to realize that his affirmation of a nature that was "quite independent of our observation," "something other" than ourselves, demanded a greater vision of reality, which extended to the way in which we think and reason. Lewis came to the conclusion – already familiar to him from his studies of classic Greek philosophy – that there was some "first principle" embedded within the universe and human reason, that enabled it to reason aright, in conformity with a deeper vision of reality. "Our logic was participation in a cosmic *Logos*."[48]

This insight did not lead Lewis to theism, still less to Christianity. Perhaps we might suggest that Lewis's view of God was similar to that found in Cambridge Platonism, especially the writings of Henry More (1614–87), which Lewis studied in some detail in 1924.[49] This new "philosophical monism"[50] seems to have led him to realize the importance of an overall vision of reality – a Platonic *synoptikon* – that could weave together rational, moral, and aesthetic threads into a coherent whole, holding them together in a unified manner, rather than as a loose and unconnected bundle. This colligatory vision would enable the "reconciliation of all contraries, the transcendence of all finitude."[51] Yet although this idea was not theistic in nature, it ultimately proved for Lewis to be theistic in its outcomes.

The critical issue was whether this cosmic *Logos* was simply a quiescent intellectual principle, or an active agent. In view of the importance of this theme to Lewis's changing "look," we shall consider this in more detail.

The "Treaty with Reality"

One aspect of Lewis's realism has not received the attention that it demands – namely, his attempts to limit reality to the intellectually manageable and controllable. Recent works on human resilience in the face of trauma have emphasized the importance of sustaining a sense of coherence as a means of coping with seemingly senseless or irrational events, particularly those which involve suffering.[52] As many such studies have suggested, the maintenance of sanity is often dependent on being able to sustain a "sense of coherence" – for example, by discerning meaning within traumatic events, or controlling or repressing a sense of incoherence.[53]

Lewis's "treaty with reality" appears to be an example of this kind of coping strategy, whether Lewis explicitly devised it for such purposes or not. This theme of limiting the impact of disturbing ideas first emerges in Lewis's correspondence during the Great War, and plays an important role in his initial resistance to Christianity. During the early 1920s, Lewis saw philosophy not simply as a human attempt to understand reality, but as a means of modulating its impact. Like T. S. Eliot, Lewis appears to have realized that "Humankind cannot bear very much reality."[54] Reality had to be filtered or tempered, in order for human beings to cope with it – especially when it seemed meaningless and pointless. Many who experienced the horror and trauma of the Great War experienced such thoughts, and found them to be destructive. Lewis kept the memory of that war at a safe distance, as he explains in *Surprised by Joy*.[55]

> I put the war on one side to a degree which some people will think shameful and some incredible. Others will call it a flight from reality. I maintain that it was rather a treaty with reality, the fixing of a frontier.

The highly suggestive phrase "a treaty with reality" – which occurs four times around this point in *Surprised by Joy* – merits closer reflection. This potent image concerns the fixing and patrolling of borders, ensuring that potentially disturbing and destructive thoughts do not gain entry, capturing the soul. One of the themes that Lewis recalls as being of importance to the period of his "New Look" is personal autonomy. Lewis wished to be in control of things – of his life, and his thoughts. Lewis persuaded himself that he was not indulging in any kind of escapism. He was not *denying* reality; he was simply limiting its impact.

Lewis's narrative of his conversion in *Surprised by Joy* makes much of this theme. The image of a "treaty with reality" suggests a radical and comprehensive compartmentalization of thought that enables troubling and disturbing thoughts to be locked away, so that they did not disturb everyday life.[56] Lewis's "New Look" shaped what he saw, preventing him from appreciating the significance of what he read. It was a filter, which protected him by constant reinterpretation of observation, limiting its capacity to subvert. Yet in the end, the illusion could not be maintained. As Lewis later reflected, "I must have been as blind as a bat not to have seen, long before, the ludicrous contradiction between my theory of life and my actual experiences as a reader."[57]

Yet this failure makes perfect sense, if Lewis's ability to "see" – note Lewis's characteristic use of an ocular metaphor (to be discussed further at 83–104) – was inhibited by a controlling worldview which, in effect, *determined* what he saw. Reality might be observed; it would not be allowed to interfere with his settled pattern of thought. Lewis believed that he had established firm and inviolable intellectual frontiers, which insulated him from ideas that might overwhelm him – such as God. Yet such a treaty could only work if Lewis was able to control ideas. What if God were an active agent? If God were to assault and infiltrate Lewis's intellectual frontiers?

The essential point to appreciate here is that Lewis's "treaty with reality" was unilateral. It was constructed, imposed, and policed by Lewis himself, on the tacit understanding that reality was passive, and Lewis was active. Lewis was in control; there would be no "interference" – a notion that Lewis loathed – from outside. The nature of reality might at times impose limits on what Lewis could think; nevertheless, it was evident that Lewis was the active agent in this process of evaluation, determining how he would assess and respond to the external world.

So what if reality – or a significant element of reality – were *active*? What if Lewis's implicit assumption of the unilateral activity and autonomy of the thinking agent were incorrect? What if God were not an additional item in the inventory of the universe, like some teapot orbiting the sun, but was a transcendent, active agent? If this were the case, Lewis's "treaty with reality" was vulnerable. For in the end, this was a treaty Lewis had made with himself; reality had not been consulted.

In *The Abolition of Man*, Lewis explores two radically opposed understandings of how the human mind responds to reality – to respond, and to control. On the one hand are those who allow their thinking to be shaped by reality, irrespective of what they wish to be true; on the other are those who already know what form reality must take, and see only what they wish to see. For one, theory is shaped by reality; for the other, reality is determined by theory.[58]

> There is something which unites magic and applied science while separating both from the "wisdom" of earlier ages. For the wise men of old the cardinal problem had been how to conform the soul to reality, and the solution had been knowledge, self-discipline, and virtue. For magic and applied science alike the problem is how to subdue reality to the wishes of men.

The views that Lewis criticizes in this important analysis seem to be those he himself adopted as a younger man. In *Surprised by Joy*, Lewis attributes the final stage in the collapse of his intellectual "treaty with reality" to reading the French philosopher Henri Bergson (1859–1941), which finally put paid to "any idea of a treaty or compromise with reality."[59]

In the mid-1920s, Lewis saw the safeguarding of his personal autonomy as demanding a policed frontier, a carefully controlled threshold to his soul. One enemy remained. One threat to his autonomy could not be ignored. For Lewis, the Christian notion of God entailed interference with his thoughts – even an invasion of his soul.[60]

> No word in my vocabulary expressed deeper hatred than the word *Interference*. But Christianity placed at the centre what then seemed to me a transcendental

Interferer. If its picture were true then no sort of "treaty with reality" could ever be possible.

In the narrative of his conversion, Lewis increasingly refers to an active and *questing* God, pounding on the door of Lewis's mind and his life, refusing to respect any "treaty with reality." Reality was imposing itself upon him, vigorously and aggressively demanding a response. "Amiable agnostics will talk cheerfully about 'man's search for God'. To me, as I then was, they might as well have talked about the mouse's search for the cat."[61] In early 1930,[62] Lewis discovered that he could no longer domesticate reality. Like a tiger, it refused to be constrained by its artificial cage. It broke free, and overwhelmed its former captor. "The reality with which no treaty can be made was upon me."[63]

Lewis's recovery of belief in God also reflects his growing realization that the ideas of the past are not necessarily to be dismissed as outdated and defunct; they are sometimes rejected by modernity precisely because they pose a threat to its intellectual hegemony, raising awkward questions about the defensibility of his ideas. In what follows, we shall consider Lewis's growing realization of the shallowness of what he famously termed "chronological snobbery."

Chronological Snobbery

For many in the 1920s – such as the "Bright Young People" – it was obvious that the latest was the best. Old ideas and values were dismissed as outmoded and discredited, retaining their cultural credibility only through an indefensible amalgam of cultural nostalgia and intellectual laziness. As a teenager, Lewis deployed the latest scientific theories about the origins of religion to ridicule the beliefs of his confidant, Arthur Greeves (1895–1966). All religions, Lewis declared in October 1916, were simply mythologies invented by human beings, usually in response to natural events or emotional needs. This, he declared, was "the recognised scientific account of the growth of religions."[64]

Lewis later came to develop a formal definition of this attitude, and give it a name – "chronological snobbery," which he defined as "the uncritical acceptance of the intellectual climate of our own age and the assumption that whatever has gone out of date is on that count discredited."[65] Lewis first became suspicious of this uncritical affirmation of the present through conversations with his close friend Owen Barfield, who raised awkward questions about its assumptions and outcomes.[66]

Was it ever refuted (and if so by whom, where and how conclusively) or did it merely die away as fashions do? If the latter, this tells us nothing about its truth or falsehood. From seeing this, one passes to the realization that our own age is also a "period," and certainly has, like all periods, its own characteristic illusions. They are likeliest to lurk in those widespread assumptions which are so ingrained in the age that no one dares to attack or feels it necessary to defend them.

The logic of Lewis's argument is difficult to refute. It marks a dawning realization that the study of the past helps us to appreciate that the ideas and values of our own age are just as provisional and transient as those of bygone ages. The intelligent and reflective engagement with the thought of a bygone era ultimately subverts any notion of "chronological snobbery." Reading past texts makes it clear that what we now term "the past" was once "the present," which proudly yet falsely regarded itself as having found the right intellectual answers or moral values that had eluded its predecessors. As Lewis later put it, "all that is not eternal is eternally out of date."[67]

Lewis realized that future historians would regard our own age as simply as a "period," with its own fixations and assumptions – whereas we tend to regard it as the privileged vantage point from which we may judge others. Instead of being at the end of the process, able to judge its ideas from a totalizing perspective, we are *within* the process, unable to discern its final outcome or consensus. Lewis's "New Look" was simply a transient moment, not a permanent and stable outcome.

For Lewis, this realization offered a double motivation for the study of the past. The *strangeness* of the past, when rightly understood, offered a confirmation of the future's perception that our own present will one day be seen in the same way. Studying the past thus subverts any pretensions to finality on the part of the present. Yet more importantly, it makes available ideas and resources which can challenge, enrich, redirect, and refresh our perceptions of reality. To make sense of the literature of the classical or Renaissance periods, we have to learn to "suspend most of the responses and unlearn most of the habits" that result from "reading modern literature" – such as an uncritical assumption of the intrinsic superiority of our own situation, and our privileged position as observers.[68]

The New Psychology

One of the most decisive influences on the shaping of western culture after the Great War was the new psychoanalytical view of Sigmund Freud

(1856–1939). For Freud himself, these theories were like a tidal wave, sweeping away naive human understandings of their own mental processes. In 1917, Freud declared that humanity had been the subject of three "narcissistic wounds" in the modern age, each of which challenged the human sense of self-importance.[69] The first such wound, Freud argued, was inflicted by the Copernican revolution, which showed that human beings did not stand at the center of the universe, but were at its periphery. The second was the Darwinian demonstration that humanity did not even have a unique place on the planet earth.

And what of the third? Freud perhaps somewhat immodestly suggested that this was his own demonstration that humanity was not even the master of its own limited realm. Ideas are shaped by hidden psychological forces, over which we have little control. According to Freud, each of these revolutions added to the pain and wounds inflicted by its predecessor, forcing a radical re-evaluation of the place and significance of humanity.

Lewis was affected by this revolution in the world of understanding our inner selves. As we noted earlier, one of Lewis's central concerns was the reliability of our intuitions. What if they were ultimately shaped by dark, irrational forces, over which we had no control, and which we did not fully understand? Freud's analysis of wish-fulfillment seemed especially destructive to Lewis. "What, I asked myself, were all my delectable mountains and western gardens but sheer Fantasies?"[70] So what Lewis had once revered, he now reviled. He had "seen through" his youthful fantasies, and discovered what they really were – dangerous deceptions and delusions. He would never, he declared, allow himself to be taken in again by such nonsense. His experience of "Joy" was merely a fantasy.

It is difficult to identify precisely when Lewis broke free from the influence of this way of thinking. Yet there is no doubt that he did. *The Pilgrim's Regress*, written in August 1932, is to be seen as Lewis's own account of his spiritual journey, in which he traveled down roads which he believed to lead to the truth, only to find they were dead ends. In the narrative, the pilgrim – John – meets old Mr Enlightenment and his son, Sigismund Enlightenment. Although it soon becomes clear the father and son have had some significant disagreements, Lewis portrays Freud – whose forename was originally "Sigismund" – as the offspring of nineteenth-century rationalism, characterized by its dismissal of everything desirable as wish-fulfillment, the "things people *wish* to believe."[71] In conversation with Sigismund, the pilgrim explains that he is seeking for a very special island. Sigismund retorts that there is no such place. Since the pilgrim desires such an island, it is really a wish-fulfillment, a figment of his imagination.

In the end, the pilgrim is thrown in jail, where he meets a young boy who has been made to learn his rationalist catechism by rote. "Argument," he recites in a parrot-like fashion, "is the attempted rationalization of the arguer's desires."[72] As such, rational argument is impossible, being simply an articulation of an unrecognized subliminal desire. This point is brought out when the pilgrim meets Reason, who explains to him how the "Spirit of the Age" is fundamentally ambivalent about reason.[73]

> If anyone argues with them they say that he is rationalizing his own desires, and therefore need not be answered. But if anyone listens to them, they will argue themselves to show that their own doctrines are true.

Reason is affirmed when it works in favor of the "Spirit of the Age," and rejected when it works against it. Puzzled, the pilgrim asks what strategy he should adopt in the face of such a bizarre argument. He receives the following reply.[74]

> You must ask them whether any reasoning is valid or not. If they say no, then their own doctrines, being reached by reasoning, fall to the ground. If they say yes, then they will have to examine your arguments and refute them on their merits: for if some reasoning is valid, for all they know, your bit of reasoning may be one of the valid bits.

Lewis's reflections on the integrity of human reasoning would later form an important element of his critique of certain forms of naturalism, to be noted in a later essay. We must now consider the final element of Lewis's "New Look" – his scientific reductionism.

Scientific Reductionism

Lewis's "New Look" can be regarded as an attempt to drill down to the bedrock of reality – to believe only that which is securely and reliably established. Anything that lay beyond the scope of rational or scientific demonstration was, in his view, to be regarded as belonging to the subjective realm of sentimentality. There would be no more "flirtations with any idea of the supernatural, no romantic delusions." Lewis was in "retreat, almost a panic-stricken flight, from all that sort of romanticism which had hitherto been the chief concern of my life."[75]

This process of developing philosophical "good sense" – which can be seen as anticipated during Lewis's years at Bookham, under the tutelage of William Kirkpatrick – led Lewis into a minimalist world, shaped by a forlorn love for things he was coming to realize were imaginary, and whose truths were defined by, and limited to, the cold realities of logic and science. Lewis realized he had "to care for almost nothing but the gods and heroes, the garden of the Hesperides, Launcelot and the Grail, and to believe in nothing but atoms and evolution and military service."[76] This reductionist resolve to "believe in nothing but atoms and evolution" was an integral part of Lewis's "New Look." Yet by 1925, Lewis was clearly in the process of putting such ideas behind him.

There are hints of such a transition in Lewis's writings of the period. In his diary entry for January 4, 1924, Lewis reflected on Bertrand Russell's atheist manifesto "The Free Man's Worship" (1903).[77] While noting that this provided "a very clear and noble statement of what I myself believed a few years ago," Lewis commented that it failed to engage "the real difficulty" – namely, that "our ideals are after all a natural product, facts with a relation to other facts, and cannot survive the condemnation of the fact as a whole." It is an important reflection, as it indicates that Lewis now regarded Russell's form of atheism as something he had left behind, and that he was alert to the vulnerability of this form of "naturalism."

Lewis's correspondence with his father portrays his break with his "New Look" in a manner that differs somewhat from the account given in *Surprised by Joy*. In a letter of August 1925 to his father, reflecting on his decision to abandon the study of philosophy in favor of English language and literature, Lewis explained something of his thinking.[78] Writing on the eve of formally becoming a Tutorial Fellow of Magdalen College, Lewis declared himself glad to have left the "bleak and questioning atmosphere" of pure philosophy. Yet he also indicated that his time reflecting on philosophical issues had helped him sort things out, liberating him from his earlier "shallow pessimisms."[79]

> I am not condemning philosophy. Indeed in turning from it to literary history and criticism, I am conscious of a descent: and if the air on the heights did not suit me, still I have brought back something of value. It will be a comfort to me all my life to know that the scientist and the materialist have not the last word: that Darwin and Spencer undermining ancestral beliefs stand themselves on a foundation of sand; of gigantic and irreconcilable contradictions an inch below the surface.

From what we know of Lewis's views in the early 1920s, it seems that he deliberately distanced himself from two highly questionable attitudes toward the natural sciences, memorably defined by Richard Olson as "science defied" and "science deified."[80] Lewis's circle in the early 1920s included thinkers – such as Owen Barfield and Cecil Harwood – who were inclined to dismiss science on the basis of their spiritual inclinations. Barfield's anthroposophy led him to be suspicious of any form of empiricism, and critical of any attempt to elevate the limited provisionalities of the natural sciences into a philosophy of life.

Others, however, took the view that science defined the foundation and limits of human knowledge. Bertrand Russell, for example, ended his famous essay on the relation of science and ethics with a bold statement to this effect: "Whatever knowledge is attainable, must be attained by scientific methods; and what science cannot discover, mankind cannot know."[81]

While Lewis was too much of a rationalist in the classic, Aristotelian sense to follow Barfield into some kind of pantheistic gnosticism, he was equally alert to the epistemological contradictions and imaginative impoverishment that radical empiricism seemed to him to entail. Lewis developed his own approach which celebrated the successes of the sciences, while criticizing inflated metaphysical doctrines or worldviews constructed on their basis. Lewis engaged in an extensive critique of various forms of reductionism, particularly during the 1940s.[82] The lines of argument used in those pieces appear to parallel those Lewis used against his own "New Look" in the early 1920s.

Perhaps the most important of these is found in his paper "The Funeral of a Great Myth,"[83] which probably dates from the late 1940s, but clearly echoes Lewis's crystallizing perceptions of the later 1920s. In this paper, Lewis argues that provisional scientific theories about evolution have been hijacked by those with social and cultural agendas, and transformed from a scientific theory into a worldview – the "Great Myth" of "popular Evolutionism."[84] A provisional scientific theory, limited in scope and open to revision in the light of evidence, is hijacked and represented as a cultural metanarrative, which holds that everything is improving, moving "onwards and upwards." Lewis sees this "popular evolutionism" mirrored and expounded somewhat uncritically in the writings of H. G. Wells (1866–1946), George Bernard Shaw (1856–1950), and Olaf Stapledon (1886–1950).[85]

Lewis's later writings show little interest in understanding recent developments in either the physical or biological sciences. His concern is not with the natural sciences as such, but with the cultural appropriation or manipulation of their methods to serve certain "imaginative and emotional needs."[86] His "Ransom Trilogy" remains one of the most discerning critiques of the moral and metaphysical inflation of scientific discourse.

Although Lewis disagreed with Barfield at points over his attitude toward the natural sciences, he had little doubt that Barfield was right in emphasizing their influence, whether direct or indirect, on shaping cultural assumptions about the world. As Barfield remarked:[87]

> You will sometimes hear people say that they have no metaphysics. Well, they are lying. Their metaphysics are implicit in what they take for granted about the world. Only they prefer to call it "common sense."

Lewis's *The Abolition of Man* explores and critiques the "scientistic" way of thinking that Lewis believed then pervaded western culture, with negative implications for the deeper way of understanding and inhabiting nature that Lewis wished to encourage.

Once more, Lewis proves to be at his most perceptive when criticizing views he once held himself. In *The Pilgrim's Regress*, Lewis engages with "false answers" to the great questions of life, noting disarmingly that one of his few qualifications for doing so is that he himself was deluded by each of them, while having "contemplated each of them earnestly enough to discover the cheat."[88] Mr Enlightenment's list of popular scientific arguments against theistic belief[89] can be seen as an expansion of Lewis's own position during the early 1920s, when he adopted the "wholesome" position that he would believe in nothing but "atoms and evolution."

Conclusion

Much research remains to be done on Lewis's changing views during the 1920s. Although there is no reason to doubt the general account of his changing ideas offered by Lewis in his autobiography *Surprised by Joy*, these reflections lack chronological specificity, and at times seem intellectually disconnected. While there is no reason to doubt that there is a coherent narrative underlying these reflections, which allows them to be woven together into a continuous account of transformation and development, it is not easy to identify all the critical landmarks along the road from the "New Look" to a recovered belief in God, nor the precise role which they played in effecting Lewis's intellectual transition. In an earlier essay, we raised concerns about reliability of Lewis's correlation of events in his inner and outer worlds (17–21), and it may be that further nuancing of Lewis's autobiographical memories will be necessary, once this more coherent narrative is established.

Any more detailed attempt to understand Lewis's "New Look" must include an assessment of the Oxford individuals known to have shaped Lewis's changing convictions, yet who have not received the critical attention due to them – most notably, the philosophers Edgar F. Carritt and John Alexander Smith. Lewis was clearly linked to a series of Oxford academic networks during the 1920s, and it is important to trace these connections as a means of assessing possible influences, and their outcomes. This short essay is intended to map out areas for further exploration, as we try to gain a more comprehensive understanding of both Lewis's intellectual development, and the Oxford academic context of the 1920s.

Yet perhaps the most important conclusion of a study of Lewis's "New Look" is this: that most of the positions that Lewis criticized so effectively, especially during the 1940s, were positions he once held himself. His critique of those positions proved plausible precisely because Lewis had developed his arguments in criticizing his own ideas. And having emerged from the "New Look," Lewis believed that he was well qualified to help others do the same – whether in breaking free from those ideas of the early 1920s, where they were still taken seriously, or in their more recent variants.

Notes

1 McGrath, *C. S. Lewis – A Life*, 44–7.

2 Peter Simkins, *Kitchener's Army: The Raising of the New Armies 1914 1916.* Manchester: Manchester University Press, 1988; Adrian Gregory, *The Last Great War: British Society and the First World War.* Cambridge: Cambridge University Press, 2008, 70–111.

3 J. M. Winter, "Oxford and the First World War." In *The History of the University of Oxford: Volume VIII: The Twentieth Century*, edited by Brian Harrison, 3–26. Oxford: Clarendon Press, 1994. For the specific situation in which University College then found itself, see Robin Darwall-Smith, *A History of University College, Oxford*. Oxford: Oxford University Press, 2008, 440–7.

4 See, for example, Paul Fussell, *The Great War and Modern Memory*. Oxford: Oxford University Press, 1975; Modris Eksteins, *Rites of Spring: The Great War and the Birth of the Modern Age*. Boston: Houghton Mifflin, 1989.

5 See the review in Belinda Davies, "Experience, Identity, and Memory: The Legacy of World War I." *Journal of Modern History* 75 (2003): 111–31.

6 Robert A. Nisbet, *History of the Idea of Progress*. New York: Basic Books, 1980, 321–2.

7 For the wider significance of Freud's influence during the inter-war period, see Mark Edmundson, *The Death of Sigmund Freud: Fascism, Psychoanalysis and the Rise of Fundamentalism*. London: Bloomsbury, 2007.

8 Carl Krockel, *War Trauma and English Modernism: T. S. Eliot and D. H. Lawrence*. New York: Palgrave Macmillan, 2011.

9   For the best account of this development and its cultural background, see Bruce L. McCormack, *Karl Barth's Critically Realistic Dialectical Theology: Its Genesis and Development 1909–1936*. Oxford: Clarendon Press, 1995, 78–202.

10   Jay Winter, *Sites of Memory, Sites of Mourning: The Great War in European Cultural History*. Cambridge: Cambridge University Press, 1995, 54–77; Alexandra Owen, *The Place of Enchantment: British Occultism and the Culture of the Modern*. Chicago: University of Chicago Press, 2004.

11   For some of the issues that led to this perception, see Shannon Ty Bontrager, "The Imagined Crusade: The Church of England and the Mythology of Nationalism and Christianity during the Great War." *Church History* 71, no. 4 (2002): 774–98.

12   Steven E. Aschheim, "Nazism, Culture and the Origins of Totalitarianism: Hannah Arendt and the Discourse of Evil." *New German Critique* 70 (1997): 117–39.

13   This radical questioning of pre-war intellectual and moral values by Oxford students in the 1920s is reflected in Christopher Hollis, *Oxford in the Twenties*. London: Heinemann, 1976. For a study of cultural trends in the younger metropolitan upper classes England during this period, see D. J. Taylor, *Bright Young People: The Lost Generation of London's Jazz Age*. New York: Farrar, Straus and Giroux, 2009. As a middle-class Ulsterman, Lewis was never part of Oxford's elitist student culture of the 1920s, famously captured in Evelyn Waugh's *Brideshead Revisited* (1945).

14   *Surprised by Joy*, 234.

15   McGrath, *C. S. Lewis – A Life*, 80–3.

16   For the works Lewis would have studied, see G. R. G. Mure, "Oxford and Philosophy." *Philosophy* 12 (1937): 291–301.

17   McGrath, *C. S. Lewis – A Life*, 80–2.

18   See H. W. B. Joseph, "The Concept of Evolution," in *Essays in Ancient and Modern Philosophy*. Oxford: Oxford University Press, 1935, 303–34; idem, *The Labour Theory of Value in Karl Marx*. Oxford, Oxford University Press, 1923.

19   McGrath, *C. S. Lewis – A Life*, 63–4, 69–70.

20   *Surprised by Joy*, 74, citing what appears to be Lewis's own translation of Lucretius, *de natura rerum*, II.180–1. For Lewis as a translator of Latin poetry, see *C. S. Lewis's Lost Aeneid: Arms and the Exile*, edited by A. T. Reves. New Haven, CT: Yale University Press, 2011.

21   Eric Baker, "Lucretius in the European Enlightenment." In *The Cambridge Companion to Lucretius*, edited by Stuart Gillespie and Philip Hardie, 274–88. Cambridge: Cambridge University Press, 2007.

22   *Surprised by Joy*, 200.

23   *Spirits in Bondage*, 25.

24   For the religious complexities of the period immediately following the Great War in England, see Alex Owen, "The 'Religious Sense' in a Post-War Secular Age." *Past and Present* 1, Supplement 1 (2006): 159–77. More generally, see Ross McKibbin, *Classes and Cultures: England 1918–1951*. Oxford: Oxford University Press, 1998, 272–95.

25 *Surprised by Joy*, 197.

26 *Surprised by Joy*, 201.

27 Letter to Leo Baker, September 25, 1920; *Letters*, vol. 1, 509.

28 *Surprised by Joy*, 264.

29 *Surprised by Joy*, 259.

30 *All My Road Before Me*, 431–2.

31 See Denys P. Leighton, *The Greenian Moment: T. H. Green, Religion, and Political Argument in Victorian Britain*. Charlottesville, VA: Imprint Academic, 2004, 129–227.

32 Paul Montagné, *Un radical religieux en Angleterre au XIXe siècle ou la philosophie de Thomas Hill Green*. Toulouse: Ouvrière, 1927; Melvin Richter, "T. H. Green and His Audience: Liberalism as a Surrogate Faith." *Review of Politics* 18 (1956): 444–72.

33 The classic paper here was G. E. Moore, "The Refutation of Idealism." *Mind* 12 (1903): 433–53. For the Edwardian background, see James Patrick, *The Magdalen Metaphysicals: Idealism and Orthodoxy at Oxford, 1901–1945*. Macon, GA: Mercer University Press, 1985, 1–22; Omar W. Nasim, *Bertrand Russell and the Edwardian Philosophers: Constructing the World*. New York: Palgrave Macmillan, 2008. The views of Samuel Alexander should be noted here, in view of Lewis's high estimation of his later distinction between "contemplation" and "enjoyment": Samuel Alexander, "The Basis of Realism." *Proceedings of the British Academy* 6 (1914): 279–314.

34 Isaiah Berlin remarked that Oxford realism developed initially from "the writings of a forgotten Oxford philosopher at the turn of the century, aimed at refutation of the prevailing Hegelian philosophy in dry Aristotelian terms." Ramin Jahanbegloo, *Conversations with Isaiah Berlin*. London: Peter Halban, 1992, 153. The "forgotten" philosopher was presumably Cook Wilson.

35 See especially H. W. B. Joseph, "The Psychological Explanation of the Development of the Perception of External Objects." *Mind* 19 (1910): 306–21; 457–69; 20 (1911): 161–80.

36 For developments at Vienna in the 1930s, see Barry Gower, "Cassirer, Schlick and 'Structural Realism': The Philosophy of the Exact Sciences in the Background to Early Logical Empiricism." *British Journal for the History of Philosophy* 8 (2000): 71–106.

37 *All My Road before Me*, 292.

38 See the definitive study of Mathieu Marion, "Oxford Realism: Knowledge and Perception." *British Journal for the History of Philosophy* 8 (2000): 299–338; 485–519.

39 Marion, "Oxford Realism," 299.

40 John Cook Wilson, *Statement and Inference*. Oxford: Oxford University Press, 1926, 802. For a useful discussion of the positions of Cook Wilson and Prichard, see Jens Kohne, *Knowledge as a Mental State? A Study on Oxford Realism*. Berlin: Logos, 2010, 39–98.

41 H. A. Prichard, *Kant's Theory of Knowledge*. Oxford, Oxford University Press, 1909, 108.

42   *Surprised by Joy*, 242.
43   H. A. Prichard, "Does Moral Philosophy Rest on a Mistake?" *Mind* 21 (1912): 21–37.
44   John Laird, "Les moralistes contemporains à Oxford et la renaissance de l'intuitionnisme." *Recherches philosophiques* 1 (1932): 235–52. Recent scholarship has seen a renewal of interest in such an approach: see, for example, Wulf Kellerwessel, "Kritische Anmerkung zur Reevaluierung des moral-philosophischen Intuitionismus." *Prima Philosophia* 17 (2004): 81–102.
45   Edgar J. Carritt, *Philosophies of Beauty from Socrates to Robert Bridges: Being the Source of Aesthetic Theory*. Oxford: Oxford University Press, 1931, 233. Note also Carritt's approving reference to Croce on intuition in art (302).
46   *Surprised by Joy*, 242.
47   *Surprised by Joy*, 242.
48   *Surprised by Joy*, 243.
49   Lewis's serious study of More began in January 1924: *All My Road before Me*, 280–1. See further James Patrick, "C. S. Lewis and Idealism." In *A Christian for All Christians: Essays in Honour of C. S. Lewis*, edited by Andrew Walker and James Patrick, 156–73. London: Hodder & Stoughton, 1990.
50   For the phrase, see *Surprised by Joy*, 243: "This sort of philosophical monism was the philosophy of my New Look."
51   *Surprised by Joy*, 244.
52   Bessel van der Kolk and Alexander McFarlane, "The Black Hole of Trauma." In *Traumatic Stress: The Effects of Overwhelming Experience on Mind, Body and Society*, edited by Bessel van der Kolk, Alexander McFarlane, and Lars Weisaeth, 3–23. London: Guildford Press, 1996; Irene Smith Landsman, "Crises of Meaning in Trauma and Loss." In *Loss of the Assumptive World: A Theory of Traumatic Loss*, edited by Jeffrey Kauffman, 13–30. New York: Brunner-Routledge, 2002.
53   See the landmark work of Aaron Antonovsky, *Health, Stress and Coping*. San Francisco: Jossey-Bass Publishers, 1979. For a recent evaluation of this approach, see Monica Eriksson and Bengt Lindström, "Validity of Antonovsky's 'Sense of Coherence' Scale: A Systematic Review." *Journal of Epidemiology and Community Health* 59 (2005): 460–6.
54   T. S. Eliot, Quartet No. 1, *Burnt Norton* (1935), part 1.
55   *Surprised by Joy*, 183.
56   There are clear parallels here with the Renaissance *ars oblivionalis*, discussed in the previous essay: 13–14.
57   *Surprised by Joy*, 248.
58   *The Abolition of Man*, 77.
59   *Surprised by Joy*, 238.
60   *Surprised by Joy*, 199.
61   *Surprised by Joy*, 265.
62   This development is traditionally dated to 1929; for the reasons for believing that it took place in 1930, see McGrath, *C. S. Lewis – A Life*, 141–5. See also the earlier essay in this collection, "The Enigma of Autobiography," 7–29.

63 *Surprised by Joy*, 265.

64 Letter to Arthur Greeves, October 12(?), 1916; *Letters*, vol. 1, 230–1.

65 *Surprised by Joy*, 241.

66 *Surprised by Joy*, 241.

67 *The Four Loves*, 166.

68 A similar point is made by Rowan Williams, *Why Study the Past? The Quest for the Historical Church*. London: Darton, Longman, and Todd, 2005, 4–31. Williams suggests that it is only when we are struck by the incongruence of the past with the present that we begin to see a need for studying history.

69 Sigmund Freud, "A Difficulty in the Path of Psycho-Analysis." *Complete Psychological Works*. London: Hogarth Press, 1955, vol. 17, 137–44. For comment, see Peter Homans, *The Ability to Mourn: Disillusionment and the Social Origins of Psychoanalysis*. Chicago: University of Chicago Press, 1989, 75–7.

70 *Surprised by Joy*, 236–7.

71 *The Pilgrim's Regress*, 59.

72 *The Pilgrim's Regress*, 62.

73 *The Pilgrim's Regress*, 71.

74 *The Pilgrim's Regress*, 71–2.

75 *Surprised by Joy*, 234.

76 *Surprised by Joy*, 201.

77 *All My Road before Me*, 281. Lewis incorrectly refers to Russell's essay from memory by the title "Worship of a Free Man." The version of the essay that Lewis would have known was almost certainly that found in the library of the Oxford Union Society: Bertrand Russell, *Mysticism and Logic, and Other Essays*. London: Longmans, Green and Company, 1918, 46–57.

78 Lewis to his father, August 14, 1925; *Letters*, vol. 1, 646–9.

79 Lewis to his father, August 14, 1925; *Letters*, vol. 1, 649.

80 Richard Olson, *Science Deified and Science Defied: The Historical Significance of Science in Western Culture*. 2 vols. Berkeley, CA: University of California Press, 1982–90.

81 Bertrand Russell, *Religion and Science*. Oxford: Oxford University Press, 1997, 243.

82 For a more recent statement of such criticisms of naturalism, see Alvin Plantinga, *Where the Conflict Really Lies: Science, Religion, and Naturalism*. New York: Oxford University Press, 2011.

83 "The Funeral of a Great Myth"; *Essay Collection*, 22–32.

84 "The Funeral of a Great Myth," 24. For a more detailed examination of recent metaphysical inflations of Darwinism, see Alister E. McGrath, *Darwinism and the Divine: Evolutionary Thought and Natural Theology*. Oxford: Wiley-Blackwell, 2011, 27–40. Bertrand Russell's advocacy of the sterilization of the "mentally defective" in the 1920s represents a moral application of this "great myth": see Stephen Heathorn, "Explaining Russell's Eugenic Discourse in the 1920s." *Russell: The Journal of Bertrand Russell Studies* 25 (2005): 107–39.

85 Lewis's three works of science fiction engage their leading ideas. See David C. Downing, *Planets in Peril: A Critical Study of C. S. Lewis's Ransom Trilogy*.

Amherst, MA: University of Massachusetts Press, 1992; Sanford Schwartz, *C. S. Lewis on the Final Frontier: Science and the Supernatural in the Space Trilogy*. Oxford: Oxford University Press, 2009. Although Wells, Shaw, and Stapledon provided Lewis with a theological foil, there is little doubt that his own positive approach was shaped by David Lindsay's *Voyage to Arcturus* (1920).

86   "The Funeral of a Great Myth"; *Essay Collection*, 23.
87   Owen Barfield, *History, Guilt and Habit*. Middletown, CT: Wesleyan University Press, 1979, 15.
88   *The Pilgrim's Regress*, 8.
89   *The Pilgrim's Regress*, 35–7.

3

A Gleam of Divine Truth: The Concept of Myth in Lewis's Thought

"On the one side a many-islanded sea of poetry and myth; on the other a glib and shallow 'rationalism.'"[1] With these words in *Surprised by Joy* (1955), Lewis summarized the dilemma in which he found himself as a young man. His rationalism led him to deny what reason could not affirm; yet his imagination cried out for something deeper and more satisfying than the thin view of reality that this same rationalism offered.

Lewis's summary of his dilemma is, of course, framed in terms of later developments in his thought. The term "myth" in this statement has the developed, nuanced sense which Lewis adopted in the 1930s; in the 1910s and early 1920s, Lewis tended to use the word "myth" primarily in its popular sense, to mean a fabricated untruth, a story that was devoid of historical basis or rational significance. In bringing the "thin artillery of a seventeen year old rationalist"[2] to bombard the Christian faith of his friend Arthur Greeves, Lewis regularly used the term "myth" or "mythology" in this rationalist sense. In the modern age, Lewis declares, it is ridiculous to expect "educated and thinking" people to believe in "any old (& already decaying) superstition."[3]

Lewis's correspondence of the 1910s confirms the general themes that he later set out in *Surprised by Joy*. The young Lewis increasingly found himself torn between the intellectually parsimonious and the imaginatively rich – between a purely rational and historical account of things, which dismissed myths as primitive superstitions, and an awareness of their compelling imaginative power and beauty. They might be untrue; indeed, they might even have been contrived with the deliberate intention of deceiving. Nevertheless, they were lies "breathed through silver."[4]

The Intellectual World of C. S. Lewis, First Edition. Alister E. McGrath.
© 2014 John Wiley & Sons, Ltd. Published 2014 by John Wiley & Sons, Ltd.

At this point in his development, Lewis had clearly absorbed some key themes of the Enlightenment metanarrative, especially its belief in a linear trajectory of intellectual development away from primitive ways of thinking ("superstition" and "myth") toward an enlightened rationalism ("reason" and "science").[5] Myth was simply a primitive way of understanding and representing reality, which could be dispensed with in the light of modern knowledge. The Enlightenment proposed a rationalizing counter-narrative to its mythological antecedents, in effect dismissing the contemporary relevance of the category of "myth" on rhetorical as much as rational grounds.[6]

Yet this rationalist development left many dissatisfied, partly on account of its "thin" notion of rationality, and more significantly because of its obvious imaginative and aesthetic deficits.[7] English Romantic writers – such as John Keats (1795–1821) – realized both the imaginative and aesthetic potential of classical myths, and saw "remythologization" as a major constructive literary tool.[8] However, the lure of mythology was at its greatest in German Romanticism, which appealed to myths as a means of recovering and renewing a deeper mode of engagement with fundamental human questions, yearnings, and imaginative questings.[9] Greek and German myths were seen as embodying the deepest insights of humanity, which were deemed to be inaccessible to modernist rationalism.[10] August Wilhelm Schlegel (1767–1845) caught the mood of the age in 1811: "The poetry of the ancients was that of possession; ours is that of longing. The former stands on the ground of the present; the latter hovers between memory and anticipation."[11]

Although the cultural influence of this development can be seen in many German writers of the nineteenth century, it is perhaps seen at its most influential in the operas of Richard Wagner (1813–83). Wagner's notion of the *Gesamtkunstwerk* – a "total work of art" – can be seen as developing Schlegel's ideas at the musical, poetic, and dramatic levels.[12] In his operatic cycle *The Ring of the Nibelungs* (1848–74), Wagner created a mythical narrative of sin and redemption with immense imaginative appeal. One of those to be enchanted by its power was the young C. S. Lewis.

Lewis's correspondence with Arthur Greeves in the mid-1910s makes it clear that his imagination had been captivated by the rich mythology of Wagner's *Ring of the Nibelungs*.[13] Arthur Rackham's highly evocative illustrations to Wagner's libretto proved to be a powerful imaginative stimulus to Lewis, causing him to be overwhelmed by an experience of desire.[14] He was engulfed by "pure Northernness" – by a vision of "huge, clear spaces hanging above the Atlantic in the endless twilight of Northern summer."[15] Wagner's myth might be untrue, a mere artful product of human genius – but it seemed to hint at something deeper, lying beyond the narrow boundaries of Lewis's early rationalism.

Lewis's sense of liminality – of standing on the threshold of some greater vision of reality – was heightened further early in March 1916, when he read George MacDonald's fantasy novel *Phantastes*.[16] Somehow, MacDonald's prose enabled Lewis to trespass into the rationally forbidden, tasting its fruits before he realized the enormity of what he had done. "It is as if I were carried sleeping across the frontier, or as if I had died in the old country and could never remember how I came alive in the new."[17] MacDonald's narrative was like "the voice of the sirens," causing Lewis to crash against the rocks of a deeper vision of reality, his rationalism overwhelmed by the sheer beauty of its "bright shadow." The episode crystallized, without exhausting, Lewis's perception of his intellectual dilemma: "Nearly all that I believed to be real I believed to be imaginary; nearly all that I believed to be real I thought grim and meaningless."[18]

Lewis never succeeded in reconciling the tension between reason and imagination at this time. By the early 1920s, his atheism hardened by his experiences of the Great War, Lewis had arrived at what can only be described as an unstable intellectual equilibrium – a resting place, but not a resolution. How, Lewis wondered, could someone remain rational, while incorporating these deep longings and yearnings, these profound imaginative impulses, within a coherent way of thinking?

The answer lay ahead of him – largely, but not entirely, in a new way of understanding the nature of myths, and their role in human reflection on meaning and significance.[19] The literary concept of "myth" is of central importance to any understanding of Lewis's theological views, and their expression in his literary works. Lewis was aware of the limits and unhelpful associations of the word "myth," yet was not able to identify an existing word which denoted what he had in mind, nor to coin a new word adequate to his imaginative vision.[20]

While some popular Christian readers of Lewis, familiar only with the conceptually emaciated notion of myth as "fiction," regard this aspect of Lewis's thought with some apprehension and concern, it is seen by those familiar with the deeper meaning of the term as one of Lewis's most important and significant contributions, particularly to Christian theology and apologetics. It is generally accepted that the realization that the story of Christ was "God's myth" was instrumental in bringing about Lewis's conversion to Christianity in the autumn of 1931.[21]

Myth at Oxford, 1880–1930

To understand Lewis's intellectual breakthrough, we need to appreciate that Oxford University was the center of intensive reflection on the nature of myth in the late nineteenth and early twentieth centuries. As we noted earlier, cultural interest in comparative mythology had its origins in Germany during the late eighteenth and early nineteenth century, and is linked with the cultural history of the period – such as its aesthetic sympathies for classical Greek culture, and its dominant historical narrative of progress from superstition to reason.[22] There is little evidence of serious interest in these questions at Oxford, until the arrival of Max Müller (1823–1900).

Müller had studied Sanskrit at Leipzig and Berlin, and moved to England in 1846 in order to study some Sanskrit texts held in London at the offices of the East India Company.[23] This led to invitations to speak at Oxford, which led to several appointments at the university, including Oxford's first Professor of Comparative Philology (1868–75). Müller's work generated both interest and debate at Oxford on the nature and significance of myth. One of Müller's most influential ideas was that of the "solar myth," which held that the sun, dawn, morning, day, light, and energy (or their absence) were the core topics of Indo-European mythology.[24]

> The whole theogony and philosophy of the ancient world centred in the Dawn, the mother of the bright gods, of the sun in his various aspects, of the morn, the day, the spring; herself the brilliant image and visage of immortality.

Müller's research was primarily concerned with the origins of myth, rather than its literary impact. While Andrew Lang (1844–1912), a Fellow of Merton College, Oxford, from 1865 to 1874,[25] was severely critical of Müller's approach, he retained Müller's emphasis on the importance of accounting for the historical origins of myths, rather than exploring their imaginative and literary appeal.

Such historical approaches began to lose ground at Oxford after the Great War of 1914–18, as others began to emerge. Perhaps the most interesting of these was due to Clement C. J. Webb (1865–1954), tutor in philosophy at Magdalen College,[26] who devoted an extended discussion to the notion of "myth" in his classic work *God and Personality* (1919). For Webb, a myth is essentially a story – a "surrogate" for history which may not convey truth, but nevertheless conveys something "like the truth."[27] Webb's analysis of the use of myths in Plato's dialogues is suggestive, opening up the question of whether they can be dismissed with quite the ease that some supposed.[28]

Yet the Oxford scholar who arguably had the greatest impact on the academic discussion of the literary significance of myth was J. R. R. Tolkien, who took up the Rawlinson and Bosworth Professorship of Anglo-Saxon at Oxford in 1925, and remained at Oxford for the remainder of his academic career. Tolkien had little time for the historical task of accounting for the origins of myths; his interest lay in their literary function. For Tolkien, the distinct qualities of a fairy-story – the type of "myth" with which he was most familiar – were to be discerned through their impact on their readers, rather than through an understanding of their historical origins.[29] They evoked:[30]

> . . . a catch of the breath, a beat and lifting of the heart, near to (or indeed accompanied by) tears, as keen as that given by any form of literary art, and having a peculiar quality . . . we get a piercing glimpse of joy, and heart's desire, that for a moment passes outside the frame, rends indeed the very web of story, and lets a gleam come through.

Myth, for Tolkien, is a story which evokes *Sehnsucht*, a sense of the "numinous."

Where other writers of the age tended to use myths as framing devices for their own literary creations – such as James Joyce's *Ulysses* (1922) or Eugene O'Neill's *Mourning Becomes Electra* (1931) – Tolkien believed that it was necessary to create new myths to sustain their literary impact.[31] Since humanity was created in the "image of God," the capacity to create stories which in some way reflect the divine rationality remained embedded within humanity, despite the Fall.[32]

> Fantasy remains a human right: we make in our measure and in our derivative mode, because we are made: and not only made, but made in the image and likeness of a Maker.

This theology of "sub-creation" – set out especially in the poem *Mythopoeia* – led Tolkien to develop a sophisticated yet subtle theology of religion.[33] By offering "a far-off gleam or echo of *evangelium* in the real world,"[34] pagan myths elicit wonder and longing, creating both an appetite and an opening for the discovery of the deeper truth that underlies all truth, however fragmentary and veiled.[35]

Lewis's Exploration of Myth, 1920–30

Classical scholarship has always been an integral part of Oxford University's academic culture. Lewis won a scholarship to University College, Oxford, in December 1916 to study classics. Although his studies were disrupted by the Great War, Lewis went on to achieve a "double First" – that is to say, securing First Class Honors in both honors moderations, and the final examination in *Literae Humaniores*. Lewis's studies of classic Greek literature and philosophy, which began seriously in 1919, would allow him to appreciate that the Greek term *mythos* was originally understood as a true story, a narrative that unveiled the true origin of the world and human beings. However, two trends of thought emerged which undermined the status of myth in Greek culture: history (as in the works of Thucydides and Herodotus) and philosophy (especially in Aristotle). Both these modes of discourse presented themselves as naturalistic alternatives to myths.

A clear tension is evident in writings of the fifth century BC between *mythos* and *logos*, between poetic accounts of reality and their rational alternatives. Although some writers of this age – most notably Plato – managed to incorporate some myths into their philosophical reflections,[36] the term *mythos* was well on its way to acquiring its modern sense as a primitive, evidentially, and rationally unsubstantiated account of reality.

Lewis began the serious and systematic study of English literature at Oxford in October 1922, taking First Class Honors in the summer of 1923.[37] This forced immersion in the classics of English literature led him to reflect on the quality of literary representations of reality. Lewis later recalled that modernist writers such as George Bernard Shaw (1856–1950) and H. G. Wells (1866–1946) "seemed a little thin"; there was "no depth in them"; they were "too simple." The rationalist outlook they represented seemed unable to cope with the "roughness and density of life."[38] Yet "the Christian mythology" – as expressed, for example, in the writings of the Christian poet George Herbert (1593–1633) seemed to Lewis to excel as a medium for "conveying the very quality of life as we actually live it."[39] Lewis was particularly impressed by Dante's *Divine Comedy*, richly steeped in a Christian vision of reality, which showed "a unity of the highest order, because it embraces the greatest diversity of subordinated detail."[40] While Lewis failed to deal with "the ludicrous contradiction between my theory of life and my actual experiences as a reader"[41] at this stage, it was clear that he was becoming increasingly aware of the importance of a myth, both in generating imaginative appeal and in providing a narrative framework for making sense of things, and holding a more complex vision of reality together as a coherent whole.

Lewis resists offering a precise definition of "myth," partly because he is aware that the criteria that must be deployed in any such attempt to define its essence are incorrigibly subjective. (Tolkien made a similar point, when he remarked that "it is one of its qualities to be indescribable, though not imperceptible."[42]) In a late essay, Lewis offered a description of myth based on six core elements, which relate mainly to the impact that such a story has upon its readers:[43]

1. Myth is an "extra-literary" phenomenon, in that its distinct identity lies in the "mythical experience" it evokes in its readers.
2. Myths have very little to do with suspense or surprise, but rather introduce us to a permanent object of contemplation – "more like a thing than a narration" – which works upon us by its peculiar flavor or quality;
3. Myths focus on characters who seem distant from us, "like shapes moving in another world," yet whose movements are seen to have "a profound relevance to our own life."
4. Myth is fantastic, dealing with "impossibles" and "preternaturals."
5. Myth allows its readers access to an experience that may be sad or joyful, but always grave and never comic.
6. Myths have the capacity to inspire awe on account of their numinous qualities.

This sixth point is of particular importance, not least on account of Lewis's own youthful experience of the capacity of such myths to enthrall and enchant. "It is as if something of great moment has been communicated to us." Recent studies in the psychology of awe have confirmed and clarified Lewis's point.[44] Awe is evoked by a sense of vastness, which the human mind finds difficult to accommodate – whether this sense is evoked spatially (a range of mountains, the night sky), imaginatively (a vision of reality which creates vast mental landscapes), or theoretically (a comprehensive theory, able to embrace the complexities of observation). It is important to note how Lewis's accounts of his early experiences of "pure Northernness" are often framed in terms of immensity and vastness – for example, visions of "huge, clear spaces hanging above the Atlantic in the endless twilight of Northern summer."[45]

Yet Lewis was aware that his attempt to "define myths by their effect on us" introduces an element of subjective judgment into the discussion. What if one person experiences a narrative as a myth, and another simply as a dull and somewhat improbable story? Lewis was quite clear in recognizing this problem, and accepting its implications: "the same story may be a myth to one man and not to another."[46] The same book "can be merely an exciting 'yarn' to one and convey a myth, or something like a myth, to another."[47]

Lewis and the Christian Myth: Conversion

Lewis's outlook on life changed radically in the late spring or early summer of 1930. Traditionally, this conversion is held to have taken place in

Oxford's Trinity Term 1929; the evidence clearly points to a later date – probably the Trinity Term of 1930.[48] In a letter to Owen Barfield of February 1930, Lewis speaks of God advancing upon him, in terms that parallel Lewis's account of his conversion in *Surprised by Joy*.[49] Lewis began to attend college chapel from October 1930,[50] as an outward expression of his changed inward world. Yet this decision was not complete in itself. In many ways, it can be seen as a reopening of some questions, and a deeper exploration of others. One of those concerns Lewis's reflections on the relation between a somewhat generic belief in God, and a more specific belief in Christianity. As Lewis explained to his confidant Arthur Greeves, he could not make sense of core Christian beliefs, such as "redemption."[51]

> What had been holding me back [from embracing Christianity] has not been so much a difficulty in believing as a difficulty in knowing what the doctrine *meant*: you can't believe a thing while you are ignorant *what* the thing is. My puzzle was the whole doctrine of Redemption: in what sense the life and death of Christ "saved" or "opened salvation to" the world.

Lewis's views on this matter were transformed by a night-time conversation with Hugo Dyson and J. R. R. Tolkien on Saturday September 19, 1931,[52] which helped Lewis to realize that myths – in the technical sense of the term – were "profound and suggestive of meanings" that lay beyond his grasp, so that he was unable to state in plain language "what it meant." We have already explored something of Tolkien's views on myths, noting both their imaginative appeal and their capacity to open up a broader vision of reality. Tolkien held that the gospels contained "a story of a larger kind," which embraced what Lewis found good, true, and beautiful in the great myths of literature, expressing it as "a far-off gleam or echo of *evangelium* in the real world."[53] There seems little doubt that this way of thinking helped Lewis to get over "the last stile"[54] on his road to faith. Tolkien seems to have removed the final barrier between Lewis and the Christian faith.

In a letter written two weeks after this conversation, Lewis told Greeves that he had now "passed on from believing in God to definitely believing in Christ."[55] The decisive insight was that Christianity was not a set of doctrines or moral principles, but a controlling grand narrative – a myth, in the true sense of the term – which generated and sustained such ideas and values.

The story of Christ was thus a "true myth" – that is to say, a myth which functions in the same manner as other myths, yet which *really happened*. Christianity possessed the literary form of a myth, with the

critical difference that it was true. The story of Christ is thus to be understood as "God's myth" where the great pagan narratives are "men's myths."[56]

> The Pagan stories are God expressing Himself through the minds of poets,
> using such images as He found there, while Christianity is God expressing
> Himself through what we call "real things." Therefore, it is *true*, not in the
> sense of being a "description" of God (that no finite mind could take in)
> but in the sense of being the way in which God chooses to (or can) appear
> to our faculties. The "doctrines" we get *out of* the true myth are of course
> *less* true: they are translations into our *concepts* and *ideas* of that wh. God
> has already expressed in a language more adequate, namely the actual
> incarnation, crucifixion, and resurrection.

Lewis expresses this same idea in *The Pilgrim's Regress*, written in August
1932, in which he set out an allegorical account of his own spiritual and
intellectual meanderings, eventually leading him to rediscover God, and
see the world through new eyes in the light of this development. One of
the novel's allegorical characters – "Wisdom," a personification of forms
of philosophical Idealism which hold that the Absolute is impersonal –
dismisses the significance of John's "discovery," telling him that he has
merely lapsed into some form of mythology. This provokes the following
response from God, summarizing and extending Lewis's thoughts of September and October 1931:[57]

> Child, if you will, it *is* mythology. It is but truth, not fact: an image, not the
> very real. But then it is My mythology. The words of Wisdom are also myth
> and metaphor: but since they do not know themselves for what they are,
> in them the hidden myth is master, where it should be servant: and it is
> but of man's inventing. But this is My inventing, this is the veil under which
> I have chosen to appear even from the first until now. For this end I made
> your senses and for this end your imagination, that you might see My face
> and live.

For Lewis, a myth is a story which evokes awe, enchantment, and inspi-
ration, and which conveys or embodies an imaginative expression of the
deepest meanings of life – meanings that prove totally elusive in the face
of any attempt to express them abstractly or conceptually. Lewis attempted
to explain this point in his 1944 essay "Myth Became Fact." His reflections merit extensive citation:[58]

> In the enjoyment of a great myth we come nearest to experiencing as a
> concrete what can otherwise be understood only as an abstraction...When
> we translate we get abstraction – or rather, dozens of abstractions. What

flows into you from the myth is not truth but reality (truth is always *about* something, but reality is that *about which* truth is), and, therefore, every myth becomes the father of innumerable truths on the abstract level. Myth is the mountain whence all the different streams arise which become truths down here in the valley; *in hac valle abstractionis*. Or, if you prefer, myth is the isthmus which connects the peninsular world of thought with that vast continent we really belong to. It is not, like truth, abstract; nor is it, like direct experience, bound to the particular.

Lewis came to see that myths possess an innate capacity to expand the consciousness and imaginations of their readers. A myth awakens imaginatively a longing for something that lies beyond the grasp of reason. Like Tolkien, Lewis came to hold that myths offered a "real though unfocused gleam of divine truth falling on the human imagination."[59] Christianity, rather than being one myth alongside many others, is thus to be seen as representing the fulfillment of all myths – the "true myth" toward which all other myths merely point. Christianity thus tells a true story about humanity, which makes sense of all the stories that humanity tells about itself. One of Lewis's most significant insights concerning the grand themes of the Christian narrative is that, if ever a myth were to be realized in historical time and space, "it would be just like this."[60]

For Lewis, God *authorizes* the use of myth as a means of captivating the human imagination and engaging the human reason. Since "God chooses to be mythopoeic," then we in our turn must be "mythopathic" – that is to say, receptive to God's myth, recognizing and acknowledging its "mythical radiance," and offering it an "imaginative welcome."[61] And, since God uses myths as a means of communicating both truth and meaning, why should not humans do the same? Particularly those wishing to encourage their culture to offer an "imaginative embrace" to the Christian faith?

Lewis declares that human beings construct myths because they are *meant* to. They have been created by God with an innate capacity to create myths as echoes of a greater story or "story of a larger kind." In that human beings bear God's image, human beings are endowed with the Creator's capacity to create, in a suitably accommodated and reduced manner. Human beings are thus "sub-creators," empowered and envisioned to create art, culture, and technology – including literature, particularly myth and fantasy, as we find these in fairy-tales. When a "story-maker" creates a believable world, Tolkien remarks, what really happens is that he:[62]

> . . . proves a successful "sub-creator". He makes a Secondary World which your mind can enter. Inside it, what he relates is "true": it accords with the

laws of that world. You therefore believe it, while you are, as it were, inside. The moment disbelief arises, the spell is broken; the magic, or rather art, has failed. You are then out in the Primary World again, looking at the little abortive Secondary World from outside.

It has not been adequately appreciated that Lewis supplements the classic Stoic notion of the *logos spermatikos* with that of *mythos spermatikos* – a narrative embedded within the deeper structures of the created order, which enables, shapes, and moulds the construction and narration of human stories.[63] Just as patristic writers argued that the seeds of divine reason were scattered throughout the creation,[64] Lewis and Tolkien suggest, without recourse to detailed analysis, that the structures and themes of the divine narrative are found within the created order, especially the human imagination. For Tolkien, human beings are "sub-creators" and "legend-makers," who "make still by the law in which we're made."[65]

So what are the implications of this understanding of a myth? In what follows, we shall consider three main outcomes of Lewis's views on myths, and their wider implications for his intellectual vision.

Lewis's Understanding of Myth: Three Consequences

Lewis's 1931 conversation with Dyson and Tolkien set in place a transformation of his intellectual vision, which arguably underlies his literary and theological endeavors from that point onward. It is clear that many of the main themes of this new way of seeing things were in place by August 1932, when Lewis dashed off *The Pilgrim's Regress* in a mere two weeks. Other aspects of Lewis's approach took longer to develop, even though their origins can clearly be traced back to the conversations of September 1931.

Three main outcomes of Lewis's changed outlook will be considered here. Before going any further, we must reiterate that the term "myth" is being used in its technical, literary sense.

1. His realization that this approach allowed paganism to be seen as an imperfect grasping toward the truth, which reaches its culmination in Christianity.
2. His emphatic insistence that Christian doctrines are subordinate to the greater reality that is articulated in the Christian "myth" or grand narrative.

3.   A rejection of any idea that Christian ideas or values can be detached
     from the myth that gives them their distinct identity and hue. What
     the German New Testament scholar Rudolf Bultmann (1884–1976)
     provocatively termed "demythologization" is a literary and theologi-
     cal impossibility.

We shall consider each of these points further in what follows.

1. Christianity as the fulfillment of human myths

One of the arguments that Lewis used to defend his early atheism in the
mid-1910s, both to himself and Arthur Greeves, was that the rich tapestry
of human religious beliefs consisted of a multitude of irreconcilable and
mutually contradictory assertions. While still a schoolboy, Lewis came to
the view that religion was a natural (though totally false) phenomenon,
"a kind of endemic nonsense into which humanity tended to blunder."[66]
Christianity was just one of a thousand religions, all claiming to be true.
So why should he believe this one to be right, and the others wrong? To
affirm that Christianity was right immediately implied that all the remainder were false – which seemed to Lewis to be an attitude that was as
morally arrogant as it was intellectually wrong.

Yet Lewis's grasp of the notion of the Christian myth forced him to
revise this view completely. Tolkien's way of looking at things gave Lewis
a lens which allowed him to see Christianity as bringing to fulfillment
such echoes and shadows of the truth that arose from human questing
and yearning. Such myths offer a fragment of that truth, not its totality.
They are like splintered fragments of the true light.[67] Yet when the full
and true story is told, it is able to bring to fulfillment all that was right
and wise in those fragmentary visions of things. For Tolkien, Christianity
provided the total picture, which both unified and transcended these
fragmentary and imperfect insights.

Lewis rightly saw that this distinction between "God's myth" and
"human myths" offered an intellectual and imaginative framework that
destroyed his earlier objection to Christianity. Lewis realized the great
myths of ancient Greece or Nordic legend did not have to be dismissed
as *totally false*; they were to be seen as echoes or anticipations of the full
truth, which was made known only in and through the Christian faith.
The Christian narrative brings to fulfillment and completion imperfect
and partial insights about reality, scattered abroad in human culture. If
Tolkien were right, similarities between Christianity and pagan religions
"*ought* to be there."[68] In fact, the problems would arise if such similarities
did *not* exist, as this would be to imply that "God's myth" left "human

myths" untouched. The great pagan myths, Lewis suggested, were "dim dreams or premonitions" of the greater and fuller truth of the Christian gospel.[69]

> The Divine light, we are told, "lighteneth every man." We should, therefore, expect to find in the imagination of great Pagan teachers and myth-makers some glimpse of that theme which we believe to be the very plot of the whole cosmic story – the theme of incarnation, death, and rebirth.

Lewis uses a series of images to try and clarify this critically important point.[70] It is not a simple question of truth and falsehood; *this* is right, but that is *wrong*. Rather, it is about a clearer and fuller vision of things, which allows shadows, dreams, and rumors to be seen as premonitions and hints of a greater truth – but a truth they were not able to formulate, disclose, or embody. "It is like watching something come gradually into focus." Seeing the full picture helps us make sense of previous hazy, fuzzy, confused, and fragmentary accounts of it, allowing these fragments to be colligated within a larger vision of things, which lent coherence to the individual parts that they lacked when considered on their own.

Yet Lewis's use of myth does more than enable us to grasp the coherence of such narratives; it enables a deeper level of engagement with them. Lewis's appeal to myth is not to be seen as a rejection of his earlier mode of argument or reflection, but as "an effort to go beyond it," offering his readers "not 'knowledge' of God but a 'taste' of the Divine Reality."[71]

This standpoint opened up important apologetic approaches. Although Lewis's first work of apologetics – *The Problem of Pain* (1940) – did not use such an approach, it is deeply embedded within the "Chronicles of Narnia." The story of Narnia evokes the memory of and desire for a greater narrative on the part of the reader. As Lewis put it in *The Voyage of the "Dawn Treader,"* "what Lucy means by a good story is a story which reminds her of the forgotten story in the Magician's Book."[72]

This theme of Christianity as "fulfillment" of the hopes of humanity is deeply grounded in the Christian tradition. Although Lewis makes little reference to these historical roots, this approach was seen by early Christian apologists – such as Justin Martyr and Clement of Alexandria – as a way of explaining the relation of Christianity to classical culture, particularly in its more explicitly Platonic forms.[73] The theme re-emerged as significant in missionary theology in the early 1900s, and played a particularly important role at the celebrated World Missionary Conference, held at Edinburgh in 1910.[74] Lewis's apologetic approach is easily aligned with these earlier models, despite its more literary orientation. There is clearly more work that could be done to explore the potential relevance of this model.

2. Christianity is primarily about a "myth," and secondarily about doctrines
One of Lewis's most distinctive themes concerns the secondary nature of Christian beliefs. These, he argues are "translations into our *concepts* and *ideas*" of that which God has already expressed in a "more adequate" language – namely, the "grand narrative" of the Christian faith itself.[75] This theme is developed at several points, perhaps most significantly in *Mere Christianity*. Lewis is emphatic that we are not asked to accept Christian *theories* about – for example – the atonement; we are asked to embrace the atonement itself, as a greater reality.

This leads Lewis to argue that "the theories are not themselves the thing you are asked to accept." Using a scientific analogy, Lewis points to scientific models, which are intended to help us construct a "mental picture." Yet this mental picture is not what the scientists believe. "What the scientists believe is a mathematical formula," something abstract that calls out to be expressed in a more accessible form. Yet these models or pictures "do not give you the real thing but only something more or less like it; they are only meant to help and if they do not help, you can dump them."[76]

The point that Lewis is making will be familiar to students of quantum theory during the 1920s and 1930s. Niels Bohr (1886–1962) and Werner Heisenberg (1901–76) made substantial theoretical contributions to this discipline, of such mathematical abstraction that they were virtually impossible for many to understand.[77] There was a need for what Heisenberg described as *Anschaulichkeit* – "visualizability," the ability to render mathematical abstractions in visible forms.[78] Heisenberg here developed a major theme drawn from literary and aesthetic scholarship,[79] and applied it to the representation of reality at the quantum level. Lewis recognizes the importance of what Heisenberg terms *Anschaulichkeit*, while insisting that any ensuing "mental pictures" are not to be confused with what they really represent. They are only intermediaries for an encounter with reality, offering ancillary rather than magisterial accounts of what they depict. Second-order levels of engagement with reality may be neat, crisp, and admirably logical. Yet these fall short of what true Christianity is all about – an encounter with the living God, something than can never be accommodated without radical imaginative loss. *Si comprehendis, non est Deus.*[80]

This has important implications, not least for apologetics. For Lewis, outsiders should not be asked to accept the truth of Christian beliefs in order to discover the vibrancy of the Christian faith. They need to discover the "myth," the grand narrative, the "big picture" – and then to appreciate the role played by beliefs in sustaining and representing this grand narrative.

3. The impossibility of demythologizing the New Testament

On June 4, 1941, the German New Testament scholar Rudolf Bultmann delivered a lecture entitled "The New Testament and Mythology," which introduced a phrase into the vocabulary of theology and New Testament scholarship: the "demythologization of the New Testament" (*die Entmythologisierung des Neuen Testaments*).[81] So what did Bultmann mean by this dramatic phrase?

The fundamental contention of Bultmann's controversial lecture of 1941 was that the New Testament proclamation or *kerygma* concerning Christ is stated and understood in mythological terms. Borrowing on questionable ideas deriving from the "History of Religion School," Bultmann argued that this myth derived from Jewish apocalyptic and Gnostic redemption myths which, although perfectly legitimate and intelligible in the first century, cannot be taken seriously today.

Bultmann insisted that, since the human understanding of the world and of human existence had changed radically since the first century, modern humanity now finds the mythological worldview of the New Testament unintelligible and unacceptable.[82] A worldview is given to people with the age in which they live, and they are in no position to alter it. The modern scientific and existential worldview means that that of the New Testament is now discarded – and with it, the gospel proclamation.[83]

Bultmann's account of the nature of "myth" is clearly somewhat confused, perhaps because it lacks any serious engagement with literary scholarship dealing with the genre. Bultmann seems to understand "myth" to refer both to a specific genre of representation of the divine in human language and imagery, and to the somewhat different matter of the worldview (*Weltanschauung*) embedded within a particular time and place. "Myth lives not only in stories of the gods but also in the worldview presupposed by them."[84] Bultmann's solution to the historical distance of the biblical narrative, its rootedness in an alien culture, and its use of outmoded scientific ideas such as a "three-decker universe" was to propose a restatement of the gospel's fundamental themes in existential categories,[85] discarding what he regarded as outmoded and outdated ideas, while retaining their deeper existential significance.

But *can* this be done? *Should* it be done? Bultmann believed that it was possible to extract the true meaning of the Christian faith from its historically situated vehicles of embodiment and transmission. Many would argue that, far from demythologizing the New Testament, Bultmann actually remythologized it – that is to say, recast its ideas using a "myth" which he believed carried cultural weight in the first half of the twentieth century.[86] Yet irrespective of what Bultmann believed needed to be done, and whether he succeeded in achieving this, a fundamental question remains open. Can the gospel be detached from the "myth" which conveys it? Can some abstract and universal message be extracted from its historically given form?

Lewis's reply was simple and emphatic: No. "We are invited to restate our belief in a form free from metaphor and symbol. The reason why we don't is that we can't."[87] For Lewis, Christianity is best understood as a "true myth," and cannot be framed in other ways without loss of its capacity to render the world truthfully and realistically. It is impossible to eliminate narrative, metaphor, and imagery from the Christian proclamation without deforming and distorting it. The Christian proclamation is not to be framed in terms of disembodied abstractions, even the beliefs of the creeds. However valuable these may be, they are secondary to the reality that is expressed in the form of a myth, and which captivates the human imagination precisely because it takes this literary form.

Furthermore, Lewis suggests, it is in any case quite unnecessary. To "demythologize" is to break the link between the Christian faith and the realizing imagination, and substitute something of lesser significance. "We desire, like St. Paul, not to be un-clothed but to be re-clothed: to find not the formless Everywhere-and-Nowhere but the promised land."[88] The "myth" that Bultmann regarded as a contingent liability for faith was seen by Lewis as a necessary and positive aspect of the Christian story. Underlying Lewis's critique of Bultmann is a pervasive, though understated, suspicion that Bultmann is an amateur when it comes to questions of literary theory and scholarship.[89]

And what of the suggestion that the "myth" of the New Testament is simply a historically conditioned shell, containing the eternal kernel of the true Christian faith? This image was widely used in German New Testament scholarship from about 1890. Bultmann, for example, argued that we had to crack and discard the mythological shell of the gospel proclamation, and feast on its kerygmatic core. Lewis would have none of this.[90]

> The earliest Christians were not so much like a man who mistakes the shell for the kernel as like a man carrying a nut which he hasn't yet cracked. The moment it is cracked, he knows which part to throw away. Till then, he holds on to the nut: not because he is a fool but because he isn't.

This fundamental belief lies behind his realization of the apologetic and theological potential of stories, evident in both the "Ransom Trilogy" and the "Chronicles of Narnia." Since the gospel takes the literary form of *mythos* rather than *logos*, Lewis seems to have concluded that the best apologetic might take the form of an imaginative narrative transposition of the Christian story, rather than its reduction to ideas and beliefs. For Lewis, what is required is the transposition of theological themes through *remythologization*, in which the genre of myth is used to display most effectively the imaginative, poetic, and intellectual dimensions of the Christian faith.

Lewis's Attitude to Myth Contextualized: The "Dialectic of Enlightenment" (1944)

So how does Lewis's attitude to myth fit into a wider historical pattern? How is he to be positioned against the backdrop of European debate about the nature and significance of myth from the dawn of the Enlightenment to the waning of the modern period?[91] We have already seen how the Enlightenment regarded itself as the critic of outmoded mythologies. The genre of myth was to be seen as a cultural anachronism, which would be eclipsed and displaced by the cultural climate of Modernism, with its emphasis upon reason and science. This narrative of the gradual oblivion of myth dominated the outlook of the Enlightenment during the eighteenth and nineteenth centuries, and persisted until the first half of the twentieth century.[92]

Many Romantic writers argued that this criticism of myth ultimately rested on a misunderstanding of its fundamental nature. "Myth" was here being (mis)understood as an archaic form of knowledge of the external world, whose implausibility reflected both its content and form. Rather, myth was to be seen as a tool for the expression and exploration of human subjectivity. The genre functioned both as a source and manner of expression of most intimate and subjective themes of the human mind and human culture.[93]

Lewis clearly echoes some aspects of the Romantic affirmation of the concept of myth. Like his fellow-Irishmen, W. B. Yeats (1865–1939) and James Joyce (1882–1941), Lewis realized that mythology retained a deep appeal to the human imagination, capable of literary embrace and ideological exploration.[94] Myth was seen as something rather more than a form of poetical decoration, being recognized as embodying an archetypal literary structure.[95] Earlier, we noted how Lewis's reflections on the nature of myth often involve focusing on the subjective impact of the genre, thereby leading to the conclusion that it is impossible to give an "objective" definition of myth. A myth is to be understood as something which is perceived to have a "mythical quality."

Yet Lewis does not see the subjective aspects of "mythical quality" as compromising its capacity to allow a deeper engagement with reality. A "myth" is "the veil under which [God has] chosen to appear." The myth offers a way of seeing things, which allows them to be seen more clearly, and in a new light. Lewis made this point more fully in a review of Tolkien's *Lord of the Rings*, in which Lewis seeks to account for the power of Tolkien's epic narrative – Lewis termed it a "romantic trilogy"[96] – in terms of its quality as a myth.[97] For Lewis, the value of myth lies in its capacity to take "all the things we know," and restore to them their "rich significance" which has been obscured by "the veil of familiarity." "By dipping them in myth," Lewis suggested, "we see them more clearly."

Lewis thus sees myth as a tool for the exploration of inner subjective realities, as well as enabling a broader and deeper understanding of the world around us. Christianity is a "true myth," which enables us to make sense of both what we see around us and experience within us – including its ability to position and hence to interpret other myths. Lewis's notion of myth interprets both our external and internal worlds, allowing us to see them in the light of the distinct rationality affirmed by the Christian myth. This understanding of myth straddles the rival visions of the Enlightenment and Romanticism, raising the question of whether Lewis is eclectic or inconsistent – or whether the recent history of the concept of myth may have taken a false turn, which Lewis corrected.

Lewis was not alone at this time in seeking to transcend the obvious limits of the great eighteenth- and nineteenth-century debates about the nature of myth. This debate began to move in new directions in 1944, with the publication of the *Dialectic of Enlightenment* by Theodor Adorno and Max Horkheimer.[98] This immensely original work argued for the rational basis of myth and the mythical basis of rationality, in effect dismantling the traditional distinction between the two notions. Adorno and Horkheimer argue that one of the core distinguishing features of modernity is the notion of instrumental rationality. Yet this, they suggest, is itself a modern myth, which asserts that the world is totally subjugated to human control. Instrumental reason may ridicule mythical language, but it replicates its distinctive themes. The Enlightenment, on this reading of things, thus does not liberate us from myth, but merely changes its form.

This suggestion of the "entwinement of myth and Enlightenment" caused concern to some. Jürgen Habermas, for example, argued that Adorno and Horkheimer offered a criticism of instrumental reason which ultimately depended on the same rationality that it was meant to criticize.[99] Yet others have suggested that their analysis, while requiring correction at points, offers an important corrective to the prevailing understanding of the relation between myth and reason on the one hand, or Enlightenment and Rationalism on the other.

Bruce Lincoln has argued that "myth" is ultimately an ideology which, unlike other forms of ideology, is presented in the form of a narrative.[100] Eric Csapo agreed that a mythology is an ideology expressed in narrative form, but suggested that its narrative form made it open to multiple readings. Noting that there "has been a general coalescence of the concept of myth with the concept of ideology" in more recent thinking,[101] Csapo makes the point that the notion of "myth" is no longer limited to significant stories sourced from "ancient" or "primal" cultures, but now extends to modern narratives of identity and value – including those of the Enlightenment itself.

Myth and the Recapturing of the Secular Imagination

Lewis's apparently idiosyncratic approach to the notion of myth, which might seem to some as representing an awkward eclecticism, thus fits into a broader pattern of reflection on the nature and significance of myth. No longer is the term regarded as designating a narrative that is presumed to be antiquated and fictional; there is a growing realization that a myth is a narrative embodying and exhibiting its own criteria of rationality, capable of "fitting in" what we seen around us and experience within us. For Lewis, a myth weaves together truth and meaning, engaging with both our reason and imagination.[102]

For in the end, what distinguishes a myth from an argument or a worldview is its capacity to engage the imagination. Like a spell, it enchants us, drawing us to it by its intrinsic lure and beauty, causing us to question existing commitments and outlooks. Only a greater myth can liberate us from the thrall of a lesser one. "You and I have need of the strongest spell that can be found to wake us from the evil enchantment of worldliness which has been laid upon us."[103]

Lewis's analysis of the limits of reason makes it clear that we need more than rational arguments to challenge the "spirit of the age." If a myth is "caught," it begins to work its magic of intellectual and moral transformation. In one sense, Lewis's apologetics can be seen as commending and offering counter-narrations rather than counter-arguments against the naturalism and secularism of our age. In speaking of the transformative capacity of the Christian gospel, Lewis supplements his theory of myth with a generous dose of Christian theology, focusing especially on what Augustine would call the "prevenience of grace."

Yet Lewis's emphasis does not here fall on divine grace, nor the mysterious workings of the Holy Spirit, even if these are clearly and necessarily presupposed. Lewis's point is that we must recognize that "myth" constitutes a literary genre that holds the key to liberation from our cultural captivation. For Lewis, Christian apologetics (129–46) is thus at its best when it out-narrates the ideologies of the world, by showing that the Christian story and its retellings, having captivated our imaginations, also enlighten our minds, and shape our moral vision.

Conclusion

Lewis's musings on myth have alarmed some of his less literate admirers, just as they have riled his less literate critics, who both misunderstand his language, believing it to imply the factual falsity of the Christian faith. We must therefore allow Lewis to define the term "myth" for us, if we are to understand why it came to be of such critical importance in bringing about his conversion to Christianity, and in shaping his later formulations and presentations of the Christian faith.

Whatever term we might use to refer to what Lewis designated "myth," it remains an inalienable element of his vision of the Christian faith – not a dispensable husk, which is cast to one side once the kernel has been extracted,[104] but a vehicle of imaginative truth, integral to the effective transmission of that truth. If, as some have argued, a myth is fundamentally "a story that is always true,"[105] Lewis can be seen to have shown how both Christian theology and apologetics can be enriched by an appreciation of the literary character of its central narrative.

For Lewis, a "myth" speaks to people in a mysterious, luminous, and powerful way, opening their minds and hearts to new ways of thinking. Myths expose the imaginative limitations of rationalism, by opening up new ways of encountering and experiencing truth.[106]

> Hitherto you have experienced truth only with the abstract intellect. I will bring you where you can taste it like honey and be embraced by it as by a bridegroom. Your thirst shall be quenched.

Notes

1   *Surprised by Joy*, 197. For comment on some of the historical and literary issues raised by this work, see the first essay in this volume.

2   W. H. Lewis, ed., *The Lewis Papers: Memoirs of the Lewis Family 1850–1930*. 11 vols. Unpublished typescript held in the Wade Center, Wheaton College, and the Bodleian Library, Oxford, vol. 10, 219. Lewis's comments are found in a three-page reflection on Greeves, possibly written around 1935: *Lewis Papers*, vol. 10, 218–20.

3   Letter to Arthur Greeves, October 12(?), 1916; *Letters*, vol. 1, 230–1.

4   Tolkien recalled Lewis describing the making of fairy-stories as "breathing a lie through silver": J. R. R. Tolkien, "On Fairy Stories." In *Tree and Leaf*. London: HarperCollins, 2001, 54.

5   For an assessment of this development, see Bruce Lincoln, *Theorizing Myth: Narrative, Ideology, and Scholarship*. Chicago: University of Chicago Press, 1999. See also the older study of Otto Gruppe, *Geschichte der klassischen Mythologie und Religionsgechichte während des Mittelalters im Abendland und während der Neuzeit*. Leipzig: B. G. Teubner, 1977.

6   A point made by Hans Erich Bödeker, "Die Religiosität der Gebildeten." In *Religionskritik und Religiosität in der deutschen Aufklärung*, edited by Karlfried Gründer and Karl Heinrich Rengstorf, 145–95. Heidelberg: Schneider, 1989.

7   Christopher Jamme, "Portraying Myth More Convincingly: Critical Approaches to Myth in the Classical and Romantic Periods." *International Journal of Philosophical Studies* 12, no. 1 (2004): 29–45. For the appeal to myth in the Renaissance, see Jean Seznec, *La survivance des dieux antiques: Essai sur le rôle de la tradition mythologique dans l'humanisme et dans l'art de la Renaissance*. Paris: Flammarion, 1980.

8   Diane Brotemarkle, *Imagination and Myths in John Keats's Poetry*. San Francisco: Mellen Research University Press, 1993, 107. On myths in English Romanticism, see Marilyn Butler, "Myth and Mythmaking in the Shelley Circle." *ELH* 49, no. 1 (1982): 50–72; Paul Cantor, *Creature and Creator: Myth-Making and English Romanticism*. Cambridge: Cambridge University Press, 1984; Anthony John Harding, *The Reception of Myth in English Romanticism*. Columbia, MO: University of Missouri Press, 1995.

9   George S. Williamson, *The Longing for Myth in Germany: Religion and Aesthetic Culture from Romanticism to Nietzsche*. Chicago: The University of Chicago Press, 2004.

10 For the development of "scientific mythology" around this time, and its cultural significance, see Josine H. Blok, "Quests for a Scientific Mythology: F. Creuzer and K. O. Müller on History and Myth." *History and Theory* 33, no. 4 (1994): 26–52.

11 August Wilhelm Schlegel, "Vorlesungen über dramatische Kunst und Literatur"; *Sämmtliche Werke*. 12 vols. Leipzig: Weidmann, 1846–7, vol. 5, 16. For the link between *mythos* and *Sehnsucht*, focusing particularly on the work of Johann Joachim Winckelmann (1717–68), see Raimund M. Fridrich, *Sehnsucht nach dem Verlorenen: Winckelmanns Ästhetik und ihre frühe Rezeption*. Berlin: Peter Lang, 2003.

12 See the discussion in Wolf-Daniel Hartwich, *Deutsche Mythologie: Die Erfindung einer Kunstreligion*. Berlin: Piper, 2000.

13 McGrath, *C. S. Lewis – A Life*, 28–9.

14   *Siegfried and The Twilight of the Gods*, illustrated by Arthur Rackham. London: Heinemann, 1911.

15   *Surprised by Joy*, 62.

16   *Surprised by Joy*, 207–9. Lewis's account here incorrectly dates this as taking place in August 1915.

17   *Surprised by Joy*, 207.

18   *Surprised by Joy*, 197.

19   A further element of importance is Lewis's growing conviction that "all things, in their way, reflect heavenly truth, the imagination not least." *Surprised by Joy*, 193–4.

20   *An Experiment in Criticism*, 43. For the distinction between "myth" and "allegory," see Paul Piehler, "Myth or Allegory? Archetype and Transcendence in the Fiction of C. S. Lewis." In *Word and Story in C. S. Lewis*, edited by Peter J. Schakel and Charles A. Huttar, 199–212. Columbia, MO: University of Missouri Press, 1991.

21   Letter to Arthur Greeves, October 18, 1931; *Letters*, vol. 1, 977. For the critical role of myth in Lewis's writings, see Irène Fernandez, *C. S. Lewis – mythe, raison ardente*. Geneva: Ad Solem, 2005, 174–459.

22   Suzanne L. Marchand, *Down from Olympus: Archaeology and Philhellenism in Germany, 1750–1970*. Princeton, NJ: Princeton University Press, 1996.

23   The best recent study is Lourens van den Bosch, *Friedrich Max Müller: A Life Devoted to Humanities*. Leiden: Brill, 2002.

24   Max Müller, *Lectures on the Science of Language*. 2 vols. London: Longmans, 1961–4, vol. 2, 498.

25   Roger Lancelyn Green, *Andrew Lang: A Critical Biography*. Leicester: E. Ward, 1946, 25–9.

26   For a discussion, see James Patrick, *The Magdalen Metaphysicals: Idealism and Orthodoxy at Oxford, 1901–1945*. Macon, GA: Mercer University Press, 1985, 23–46.

27   C. J. J. Webb, *God and Personality*. London: Allen & Unwin, 1919, 169.

28   For an excellent re-evaluation of myth in the classical age, and its later reappropriation, see Luc Brisson, *How Philosophers Saved Myths: Allegorical Interpretation and Classical Mythology*. Chicago: The University of Chicago Press, 2004.

29   For studies of Tolkien's concept of myth, see Richard L. Purtill, *J. R. R. Tolkien: Myth, Morality, and Religion*. San Francisco: Ignatius Press, 2003; Jane Chance, ed., *Tolkien and the Invention of Myth*. Lexington, KY: University Press of Kentucky, 2004.

30   Tolkien, "On Fairy Stories," 69–70.

31   Patchen Mortimer, "Tolkien and Modernism." *Tolkien Studies* 2 (2005): 113–29.

32   Tolkien, "On Fairy Stories," 56.

33   For Tolkien's notion of Mythopoesis, see Kirstin Johnson, "Tolkien's Mythopoesis." In *Tree of Tales: Tolkien, Literature, and Theology*, edited by Trevor Hart and Ivan Khovacs, 25–38. Waco, TX: Baylor University Press, 2007.

34   Tolkien, "On Fairy Stories," 71.

35 See the careful exploration of these ideas in Verlyn Flieger, *Splintered Light: Logos and Language in Tolkien's World*. Kent, OH: Kent State University, 2002. For Christological prefigurements in Middle Earth, see Jonathan Padley and Kenneth Padley, "'From Mirrored Truth the Likeness of the True': J. R .R. Tolkien and Reflections of Jesus Christ in Middle-Earth." *English* 59, no. 224 (2010): 70–92.

36 Kathryn A. Morgan, *Myth and Philosophy from the Presocratics to Plato*. Cambridge: Cambridge University Press, 2000; R. G. A. Buxton, ed. *From Myth to Reason? Studies in the Development of Greek Thought*. Oxford: Oxford University Press, 1999. See also the older study of G. E. R. Lloyd, "Plato on Mathematics and Nature, Myth and Science." In *Methods and Problems in Greek Science*. Cambridge: Cambridge University Press, 1991, 333–51.

37 McGrath, *C. S. Lewis – A Life*, 98–108.

38 *Surprised by Joy*, 249.

39 *Surprised by Joy*, 249.

40 *The Allegory of Love*, 142.

41 *Surprised by Joy*, 248.

42 Tolkien, "On Fairy Stories," 10. For the intellectual relationship of Tolkien and Lewis, see Ralph C. Wood, "Conflict and Convergence on Fundamental Matters in C. S. Lewis and J. R. R. Tolkien." *Renascence: Essays on Values in Literature* 55 (2003): 315–38.

43 *An Experiment in Criticism*, 43–4.

44 See especially Dacher Keltner and Jonathan Haidt, "Approaching Awe: A Moral, Spiritual and Aesthetic Emotion." *Cognition and Emotion* 17 (2003): 297–314.

45 *Surprised by Joy*, 62.

46 *An Experiment in Criticism*, 45.

47 *An Experiment in Criticism*, 48.

48 For the evidence, see McGrath, *C. S. Lewis – A Life*, 141–5.

49 Letter to Owen Barfield, February 3, 1930; *Letters*, vol. 1, 882–3.

50 Letter to Arthur Greeves, October 29, 1930; *Letters*, vol. 1, 942.

51 Letter to Arthur Greeves, October 18, 1931; *Letters*, vol. 1, 976.

52 For details, see McGrath, *C. S. Lewis – A Life*, 146–51.

53 Tolkien, "On Fairy Stories," 71–2.

54 *Surprised by Joy*, 252.

55 Letter to Arthur Greeves, October 1, 1931; *Letters*, vol. 1, 974.

56 Letter to Arthur Greeves, October 18, 1931; *Letters*, vol. 1, 977.

57 *The Pilgrim's Regress*, 171.

58 "Myth Became Fact"; *Essay Collection*, 140–1. The Latin tag Lewis cites is to be translated as "in this valley of abstraction," or perhaps "in this valley of separation."

59 *Miracles*, 218 n. 1.

60 For the strong "sense of place" that is so characteristic of some myths, see Fabienne Claire Caland, "De Bifröst à Gjallarbrú, deux lieux fédérateurs dans la mythologie nordique." In *Le lieu dans le mythe*, edited by Juliette

Vion-Dury, 89–98. Limoges: Presses Universitaires de Limoges et du Limousin, 2002.

61   "Myth Became Fact"; *Essay Collection*, 142.

62   Tolkien, "On Fairy Stories," 37.

63   Fabienne Claire Caland, "Le mythos spermatikos." In *Horizons du mythe*, edited by Denise Brassard and Fabienne Claire Caland, 7–32. Montréal: Cahiers du CELAT, 2007.

64   The writings of Justin Martyr should be noted here: Ragner Holte, *"Logos Spermatikos*: Christianity and Ancient Philosophy According to St. Justin's Apologies." *Studia Theologica* 12 (1958): 109–68; Jan H. Waszink, "Bemerkungen zu Justins Lehre vom *Logos Spermatikos.*" In *Mullus: Festschrift Theodor Klauser*, edited by Alfred Stuiber and Alfred Hermann, 380–90. Münster: Aschendorffsche Verlagsbuchhandlung, 1964; Mark J. Edwards, "Justin's *Logos* and the Word of God." *Journal of Early Christian Studies* 3 (1995): 261–80.

65   This is a central theme of Tolkien's poem *Mythopoeia*: see Tolkien, *Tree and Leaf*, 87–8.

66   *Surprised by Joy*, 71.

67   See P. H. Brazier, "C. S. Lewis and Christological Prefigurement." *Heythrop Journal* 48 (2007): 742–75. For this theme in Tolkien, see Flieger, *Splintered Light: Logos and Language in Tolkien's World*. For a useful comparison of Lewis and Tolkien on this theme, see Martha C. Sammons, *War of the Fantasy Worlds: C. S. Lewis and J. R. R. Tolkien on Art and Imagination*. Santa Barbara, CA: Praeger, 2010, 21–43; 117–33.

68   "Myth Became Fact"; *Essay Collection*, 142.

69   "Is Theology Poetry?"; *Essay Collection*, 16. Lewis here quotes from John 1:9 in the King James translation of 1611. A modern translation of this verse would read: "The true light, which enlightens everyone, was coming into the world."

70   For what follows, see "Is Theology Poetry?"; *Essay Collection*, 16.

71   Peter J. Schakel, *Reason and Imagination in C. S. Lewis: A Study of Till We Have Faces*. Grand Rapids, MI: Eerdmans, 1984, 150.

72   *The Voyage of the "Dawn Treader,"* 122. Lewis's use of myth in the "Chronicles of Narnia" was viewed with suspicion by Tolkien, who regarded Lewis's approach as eclectic. Tolkien was particularly concerned by the appearance of Father Christmas in *The Lion, the Witch, and the Wardrobe*, which he considered to violate the integrity of its mythic structure. For a defense of Lewis on this point, see P. H. Brazier, "Why Father Christmas Appears in Narnia." *Sehnsucht* 3 (2009): 61–77.

73   See, for example, Mark J. Edwards, "Justin's *Logos* and the Word of God." *Journal of Early Christian Studies* 3 (1995): 261–80; Andrew Walker, "Scripture, Revelation and Platonism in C. S. Lewis." *Scottish Journal of Theology* 55 (2002): 19–35.

74   The roots of this approach lay in British India in the later nineteenth century: see Eric J. Sharpe, *Not to Destroy but to Fulfil: The Contribution of*

J. N. Farquhar to Protestant Missionary Thought in India before 1914. Lund: Gleerup, 1965.

75 Letter to Arthur Greeves, October 18, 1931; *Letters*, vol. 1, 977.

76 *Mere Christianity*, 55.

77 For example, see Edward MacKinnon, "Heisenberg, Models and the Rise of Matrix Mechanics." *Historical Studies in the Physical Sciences* 8 (1979): 137–85; John Honner, *The Description of Nature: Niels Bohr and the Philosophy of Quantum Physics*. Oxford: Clarendon Press, 1987.

78 Jan Lacki, "Observability, Anschaulichkeit and Abstraction: A Journey into Werner Heisenberg's Science and Philosophy." In *100 Years Werner Heisenberg: Works and Impact*, edited by Dietrich Papenfuß, Dieter Lüst, and Wolfgang P. Schleich, 11–29. Weinheim: Wiley-VCH Verlag, 2002. For Heisenberg's original formulation of the issue, see Werner Heisenberg, "Über den anschaulichen Inhalt der quantentheoretischen Kinematik und Mechanik." *Zeitschrift für Physik* 43 (1927): 172–98.

79 For an excellent survey, see Gyburg Radke-Uhlmann and Arbogast Schmitt, eds. *Anschaulichkeit in Kunst und Literatur: Wege bildlicher Visualisierung in der europäischen Geschichte*. Berlin: de Gruyter, 2011.

80 Augustine of Hippo, *Sermo* CXVII.iii.5. As used here, the Latin term *comprehendere* is perhaps best understood as "getting your mind around."

81 Heinrich Balz, "Neues Testament und Mythologie: Rudolf Bultmanns Programm einer Entmythologisierung des Neuen Testaments." In *Mythos: Erzählende Weltdeutung im Spannungsfeld von Ritual, Geschichte und Rationalität*, edited by Gerhard Binder and Bernd Effe, 119–36. Trier: Wissenschaftlicher Verlag Trier, 1990.

82 This view is found throughout John Hick, ed. *The Myth of God Incarnate*. London: SCM Press, 1977. Myth is here generally understood as something outdated and incredible.

83 Friedrich Beißer, "Mythos und christliche Theologie." In *Bibel und Mythos: Fünfzig Jahre nach Rudolf Bultmanns Entmythologisierungsprogramm*, edited by Bernd Jaspert, 74–90. Göttingen: Vandenhoeck & Ruprecht, 1991.

84 Bultmann, Letter to Karl Barth, November 11, 1952. In Bernd Jaspert, ed. *Karl Barth–Rudolf Bultmann Letters 1922–1966*. Grand Rapids, MI: Eerdmans, 1981, 96. See further James D. G. Dunn, "Demythologising: The Problem of Myth in the New Testament." In *New Testament Interpretation: Essays on Principles and Methods*, edited by I. Howard Marshall, 285–307. Carlisle: Paternoster Press, 1979; C. Stephen Evans, "The Incarnational Narrative as Myth and History." *Christian Scholar's Review* 23, no. 4 (1994): 387–407.

85 For an assessment of Bultmann's use of Martin Heidegger's existentialism, see Hans Hübner, "'Existentiale' Interpretation bei Rudolf Bultmann und Martin Heidegger." *Zeitschrift für Theologie und Kirche* 103 (2006): 533–67.

86 Philippe Cardon-Bertalot, "Théologie et mythologie: le problème de la 'remythologisation' du discours chrétien." *Positions luthériennes* 47 (1999): 311–28.

87 "Is Theology Poetry?"; *Essay Collection*, 18.

88   *Miracles*, 264.

89   See especially Lewis's 1959 paper "Modern Theology and Biblical Criticism," subsequently published as "Fern-Seed and Elephants"; *Essay Collection*, 242–54.

90   "Is Theology Poetry?"; *Essay Collection*, 18. Lewis did not engage in detailed direct debate with Bultmann over this point; nevertheless, it is possible to suggest that he does so by proxy, through his Oxford colleague Austin Farrer, whose views on myth were similar to Lewis's. For discussion, see Brian Hebblethwaite, *The Philosophical Theology of Austin Farrer*. Leuven: Peeters, 2007, 105.

91   Hans Poser, "Mythos und Vernunft: Zum Mythenverständnis der Aufklärung." In *Philosophie und Mythos: Ein Kolloquium*, edited by Hans Poser, 130–55. Berlin: de Gruyter, 1979.

92   A number of significant scientific writers of the early modern period do not fit easily into this paradigm, including Francis Bacon: see Rhodri Lewis, "Francis Bacon, Allegory and the Uses of Myth." *Review of English Studies* 61 (2010): 360–89, especially 363: "there remains no satisfactory account of why Bacon troubled himself with myth, or of how his interest in it can be located within his broader programme of intellectual reform."

93   Heinz Gockel, *Mythos und Poesie: Zum Mythosbegriff in Aufklärung und Frühromantik*. Frankfurt am Main: Klostermann, 1981.

94   Note the use of the genre of myth in general, and certain specific Celtic myths – such as "On Baile's Strand" and "The Death of Cuchulain" – in Yeats's works: see Mary Helen Thuente, *W. B. Yeats and Irish Folklore*. Dublin: Gill and Macmillan, 1980. On Joyce, see the classic study of T. S. Eliot, "'Ulysses,' Order and Myth." In *Selected Prose of T. S. Eliot*. London: Faber and Faber, 1975, 175–8, especially 177–8. See also William O'Neill, "Myth and Identity in Joyce's Fiction: Disentangling the Image." *Twentieth Century Literature* 40, no. 3 (1994): 379–91.

95   The question of the extent to which Lewis appropriated Carl Gustav Jung's theory of archetypes needs further exploration, especially given Lewis's comments in "Psycho-Analysis and Literary Criticism," which suggest some influence of Jung on Lewis: *Selected Literary Essays*, 286–300. Yet it is possible that Lewis encountered such devices primarily in medieval literature, such as Petrarch, Dante, and Chaucer: see, for example, the suggestive study of Paul T. Piehler, "Allegory without Archetype: Image and Structure in Petrarch's *Trionfi*." In *Petrarch's Triumphs. Allegory and Spectacle*, edited by Konrad Eisenbichler and Amilcare A. Iannucci, 97–112. Ottawa: Dovehouse Editions, 1990.

96   See the unpublished letter to the Swedish Academy, dated January 16, 1961, proposing Tolkien for the 1961 Nobel Prize in Literature: text in McGrath, *C. S. Lewis – A Life*, 351.

97   "Tolkien's The Lord of the Rings"; *Essay Collection*, 524–5.

98   Avner Cohen, "Myth and Myth Criticism Following the *Dialectic of Enlightenment*." *The European Legacy: Toward New Paradigms* 15 (2010): 583–98. The

work was first published in 1944 with the title *Philosophische Fragmente*; a revised version of 1947 took the new title *Dialektik der Aufklärung*. For the institutional context within which this important work emerged, see Martin Jay, *The Dialectical Imagination: A History of the Frankfurt School and the Institute for Social Research 1923–1950*. Berkeley, CA: University of California Press, 1996, 3–40.

99 Jürgen Habermas, "The Entwinement of Myth and Enlightenment: Rereading *Dialectic of Enlightenment.*" *New German Critique* 26 (1982): 13–20.

100 Lincoln, *Theorizing Myth*, 47–140.

101 Eric Csapo, *Theories of Mythology*. Oxford: Blackwell, 2005, 292–3.

102 See Lewis's analysis in the essay "Bluspels and Flalansferes: A Semantic Nightmare": *Selected Literary Essays*, 251–65. Note particularly his suggestion that "reason is the natural organ of truth; but imagination is the organ of meaning." There are interesting resonances here with Hannah Arendt, *The Life of the Mind*. New York: Harcourt Brace Jovanovich, 1981, 15: "The need of reason is not inspired by the quest for truth but by the quest for meaning. And truth and meaning are not the same."

103 "The Weight of Glory"; *Essay Collection*, 99.

104 The view of the Enlightenment: see the classic study of Hans Frei, *The Eclipse of Biblical Narrative: A Study in Eighteenth and Nineteenth Century Biblical Hermeneutics*. New Haven, CT: Yale University Press, 1977.

105 Frederick Buechner, *Wishful Thinking*. New York: HarperCollins, 1993, 77.

106 *The Great Divorce*, 40.

4

The Privileging of Vision: Lewis's Metaphors of Light, Sun, and Sight

Wär' nicht das Auge sonnenhaft,
Die Sonne könnt es nie erblicken;
Läg nicht in uns des Gottes eigne Kraft,
Wie könnt uns Göttliches entzücken?[1]

Johann Wolfgang von Goethe

"I believe in Christianity as I believe that the Sun has risen, not only because I see it but because by it I see everything else."[2] This beautifully crafted sentence acts as both the conclusion and the climax of Lewis's remarkable paper "Is Theology Poetry?," delivered to the Socratic Club at Oxford University in 1945. Lewis's fundamental intention here was to affirm the conceptual capaciousness of the Christian faith, which he believed to be able to "fit in" science, art, morality, and other religions. Yet many, while admiring the expansive vision of Christianity that Lewis's words express, find themselves equally struck by the visual imagery through which he chose to express the thought – the sun illuminating a landscape.

Curiously, Lewis scholarship has paid surprisingly little attention to the way in which Lewis privileges metaphors relating to sun, light, vision, and shadows in his writings.[3] It is a somewhat troubling omission, for two chief reasons. First, Lewis's use of such metaphors helps us locate him within the "great tradition" of western thought; second, it clarifies Lewis's distinct approach to apologetics (see 129–46), which often focuses on the manner in which Christianity offers a new way of seeing things, which casts light on the enigmas and paradoxes of human existence,

---

The Intellectual World of C. S. Lewis, First Edition. Alister E. McGrath.
© 2014 John Wiley & Sons, Ltd. Published 2014 by John Wiley & Sons, Ltd.

allowing them to be seen in a new way. As Henry Miller (1891–1980) once remarked, both expressing and continuing this visual imagery, "One's destination is never a place, but rather a new way of looking at things."[4]

The Privileging of Ocular Metaphors: Vision, the Sun, and Light in Lewis's Writings

Lewis's clear preference for visual analogies for human thought reflect his being embedded within the classic tradition of ancient Greece, and its Renaissance reformulations.[5] This privileging of the imagery and vocabulary of sight is deeply embedded within the western scientific, religious, philosophical, and literary tradition,[6] which draws extensively on the language of sight and vision for its metaphors of truth and meaning.[7] Hannah Arendt is one of many writers to note that, "from the very outset, in formal philosophy, thinking has been thought of in terms of *seeing*."[8] Indeed, the critically important term "theory" – derived from the Greek *theoria*, which could be translated as "beholding a spectacle" – can be interpreted as "a way of seeing something."[9] This privileging of the metaphorical ocular – often referred to in recent discussion as "the hegemony of vision"[10] – has been documented and criticized by recent writers, including Michel Foucault and Jacques Derrida.[11] As Derrida points out, "starting with its first words, metaphysics associates sight with knowledge."[12] Yet, despite such criticisms, it has proved impossible to break with the ocularcentric tradition of modernity. It possesses some intuitive plausibility that defies attempts to marginalize it, or replace it with auditory or other alternatives.[13] We should not be surprised that Lewis draws on this philosophical tradition, and uses it powerfully in both his fictional and apologetic works. His preference for a metaphorics of the ocular reflects how deeply he is embedded within a broader tradition of cultural and philosophical discourse and reflection.

Yet this preference for metaphors of vision is not simply found in western philosophical writings; the theme of "seeing God" is deeply rooted in the Christian Bible,[14] and plays an important role in shaping both the conceptualities and expectations of Christian theology.[15] John Milton's preference for visual rather than auditory metaphors[16] reflects both his cultural and religious roots. Nicolas Malebranche's philosophy of religion, which makes an appeal to the problematic idea of "vision in God," echoes similar themes.[17] Lewis himself picks up on some of these biblical themes, which have clearly helped to shape his thinking.[18]

It is important to appreciate that Lewis's decision to give preference to visual imagery was not a forced choice. Auditory metaphors are widely found in religious literature in general,[19] and theological works in particular. Augustine's *Confessions*, for example, often seems to privilege auditory metaphors for truth;[20] his *City of God* makes extensive use of the musical metaphor of harmony.[21] Dante's *Divine Comedy*, highly regarded by Lewis as an exemplar of the medieval worldview, develops musical imagery at multiple locations,[22] even if the imagery of light predominates overall.[23]

Protestantism's characteristic emphasis upon the foundational role of the "Word of God" leads to a corresponding preference for auditory metaphors. Martin Luther's analysis of the doctrine of justification makes extensive use of metaphors of hearing, as Robert Jenson noted recently.[24]

> One sees how all this works together only when one notices the astonishing switch that Luther has pulled on the Greeks' ontology and epistemology. In their doctrine, the specific character of personal beings, "souls," is that their being is determined by what they, as perfect eyes, *see*. Luther switched that; for him the specific character of personal being is that we are what, as perfect ears, we *hear*.

Similar themes can easily be evidenced from within the Protestant tradition. The versions of Protestantism which emerged in Zurich in the 1550s emphasized the importance of hearing the word of God, especially through preaching.[25] For John Calvin, the church of God is the community which is generated, constituted, and maintained by the proclamation and obedient hearing of the Word of God.[26] For Karl Barth, a leading twentieth-century Protestant theologian, one of the primary characteristics of the church is its hearing and being shaped by the Word of God.[27] The celebrated "Barmen Declaration" (1934) privileged auditory metaphors in formulating its principled resistance to Adolf Hitler's Nazification of German Christianity: "Jesus Christ, as he is attested for us in Holy Scripture, is the one Word of God which we have to hear and which we have to trust and obey in life and in death."[28] Faith is here understood primarily in terms of trust and obedience, arising from hearing the Word of God.

For Luther, faith arises from *hearing the Word of God properly*; for Lewis, faith expresses itself in *seeing things rightly*. Lewis rarely uses metaphors of *hearing*; his clear preference is for metaphors of *sight*. In this essay, we shall set Lewis's reflections in their broader intellectual and cultural context, and explore the role these images play in his writings.

Lewis's works – especially the "Chronicles of Narnia" – make reference to all the human senses: seeing, hearing, smelling, touching, and tasting. Who, for example, can forget his description of Eustace sampling the

White Witch's gift-wrapped Turkish Delight? Yet it is clear that Lewis privileges ocular imagery. A fundamental theme that underlies much of Lewis's writings is the question of how we *see* things.

Recent interest in the use of medieval planetary symbolism in Lewis's writings, especially the "Chronicles of Narnia,"[29] highlights Lewis's distinctiveness at this point. Medieval discussion of the planets made extensive use of auditory symbolism – particularly the musical metaphor of "harmony" – in emphasizing the regularity of patterns disclosed by the observation of the heavens.[30] In recent years, there has been growing appreciation of the place of musical motifs and imagery in the scientific writings of Isaac Newton (1643–1727), a pioneer of the scientific revolution.[31] Yet despite the rich imaginative potential of such auditory symbols in Renaissance literature and science,[32] Lewis prefers to focus on visual imagery.

One of the more striking features of Lewis's works, both fictional and critical, is not simply his extensive use of ocular imagery; he tends to present metaphors relating to light in *a consistently positive sense*. Others, however, have noted the ambiguity of such metaphors. Light has its darker side. Before exploring Lewis's use of these ocular visions in more detail, we need to consider the ambivalence of ocular metaphors within western culture.

The Moral Ambivalence of Seeing: Reflections on Culture and Power

The western cultural tradition is saturated with the imagery of light and sight. Yet it would be a serious misjudgment to assume that light and sight are necessarily understood to play purely positive roles. In a political context, they can easily function as symbols of an open society on the one hand, and a controlled and policed society on the other. In what follows, we shall consider two ocular metaphors, and note the way they have been used in such discussions.

The fundamentally ocular metaphor of "transparency" is widely used in modern debates about an open society, in which political transactions are publicly accountable. Such metaphors can be traced back to the early Enlightenment. Jean-Jacques Rousseau (1712–78) regarded politics as a means of preserving or restoring "a compromised state of transparency."[33] The English political philosopher Jeremy Bentham (1746–1832) concurred: "In the darkness of secrecy, sinister interest and evil in every shape, have full swing."[34] The issue has become of particular importance in the contemporary political rhetoric of the United States,[35] not least in relation to identifying and neutralizing the undue influence of certain individuals and corporate interests in the public sphere.[36] Lewis is a clear advocate of such transparency, particularly in the "Ransom" trilogy.

Yet the capacity to *see* also implies a capacity to *control*. The same Jeremy Bentham who advocated transparency in public life to safeguard freedom also designed a "panopticon" as a means to allow prison guards to observe prisoners, without themselves being observed.[37] Michel Foucault famously developed this image as metaphor for the tendency of modern states to observe and normalize through processes of social surveillance.[38] For Foucault, being able to see others is a precondition for control, dominance, and the suppression of deviant behavior.[39] Bentham illustrates the fundamental ambiguity of being able to see and be seen, which easily leads from the moral high ground of political openness to the darker regions of state control of individuals.

Lewis tends not to see ocular metaphors in this more sinister manner, mainly because he tends to apply his ocular metaphors to *individuals*, who are enabled to discern more about the world around them. His Oxford colleague J. R. R. Tolkien, however, developed one of the most potent ocular images of oppression in western literature – the all-seeing "eye" of the Dark Lord Sauron, which clearly anticipates the oppressive overtones of Foucault's cultural metaphor of the "panopticon."[40] Tolkien, however, regarded this oppression as reflecting the corrupting impact of power, characteristic of *humanity*,[41] whereas Foucault regarded this form of power as an innovation, characteristic of *modernity*.

A close reading of Lewis's works, both fiction and non-fiction, suggests that two interconnected ocular images are of particular importance in his writings:

1. The imagery of "seeing" itself, focusing on how the human observer perceives things;
2. The image of the sun or illumination as enabling human knowledge, especially in revealing and illuminating the shadowlands.

We shall consider both of these in more detail in what follows.

Seeing Things as They Really Are

Lewis frequently addressed the question of the limits and reliability of human sight. How could we learn to see things as they really are? How can we discern what lies beneath mere appearances? Can our natural vision be supplemented, to allow it to reach further? Or healed, in order to extend its scope? Above all: how can we see *God*? The question of how we "see" things rightly underlies much theological reflection,[42] and is echoed in the literary works of the Middle Ages and Renaissance, which Lewis made his field of specialization.

For Lewis, the Christian faith offers us a means of seeing things properly – as they really are, despite their outward appearances.[43] This theme emerges in his first significant religious work, *The Pilgrim's Regress* (1933). Having reached the mysterious island which is the true object of his longing, the pilgrim now retraces his steps as he returns home. Yet although he walks through the same landscapes, he see the land "as it really is." "'It is just as it was when you passed it before', said the Guide, 'but your eyes are altered. You see nothing now but realities.'"[44]

This notion of seeing things in new ways is often expressed in the art, thought, and poetry of the Renaissance using the ocular metaphor of the mirror.[45] Unsurprisingly, the metaphor of a mirror and reflection are found frequently in Lewis's works, often to explain the manner in which God is known indirectly and in a scaled down manner – as seen, for example, when comparing "the Sun and the Sun's reflection in a dewdrop."[46]

Lewis uses the image of a mirror to particular effect in *The Last Battle*, the concluding book of the "Chronicles of Narnia." In trying to explain the difference of quality between the "Old Narnia" and the "New Narnia," Lewis invites his readers to imagine seeing a landscape through a window; and then to see that same landscape, but this time reflected through a mirror on the wall opposite the window. Lewis suggests that the quality of seeing is significantly different in each case:[47]

> [The images seen in the mirror] were in one sense just the same as the real ones: yet at the same time they were somehow different – deeper, more wonderful, more like places in a story: in a story you have never heard but very much want to know.

Lewis's point concerns the imaginative enhancement of vision, which allows something to be seen in a "deeper, more wonderful" manner. It is, of course, a subjective judgment; yet for Lewis, such subjective judgments are integral to the inner life of human beings. Lewis had earlier commented on the use of a similar device in Dante's *Divine Comedy*, in which the poet's imagery of light allows us to "not only understand the doctrine but see the picture."[48]

As Lewis's use of the image of the mirror makes clear, the idea of seeing things through glass – such as a mirror, telescope, or window – was clearly seen as imaginatively productive. We may fail to see God because we look through "a dirty telescope" or "a dirty lens";[49] we look through a window, the transparency of which allows us to see "the street or garden beyond it."[50]

This imagery of seeing through glass – with its associated notions of reflection, refraction, and visual enhancement[51] – is found in many medieval writings on the theory of knowledge or spiritual discernment.[52] One of its more familiar deployments is found in George Herbert's *Elixir*, which draws a fine distinction between "looking at" glass, and "looking through" it.

> A man that looks on glass,
> On it may stay his eye;
> Or if he pleaseth, through it pass,
> And then the heav'n espy.

Herbert here contrasts two quite different possible modes of engagement with a piece of glass – a "looking on," which merely focuses on the medium, and a "passing through," which allows the medium to be the gateway to what lies beyond. There are, of course parallels here – though not an identity – with Lewis's notion of "looking at" and "looking along."[53] Light is not something that we *see*; it is something *by which* we see.

This approach is deeply embedded in both classical Greek thought and in Christian theology. Plato and Aristotle both appropriated the notion of *theoria* – which originally designated spectators who watched the Olympic Games and other sacred festivals in a kind of "sacralized spectating" – to refer to a way of "seeing" reality.[54] The development of the notion of "theory" thus rests on an explicit assumption about parallels between "seeing" and "knowing," with potential implications for claims to cultural power and authority.[55]

Similar ideas were developed within the Christian tradition, particularly by Augustine of Hippo, who emphasized Christ's ability to heal "the eyes of the heart," thus enabling people to see reality properly.[56] Charles Taylor's analysis of the influence of Augustine on shaping western perceptions of the self and its capacities should be noted here:[57]

> God is not just the transcendent object or just the principle of order of the nearer objects, which we strain to see. God is also and for us primarily the basic support and underlying principle of our knowing activity. God is not just what we long to see, but what powers the eye which sees. So the light of God is not just "out there", illuminating the order of being, as it is for Plato; it is also an "inner" light. It is the light "which lighteth every man that cometh into the world." It is the light in the soul.

So does Lewis adopt a "spectator theory of knowledge" in which the mind is compared to a blank slate, on which reality impresses itself, or a dark chamber, into which the light of experience streams? Such approaches, based on the analogy of vision, were criticized by American pragmatist philosophers in the late nineteenth and early twentieth centuries. John Dewey, for example, advocated an "experimental theory of knowledge," in which the mind actively constructed its view of reality. Knowledge is the product of inquiry, a problem-solving process in which we move from doubt to belief. For Dewey, any theory of knowledge which proposes an analogy with the process of seeing is necessarily deficient.[58]

> The theory of knowing is modelled after what was supposed to take place in the act of vision. The object refracts light and is seen; it makes a difference to the eye and to the person having an optical apparatus, but none to the thing seen. The real object is the object so fixed in its regal aloofness that it is a king to any beholding mind that may gaze upon it. A spectator theory of knowledge is the inevitable outcome.

Who does Dewey have in his gunsights here? There is little doubt that his primary targets are writers such as Plato and Aristotle, who he regards as privileging theory over practice, and failing to appreciate the internal struggles and debates that must take place before we "know" something.

Dewey is clearly concerned about a passive theory of the acquisition of knowledge, as if this were imprinted on the mind by analogy with a photographic image. Yet it would be ridiculous to accuse Aristotle or Plato of any such theory of knowledge. Neither treat knowledge as the outcome of an "instant ocularity." Both Aristotle and Plato, in their different ways, clearly assume that the thinking individual must exercise judgment, wisdom, and above all intellectual energy in working out, from an observation of the world, precisely what can be "known" about it, and how reliable this "knowledge" might be. Similarly, Lewis's privileging of visual metaphors for knowledge does not entail the absence of critical engagement with possible modes of vision – a point which becomes particularly clear when reading his autobiography, *Surprised by Joy*.

Readers of *Surprised by Joy* are in a privileged position, as they can study at least something of Lewis's thought processes as he navigated his way from atheism to a form of idealism, to theism, and finally to Christianity.[59] There is no way in which Lewis's preference for visual analogies of the process of knowing implies a passive "spectator theory of knowledge." As we noted earlier, Lewis's mature understanding of reality was not gained by an instant exposure to reality, captured once and for all in an unambiguous image, but through an extended and sustained process of reflection about which way of "seeing" reality seemed best adapted to its accommodation and representation (120–2).

Yet perhaps the most important point to be made concerning the importance of "seeing" for Lewis is this: a failure to *understand* is ultimately a failure to *see*. Lewis rightly realized that many people frame their accounts of things analogically, using what Hilaire Belloc called "parallelism" – that is to say, the "illustration of some unperceived truth by its exact consonance with the reflection of a truth already known and perceived."[60] The perception of a cognitive dissonance with a theological notion – such as the Trinity – may thus arise from the use of an inadequate analogy or the deployment of an inappropriate "way of seeing," rather than a fundamental difficulty with the idea itself. We may be looking at things through the wrong set of spectacles; a different set allow us to see things in a new way, bringing into focus what once seemed blurred and confusing.

Lewis's commendation of the Christian faith rests partly in his belief that it offers a capacious and deeply satisfying vision of reality – a way of looking at things that simultaneously allows both discernment of its complexity and affirmation of its interconnectedness. The human imagination plays a leading role in grasping this "big picture," in that it is more easily perceived than understood. Here is what we might call a "religious imaginary"[61] – a "way of living, seeing and making,"[62] grounded in the Christian vision of reality, which lends coherence to the whole picture of existence.

One of the most striking aspects of Lewis's thought is his emphatic insistence on the coherence of the Christian way of seeing things. In his *Republic*, Plato used the ocular term *synoptikos* as a way of denoting the ability – which he holds to be characteristic of a philosopher – to "see the whole together" or "see things in a unified manner."[63]

Lewis follows Plato in using a visual image to express this fundamental theme of coherence – whether he finds it within the Christian faith itself, or within the canon of western literature. Citing Dante's *Divine Comedy*, Lewis argues that coherence is observed when every individual part of the whole shines on and thereby illuminates the others: *ogni parte ad ogni parte splende*.[64] The interconnectedness of this literary canon, Lewis declares, is such that "it does not matter at what point you first break into the system of European poetry," in that "everything will lead you to everything else in the end."[65] It is the same with Christianity; everything is interconnected.

Lewis is clear that the act of "seeing" is ultimately about discernment; "looking at" is not the same as "beholding." There are points at which Lewis echoes the ocular imagery of John Ruskin (1819–1900), who held that "the greatest thing a human soul ever does in this world is to see something, and tell what it saw in a plain way...To see clearly is poetry, prophecy, and religion – all in one."[66] This naturally raises the theological question of whether this process of seeing properly is to be calibrated and corrected as if it were a purely human technique, or whether it is to be seen as the outcome of divine grace and transformation.

The New Testament speaks, not so much of the training of the human eye, as of the healing of human blindness, or the divine removal of a veil that prevents us from beholding reality (Acts 9:9–19; 2 Corinthians 3:13–16). The mere opening of eyes does not ensure that we see things correctly.[67] The human eye must itself be healed by grace if the world is to be seen properly. Writers such as Augustine stressed that the Christian way of "seeing" reality is neither naturally acquired nor naturally endorsed. It comes about through the Christian revelation, which brings about a transformation of our perception of things.[68] Lewis appears to echo such views in *Surprised by Joy*, where he portrays the emergence of his new way of seeing things in terms of a series of moves made against him by God. Yet elsewhere, Lewis suggests that while God is both source and cause of the healing of our sight and minds, we must respond in such a way as to make this effective in our lives. God has made salvation possible; "we individuals have to appropriate that salvation."[69] It is like a "good infection"; we must "catch it," if we are to be healed.

The Sun and Illumination as the Enablers of Knowledge

Lewis's writings make frequent use of the analogy of the sun as a source of illumination. Any association between God and the sun is conspicuously absent from the Old Testament, on account of the risk of assimilation to Canaanite nature religions, which often involved the worship of the sun and other heavenly bodies as divine.[70] The image features prominently in many classical mythologies – Egyptian, Greek, Roman, and Nordic[71] – and plays a significant role in the medieval planetary symbolism that may have influenced Lewis's construction of the "Chronicles of Narnia."[72]

The imagery of light is deeply embedded in both biblical and classical sources. At an unknown date in the late Middle Ages, Oxford University adopted as its motto the Latin tag *Dominus illuminatio mea* – "the Lord is my light" (Psalm 27:1). Lewis could hardly have failed to notice this symbolism. Throughout the Christian Bible, the iconic dialectic between darkness and light is seen as correlated with the moral dialectic between evil and good, the spiritual dialectic between unbelief and faith, and the epistemic dialectic between doubt and knowledge.[73] Although the contrast between light and dark is particularly striking in John's gospel,[74] this theme is found throughout the Bible, and subsequently in its interpretation within the Christian churches.

This imagery is, however, also found throughout the literature of the ancient world. Eastern religions make much use of the imagery of light and darkness.[75] Yet in terms of the shaping of western literary and cultural conventions, it is arguable that the use of metaphors of light in the writings of Plato have perhaps proved most significant, especially as these are developed within neo-Platonism.[76] "Light is more than just a metaphor; it is almost an instance of how intelligible reality generates its extended image."[77] Perhaps this factor, coupled with its extensive use in the Bible, led to the imagery of light or illumination being appropriated by many early Christian writers.

The most important of these is Augustine of Hippo (354–430), who made the imagery of light the cornerstone of his discussion of true knowledge, especially knowledge of divine things.[78] It is not clear whether Augustine develops a coherent account of human cognition, based on the notion of illumination, or whether he simply saw light as a useful metaphorical organizing principle for his reflections. Nevertheless, there is no doubt of the importance of his fundamental conviction that true knowledge arises through the divine illumination of the human intellect. For Augustine, God is the intelligible sun who gives light to the mind and therefore brings intelligibility to what we see.[79] At times, Augustine suggests that God illuminates the mind itself; at others, that God, like a sun, illuminates the extra-mental reality which is to be understood:[80]

> Both the earth and light are visible; yet the earth cannot be seen unless it is illuminated by light...In the same way, things cannot be understood unless they are illuminated by something else as their own sun.

There are clear parallels between Augustine and Lewis in this matter, evident in Lewis's remark that "the human mind in the act of knowing is illuminated by the Divine reason."[81] Lewis himself confessed that his "glad debts" to Augustine were "incalculable,"[82] without actually identifying what they might be. The notion of divine illumination, many would argue, would be one of them. Lewis probably echoes intermediaries at this point, especially the Cambridge Platonists,[83] which he is known to have studied in the 1920s. Yet the imagery of light and darkness is so widely found in the literature of the English Renaissance and Romanticism that it is difficult to identify the sources of Lewis's ideas.[84] Perhaps we must be realistic, and limit ourselves to exploring Lewis's use of such metaphors of light, rather than attempting to demonstrate their provenance.

We do not really find a fully developed epistemology in Lewis's writings, although the basic elements of his position may be identified with reasonable confidence. What we find instead is a series of reflections on the image of light, musings rather than sustained analyses, episodic interventions rather than an extended and focused engagement. One of the most interesting of these is Lewis's critique of the trenchant rationalism of a movement that itself appealed to the imagery of light in its self-definition and self-understanding: the Enlightenment.[85]

The term "Enlightenment" has come to be used in English as a shorthand way of referring to the "age of reason" – the cultural mood which exercised so significant an influence over western thought throughout Lewis's lifetime. The iconography of the movement was firmly established by the 1790s.[86] Writers such as Daniel Chodowiecki (1726–1802) appealed to the image of the rising sun, dispersing mists and dispelling darkness, as a superb representation of the impact of reason on ignorance and superstition.[87]

Recent scholarship has revealed this movement as rather more complex than many had realized, exposing its intellectual diversity, its suppression of liberal ideas and values now (but not then) regarded as benign, and highlighting its covert social and moral assumptions – such as the puzzling notion of "natural humanity," devoid of any cultural context or influence.[88]

The general category of "Enlightenment" turns out to be a practical necessity for holding a plurality of particulars together as different aspects of a single movement, rather than as distinguishing features of diverging movements.[89] Nevertheless, it remains fair to suggest that this movement generally regarded human reason as the key to a brighter and better future, not least in liberating humanity from what it regarded as outdated and repressive "superstitions" of "myths." Yet some argued that, while eighteenth-century rationalism might have liberated humanity from some superstitions, it ended up enslaving it to other questionable ideas and practices.[90]

Yet the most cogent and compelling English critiques of the Enlightenment came not from philosophers, but from the writers of literature. Romanticism can be seen as a protest against the spiritual, emotional, and aesthetic impoverishment of humanity within the bleak world of pure reason. William Blake, for example, protested against the human subjugation of nature, which he regarded as the inevitable outcome of the Enlightenment's emphasis on human mastery.[91] Romantic poets protested against the "disenchantment" of the world by modern science, and the excesses of scientific reductionism.[92]

Lewis subverts this rationalist outlook using the imagery of "light," making two points in particular. First, he insists that human reason does not "illuminate" reality as if it were in itself and of itself a *source* of light; rather, the ability of reason to illuminate things is itself a consequence of it already having been illumined by the Divine reason. Reason is not autonomous, especially in relation to the things of God. It must be enabled to see; otherwise, it sees only dimly, if at all. Second, Lewis argues that what the human mind apprehends when "seeing" reality is not limited to rational truths, but to a broader and deeper vision of things, engaging and involving the imagination and emotions, not merely reason. We do not simply know about things; we *know* them, at a much deeper level.

Lewis hints at both these points in a significant passage in his late work *The Four Loves*, in which the ultimate grounding of true knowledge – in both its rational and relational senses – is affirmed to lie in God's illumination of the converted human mind.[93]

> The humblest of us, in a state of Grace, can have some "knowledge-by-acquaintance" (*connaître*), some "tasting," of Love Himself; but man even at his highest sanctity and intelligence has no direct "knowledge about" (*savoir*) the ultimate Being – only analogies. We cannot see light, though by light we can see things. Statements about God are extrapolations from the knowledge of other things which the divine illumination enables us to know.

Lewis was concerned to affirm the importance of reason, while avoiding the aesthetically bleak and metaphysically austere vision of reality resulting from an exaggeration of reason's power and a failure to comprehend the importance of other human mental faculties – above all, the imagination.[94] The image of light allowed Lewis to emphasize the *derivative* ability of the mind to comprehend (it is "illuminated by the Divine reason"),[95] while at the same time expanding his understanding of what the mind actually grasped, subverting the limiting assumption that the mind was capable merely of ratiocination.

A similar point is made by David Michael Levin in making his distinction between "assertoric" and "alethic gaze."[96] The former represents a manner of looking at something which is abstracted from its context, rigid, and defined fundamentally in the thin terms of logic; the latter is a rich and complex visual encounter, which allows the beholder to appreciate the full richness of what is being seen. The former reduces reality to abstractions in order to master it; the latter tries to see something *as it really is*. (Iris Murdoch's notion of "attentiveness" makes a similar point: our responsibility is to "come to see the world as it is."[97])

So are the associations between seeing and reality, between light and goodness, arbitrary, the outcome of the unrestrained human imagination? Or are they embedded in a deeper order of things, which the human mind discerns, rather than invents?[98] While Lewis does not engage this question systematically, there are points at which he clearly intimates that such associations reflect a form of resonance between the human mind and reality. The "orderliness of Nature" is grounded in the divine Reason, from which human reason itself is derived.[99]

Yet it is not merely human reason that is guided by a deeper reality; Lewis suggests that this also extends to the imagination. In an important essay comparing the work of several poets, Lewis remarked that it was essential for poets to follow the cues of their imaginations because these "are constrained by deepest necessities."[100] It is as if, Lewis suggests, there are certain "fundamental laws of the imagination,"[101] which somehow direct our intuitions to follow the moral and rational grain of the universe.

This point is developed more fully in the difficult closing paragraph of the essay "Bluspels and Flalansferes," which hints at some kind of imaginative correspondence between human intuition and such natural qualities as light and dark. Far from being "arbitrary and fanciful," such intimations of correspondence must be seen to be rooted in something much more fundamental.[102]

> It does follow that if those original equations, between good and light, or evil and dark, between breath and soul and all the others, were from the beginning arbitrary and fanciful – if there is not, in fact, a kind of psycho-physical parallelism (or more) in the universe – then all our thinking is nonsensical. But we cannot, without contradiction, believe it to be nonsensical.

Conclusion

In this essay, we have explored Lewis's extensive use of ocular metaphors for truth. Lewis clearly believes that this highly visual way of thinking and speaking is well grounded in the Christian tradition, that it resonates with some core themes of classical philosophy, that it is echoed in the medieval and Renaissance literary traditions, and – perhaps most important of all! – that it is rationally and imaginative *useful*. He is right on all four counts. There is more that needs to be done to appreciate the subtleties of Lewis's use of ocular imagery in his writings, especially his apologetics works and the "Chronicles of Narnia." There can be no doubt of its importance for his intellectual vision, nor of the enhanced understanding of Lewis's approach that will result from closer study of his visual metaphors.

Notes

1 Johann Wolfgang von Goethe, *Werke*. Edited by Erich Trunz. Munich: Beck, 1996, vol. 1, 367. A rough translation reads: "If our eye were not sun-adapted, it could never glimpse the sun. If God's own power did not lie within us, how could we take delight in the divine?"

2 "Is Theology Poetry?"; *Essay Collection*, 21.

3 A rare exception in Michael Ward, *Planet Narnia: The Seven Heavens in the Imagination of C. S. Lewis*. Oxford: Oxford University Press, 2007, 100–20. Although Ward's emphasis lies primarily on Lewis's appeal to the sun within the medieval view of the planets and their associated symbolisms, he touches on some of the deeper questions to be considered in this essay.

4 Henry Miller, *Big Sur and The Oranges of Hieronymus Bosch*. New York: New Directions, 1957, 25.

5 See the landmark essay of Hans Jonas, "The Nobility of Sight: A Study in the Phenomenology of the Senses." *Philosophy and Phenomenological Research* 14, no. 4 (1954): 507–19. More recently, see the collection of essays in David Michael Levin, ed. *Sites of Vision: The Discursive Construction of Sight in the History of Philosophy*. Cambridge, MA: MIT Press, 1997. For Pindar's striking use of metaphors of vision, see Zsolt Adorjáni, *Auge und Sehen in Pindars Dichtung*. Hildesheim: Georg Olms Verlag, 2011; for the theme in Thomas Mann, especially in relation to Old Testament characters, see David L. Tingey, *Seeing Jaakob: The Poetics of Visuality in Thomas Mann's Die Geschichten Jaakobs*. New York: Peter Lang, 2010.

6 As noted by Paola Potestà, *Gli occhi, il sole, la luce: Metafore sulla visione tra scienza e arte dall'antichità greca al '400*. Florence: Fondazione Giorgi Ronchi, 2002. For the emblematic and metaphorical use of optical images in scientific publications of the early modern period, see William B. Ashworth, "Divine Reflections and Profane Refractions: Images of a Scientific Impasse in 17th-Century Italy." In *Gianlorenzo Bernini: New Aspects of his Art and Thought*, edited by Irving Lavin, 179–207. University Park, PA: Penn State University Press, 1985.

7 See the seminal essay by Hans Blumenberg, "Licht als Metapher der Wahrheit." *Studium Generale* 10, no. 7 (1957): 432–47. This essay is widely recognized to be of landmark significance: see Philipp Stoellger, *Metapher und Lebenswelt: Hans Blumenbergs Metaphorologie als Lebensweltthermeneutik und ihr religionsphänomenologischer Horizont*. Tübingen: Mohr Siebeck, 2000, 70–80.

8   Hannah Arendt, *The Life of the Mind*. New York: Harcourt Brace Jovanovich, 1981, 110.

9   Martin Heidegger, *The Question Concerning Technology, and Other Essays*. New York: Harper & Row, 1977, 163–4. See further Hannelore Rausch, *Theoria: Von ihrer sakralen zur philosophischen Bedeutung*. Munich: Fink, 1982, 148–52; William McNeill, *The Glance of the Eye: Heidegger, Aristotle, and the Ends of Theory*. Albany, NY: State University of New York Press, 1999, 252–79.

10   See the important collection of essays in David M. Kleinberg-Levin, ed., *Modernity and the Hegemony of Vision*. Berkeley, CA: University of California Press, 1993.

11   As noted by Martin Jay, "The Rise of Hermeneutics and the Crisis of Ocularcentrism." *Poetics Today* 9, no. 2 (1988): 307–26; Christopher Collins, *The Poetics of the Mind's Eye: Literature and the Psychology of Imagination*. Philadelphia: University of Pennsylvania Press, 1991, 1–20; Evelyn Keller and Christine Grontkowski, "The Mind's Eye." In *Discovering Reality: Feminist Perspectives on Epistemology, Metaphysics, Methodology, and Philosophy of Science*, edited by Sandra Harding and Merril B. Hintikka, 207–24. Dordrecht: Reidel, 2004. Metaphors of vision play an important role in the writings of Noam Chomsky: Chris Werry, "Reflections on Language: Chomsky, Linguistic Discourse and the Value of Rhetorical Self-Consciousness." *Language Sciences* 29 (2007): 66–87. For the religious use of metaphors of vision, see Alister E. McGrath, "The Lord Is My Light: On the Discipleship of the Mind." *Evangelical Quarterly* 83 (2011): 133–45.

12   Jacques Derrida, "The Principle of Reason: The University in the Eyes of its Pupils." *Diacritics* 13 (1983): 1–17; quote at 4.

13   See the comments of Hans-Georg Gadamer, "Über das Hören." In *Hermeneutische Entwürfe*. Tübingen: Mohr Siebeck, 2000, 48–55.

14   Mark S. Smith, "'Seeing God' in the Psalms: The Background to the Beatific Vision in the Hebrew Bible." *Catholic Biblical Quarterly* 50 (1988): 171–83. On the book of Job, see Leo G. Perdue, *Wisdom Literature: A Theological History*. Louisville, KY: Westminster John Knox Press, 2007, 102.

15   As noted by William J. Hoye, *Actualitas Omnium Actuum: Man's Beatific Vision of God as Apprehended by Thomas Aquinas*. Meisenheim: Hain, 1975.

16   John D. Schaeffer, "Metonymies We Read By: Rhetoric, Truth and the Eucharist in Milton's *Areopagitica*." *Milton Quarterly* 34, no. 3 (2000): 84–92.

17   Nicholas Jolley, "Intellect and Illumination in Malebranche." *Journal of the History of Philosophy* 32, no. 2 (1994): 209–24.

18   E.g., see *Reflections on the Psalms*, 43–4.

19   As noted by David Chidester, *Word and Light: Seeing, Hearing, and Religious Discourse*. Urbana, IL: University of Illinois Press, 1992.

20   Carl G. Vaught, *Metaphor, Analogy, and the Place of Places: Where Religion and Philosophy Meet*. Waco, TX: Baylor University Press, 2004, 61–4.

21   Augustine regarded the meter of music or poetry as reflecting a divinely established order, a theme which can be argued to be present in George Herbert's poetry: William H. Pahlka, *Saint Augustine's Meter and George Herbert's Will*. Kent, OH: Kent State University Press, 1987. For the development of

the metaphor of "harmony" in western culture, see the classic study of Leo Spitzer, "Classical and Christian Ideas of World Harmony." *Traditio* 2 (1944): 409–64; 3 (1945): 307–64.

22 Francesco Ciabattoni, *Dante's Journey to Polyphony*. Toronto: University of Toronto Press, 2010, 8–137. For Lewis's comments on Dante's views concerning the "music of the spheres," see *The Discarded Image*, 111–12.

23 For example, consider Dante's description of Hell as a region *d'ogni luce muto* (*Inferno*, V, 28), which contrasts sharply with the luminosity of Paradise. See further Hélène Domon, *Le livre imaginaire*. Birmingham, AL: Summa Publications, 2000, 70–4.

24 Robert Jenson, "Response to Tuomo Mannermaa, 'Why Is Luther So Fascinating?'" In *Union with Christ*, edited by Carl Braaten and Robert Jenson, 21–4. Grand Rapids, MI: Eerdmans, 1998. See the earlier study of Ernst Bizer, *Fides ex auditu: Eine Untersuchung über die Entdeckung der Gerechtigkeit Gottes durch Martin Luther*. Neukirchen: Neukirchener Verlag, 1966. Luther's use of Romans 10:17 is particularly important at this point.

25 Edward A. Dowey, "Das Wort Gottes als Schrift und Predigt im zweiten Helvetischen Bekenntnis." In *Glauben und Bekennen: Vierhundert Jahre Confessio Helvetica posterior – Beiträge zu ihrer Geschichte und Theologie*, edited by Joachim Staedtke, 235–50. Zürich: Zwingli Verlag, 1966.

26 John Calvin, *Institutes of the Christian Religion*, IV.i.9–10; in *Joannis Calvini: Opera Selecta*, ed. P. Barth and W. Niesel. Munich: Kaiser Verlag, 1936, vol. 5, 13–14.

27 Barth's emphasis on the slogan *Deus dixit!* is important here, not least because of its privileging of auditory metaphors: God speaks, humanity listens. See further Stephen H. Webb, *Re-Figuring Theology: The Rhetoric of Karl Barth*. Albany, NY: State University of New York Press, 1991.

28 "The Theological Clarification of the Present State of the German Evangelical Churches" (1934), 1. In W. Niesel, ed. *Bekenntnisschiften und Kirchenordnungen der nach Gottes Wort reformierten Kirche*. Zurich: Evangelischer Verlag, 1938, 335.

29 See Ward, *Planet Narnia*, 23–41.

30 Johann Kepler's work is of particular importance in this respect: see Bruce Stephenson, *The Music of the Heavens: Kepler's Harmonic Astronomy*, Princeton, NJ: Princeton University Press, 1994. For the wider use of musical and other auditory metaphors in early modern science, see Rudolf Haase, *Aufsätze zur harmonikale Naturphilosophie*. Graz: Akademische Druck- und Verlangsanstalt, 1974; Penelope Gouk, *Music, Science, and Natural Magic in Seventeenth-Century England*. New Haven, CT: Yale University Press, 1999.

31 See especially J. E. McGuire, and P. M. Rattansi, "Newton and the Pipes of Pan." *Notes and Records of the Royal Society* 21, no. 2 (1966): 104–43; Myles W. Jackson, "Music and Science During the Scientific Revolution." *Perspectives on Science* 9, no. 1 (2001): 106–15.

32 See the analysis of Fernand Hallyn, *La structure poétique du monde: Copernic, Kepler*. Paris: Editions du Seuil, 1987. On the aesthetic aspects of harmony, particularly the use of spatial metaphors to elaborate harmonic themes,

see Roger Scruton, *The Aesthetics of Music*. Oxford: Clarendon Press, 1997, 63–71.

33   Jean Starobinski, *Jean-Jacques Rousseau: Transparency and Obstruction*. Chicago: University of Chicago Press, 1988, 13. For the impact of this notion on the French Revolution, see Marc Richir, "Révolution et transparence sociale." In Johann Gottlieb Fichte, *Considérations sur la Révolution française*. Paris: Payot, 1974, 7–74.

34   Jeremy Bentham, "Constitutional Code." In John Bowring, ed., *The Works of Jeremy Bentham*. New York, Russell & Russell, 1962, vol. 9, 493. For an excellent analysis, see Robert J. McCarthy Jr, "Panopticism and Publicity: Bentham's Quest for Transparency." *Public Culture* 6, no. 2 (1994): 547–75.

35   Jonathan Marks, "Jean-Jacques Rousseau, Michael Sandel and the Politics of Transparency." *Polity* 33, no. 4 (2001): 619–42.

36   See especially Mark Fenster, "Seeing the State: Transparency as Metaphor." *Administrative Law Review* 62, no. 3 (2010): 617–72.

37   Janet Semple, *Bentham's Prison: A Study of the Panopticon Penitentiary*. Oxford: Clarendon Press, 1993.

38   Foucault Michel, *Discipline and Punish: The Birth of the Prison*. New York: Vintage Books, 1995, 195–210.

39   William Bogard, *The Simulation of Surveillance: Hypercontrol in Telematic Societies*. Cambridge: Cambridge University Press, 1996.

40   Jane Chance, *The Lord of the Rings: The Mythology of Power*. Lexington, KY: University Press of Kentucky, 2001, 1–25.

41   S. J. William Dowie, "The Gospel of Middle Earth According to J. R. R. Tolkien." *Heythrop Journal* 15, no. 1 (1974): 37–52.

42   See, for example, Robert E. Barron, *And Now I See: A Theology of Transformation*. New York: Crossroad, 1998, 1: "Christianity is, above all, a way of seeing"; Andrew Louth, "Light, Vision and Religious Experience in Byzantium." In *The Presence of Light: Divine Radiance and Religious Experience*, edited by Matthew T. Kapstein, 85–103. Chicago: University of Chicago Press, 2004; Alister E. McGrath, *The Open Secret: A New Vision for Natural Theology*. Oxford: Blackwell, 2008, 113–216.

43   These themes are often described using the images of mirrors and lamps as models of the human imagination: see the classic study of M. H. Abrams, *The Mirror and the Lamp: Romantic Theory and the Critical Tradition*. Oxford: Oxford University Press, 1953. For comment, see Richard Kearney, *The Wake of Imagination: Toward a Postmodern Culture*. London: Routledge, 1988, 155.

44   *The Pilgrim's Regress*, 176–7.

45   See Dosia Reichardt, "'Only Your Picture in My Mind': The Image, the Heart, and the Mirror in Some Seventeenth-Century Poems." *Renaissance and Reformation* 30, no. 2 (2006): 67–82. On the medieval background, see Ritamary Bradley, "Backgrounds of the Title *Speculum* in Mediaeval Literature." *Speculum* 29, no. 1 (1954): 100–15; Edward Peter Nolan, *Now through a Glass Darkly: Specular Images of Being and Knowing from Virgil to Chaucer*. Ann Arbor, MI: University of Michigan Press, 1990. For its artistic use, see, for

example, Gustav Friedrich Hartlaub, *Zauber des Spiegels: Geschichte und Bedeutung des Spiegels in der Kunst*. Munich: Piper, 1951; Heinrich Holzapfel, *Subversion und Differenz: Das Spiegelmotiv bei Freud, Thomas Mann, Rilke und Jacques Lacan*. Essen: Blaue Eule, 1986.

46 *Surprised by Joy*, 193.

47 *The Last Battle*, 160. Lewis actually uses the term "looking-glass" at several points, which was the preferred way of referring to mirrors in certain sections of British culture in the late 1940s and early 1950s: see Alan S. C. Ross, "Linguistic Class Indicators in Present-Day English." *Neuphilologische Mitteilungen* 55 (1954): 113–49. For the popular debate that ensued in England, see Nancy Mitford, ed., *Noblesse Oblige*. Oxford: Oxford University Press, 1956.

48 "Imagery in the Last Eleven Cantos of Dante's 'Comedy'"; *Studies in Medieval and Renaissance Literature*, 78–93; quote at 90.

49 *Mere Christianity*, 163.

50 *The Abolition of Man*, 81.

51 For these ideas in Tolkien, see Verlyn Flieger, *Splintered Light: Logos and Language in Tolkien's World*. Kent, OH: Kent State University, 2002. For their deeper background, see Shandi Stevenson, "The Shadow beyond the Firelight: Pre-Christian Archetypes and Imagery Meet Christian Theology in Tolkien's Treatment of Evil and Horror." In *The Mirror Crack'd: Fear and Horror in J.R.R. Tolkien's Major Works*, edited by Lynn Forrest-Hill, 93–118. Newcastle: Cambridge Scholars, 2008.

52 See especially Dallas G. Denery, *Seeing and Being Seen in the Later Medieval World: Optics, Theology, and Religious Life*. Cambridge: Cambridge University Press, 2005.

53 See "Meditation in a Toolshed"; *Essay Collection*, 607–10.

54 See the excellent study of the metaphorical foundation of philosophic *theoria* in the practice of sacralized vision in Andrea Wilson Nightingale, *Spectacles of Truth in Classical Greek Philosophy: Theoria in Its Cultural Context*. Cambridge: Cambridge University Press, 2004, 14–92.

55 A point made by Thomas Rakoczy, *Böser Blick, Macht des Auges und Neid der Götter: Eine Untersuchung zur Kraft des Blickes in der griechischen Literatur*. Tübingen: Gunter Narr, 1996. The idea of the "evil eye" – hinted at in biblical texts – can be seen as an extension of this idea: John H. Elliott, "Lecture socioscientifique. Illustration par l'accusation du 'Mauvais Oeil' en Galatie." In *Guide des nouvelles lectures de la Bible*, edited by André Lacocque, 141–67. Paris: Bayard Éditions, 2005.

56 Augustine of Hippo, *Sermon* 88.5.5. For Augustine's notion of "seeing" the things of God, see *Confessions* 7.17.23.

57 Charles Taylor, *Sources of the Self*. Cambridge, MA: Harvard University Press, 1989, 129, citing John 1:9 in the King James translation.

58 See especially his 1929 essay "The Quest for Certainty"; John Dewey, *Later Works, 1925–1953*. 17 vols. Carbondale, IL: Southern Illinois University Press, 1981, vol. 4, 19.

59   See two earlier essays in this volume: 7–29; 31–54.

60   Hilaire Belloc, *On the Place of Gilbert Chesterton in English Letters*. New York: Sheed & Ward, 1940, 37.

61   For the notion, see especially Charles Taylor, *Modern Social Imaginaries*. Durham, NC: Duke University Press, 2002.

62   Cornelius Castoriadis, *The Imaginary Institution of Society*. Cambridge, MA: MIT Press, 1987, 145.

63   Plato, *Republic*, 537C7. For the dialectical importance of this notion, see Noburu Noōtomi, *The Unity of Plato's Sophist: Between the Sophist and the Philosopher*. Cambridge: Cambridge University Press, 1999, 95–121, especially 114–17.

64   Dante, *Inferno* VII, 75; cited at *Surprised by Joy*, 60. The context makes Lewis's point more clearly: *ogni parte ad ogni parte splende, distribuendo igualmente la luce*; "every part shines on every part, distributing the light evenly."

65   *Surprised by Joy*, 60. Lewis's image of the "dance" makes a similar point: *Mere Christianity*, 175.

66   Ruskin, *Works*, vol. 5, 333. See also Susan P. Casteras, ed., *John Ruskin and the Victorian Eye*. New York: Harry N. Abrams, 1993.

67   Note the comments of Iris Murdoch: "By opening our eyes, we do not necessarily see what confronts us...Our minds are continually active, fabricating an anxious, usually self-preoccupied, often falsifying *veil* which partially conceals the world." Iris Murdoch, *The Sovereignty of Good*. London: Routledge, 1970, 84.

68   Lydia Schumacher, *Divine Illumination: The History and Future of Augustine's Theory of Knowledge*. Oxford: Wiley-Blackwell, 2011, 25–65.

69   *Mere Christianity*, 181.

70   For a detailed analysis, see Glen Taylor, *Yahweh and the Sun: Biblical and Archaeological Evidence for Sun Worship in Ancient Israel*. Sheffield: JSOT Press, 1993.

71   Jan Assmann, *Egyptian Solar Religion in the New Kingdom: Re, Amun and the Crisis of Polytheism*. London: Kegan Paul, 1995. For Greek borrowing of this Egyptian mythology, see Scott Noegel, "Apollonius' 'Argonautika' and Egyptian Solar Mythology." *The Classical World* 97, no. 2 (2004): 123–36.

72   Ward, *Planet Narnia*, 100–20.

73   See, for example, Elizabeth R. Achtemeier, "Jesus Christ, the Light of the World: The Biblical Understanding of Light and Darkness." *Interpretation* 17, no. 4 (1963): 439–49; Beverly Roberts Gaventa, *From Darkness to Light: Aspects of Conversion in the New Testament*. Philadelphia: Fortress Press, 1986; Jeffrey L. Staley, "Stumbling in the Dark, Reaching for the Light: Reading Character in John 5 and 9." *Semeia* 53 (1991): 55–80.

74   See, for example, Homer A. Kent, Jr, *Light in the Darkness: Studies in the Gospel of John*. Grand Rapids, MI: Baker, 1974.

75   As noted by David L. McMahan, *Empty Vision: Metaphor and Visionary Imagery in Mahayana Buddhism*. London: Routledge, 2002; Claudia Weber, *Die Lichtmetaphorik im frühen Mahayana-Buddhismus*. Wiesbaden: Harrassowitz, 2002.

76   For Plotinus's metaphysics of light, see Frederic Maxwell Schroeder, *Form and Transformation: A Study in the Philosophy of Plotinus*. Montreal: McGill-Queen's Press, 1992, 24–51. The reduced ontological status of "shadows" in Plato's metaphorics of vision should be noted here: Gregory Vlastos, "Degrees of Reality in Plato." In *Platonic Studies*. Princeton: Princeton University Press, 1973, 58–75.

77   John Fielder, "Plotinus' Copy Theory." *Apeiron* 11, no. 2 (1977): 1–11; quote at 6.

78   Ronald Nash, *The Light of the Mind: St. Augustine's Theory of Knowledge*. Lexington, KY: University Press of Kentucky, 2003.

79   For this Christianized version of Platonism, see Philip Cary, *Augustine's Invention of the Inner Self: The Legacy of a Christian Platonist*. Oxford: Oxford University Press, 2000, 63–76.

80   Augustine of Hippo, *Soliloquies*, I.viii.15.

81   *Miracles*, 22.

82   *The Four Loves*, 145.

83   For the use of light in relation to reason within this movement, see Dominic Scott, "Reason, Recollection and the Cambridge Platonists." In *Platonism and the English Imagination*, edited by Anna P. Baldwin and Sarah Hutton, 139–50. Cambridge: Cambridge University Press, 2005. On More's notion of the divine illumination of reason, see Michael Losonsky, *Enlightenment and Action from Descartes to Kant: Passionate Thought*. Cambridge: Cambridge University Press, 2001, 121–3.

84   For example, see the important points made in Hans Feger, "Die liebliche Sonne der Nacht: Zur Lichtmetaphorik bei Schelling und Novalis." In *Offene Formen: Beitrage zur Literatur, Philosophie und Wissenschaft im 18. Jahrhundert*, edited by Bernd Brautigam and Burghard Damerau, 288–321. Berlin: Peter Lang, 1997.

85   The movement now known in English as "the Enlightenment" is known under other images in European languages. Some retain the imagery of light (for example, the Italian term *Illuminismo* or the French terms *les Lumières* or *le siècle des Lumières*); others do not (for example, the German term *Aufklärung*).

86   See the analysis in Werner Schneiders, "Aufklärungsphilosophicn." In *Europäische Aufklärung(en): Einheit und nationale Vielfalt*, edited by Siegfried Jüttner and Jochen Schlobach, 1–25. Hamburg: Felix Meiner Verlag, 1992, especially 9–13; Hilmar Frank, *Aussichten ins Unermeßliche: Perspektivität und Sinnoffenheit bei Caspar David Friedrichs*. Berlin: Akademie Verlag, 2004, 27–32.

87   Ulrich Im Hof, *Das Europa der Aufklärung*. 2nd edn. Munich: C. H. Beck, 1993, 11–18.

88   See, for example, the issues raised by James Schmidt, *What Is Enlightenment? Eighteenth-Century Answers and Twentieth-Century Questions*. Berkeley, CA: University of California Press, 1996; Neil Postman, *Building a Bridge to the 18th Century: How the Past Can Improve Our Future*. New York: Alfred A. Knopf, 1999; Fania Oz-Salzberger, "New Approaches towards a History of

the Enlightenment: Can Disparate Perspectives Make a General Picture?" *Tel Aviver Jahrbuch für deutsche Geschichte* 29 (2000): 171–82. For more traditional accounts, see Jonathan Israel, *Radical Enlightenment: Philosophy and the Making of Modernity 1650–1750.* Oxford: Oxford University Press, 2001; Louis K. Dupré, *The Enlightenment and the Intellectual Foundations of Modern Culture.* New Haven, CT: Yale University Press, 2004.

89   See especially Sankar Muthu, *Enlightenment Against Empire*. Princeton, NJ: Princeton University Press, 2003.

90   See the trenchant analysis in John Ralston, *Voltaire's Bastards: The Dictatorship of Reason in the West*. New York: Free Press, 1992.

91   Michael Ackland, "Blake's Critique of Enlightenment Reason in *The Four Zoas*." *Colby Library Quarterly* 19, no. 4 (1983): 173–90.

92   Alison Stone, "Adorno and the Disenchantment of Nature." *Philosophy & Social Criticism* 32 (2006): 231–53.

93   *The Four Loves*, 152–3. Lewis here is exploring the relationship between various forms of human love and the love of God. There are interesting parallels here between Lewis and Bertrand Russell, which merit closer study: see, for example, Bertrand Russell, "Knowledge by Acquaintance and Knowledge by Description." In *Mysticism and Logic, and Other Essays*. London: Longmans, Green and Company, 1918, 200–21.

94   See especially Peter J. Schakel, *Reason and Imagination in C. S. Lewis: A Study of Till We Have Faces*. Grand Rapids, MI: Eerdmans, 1984. Lewis was not a solitary voice in the 1920s and beyond in making this point: see Claes G. Ryn, *Will, Imagination, and Reason: Babbitt, Croce, and the Problem of Reality*. New Brunswick, NJ: Transaction Publishers, 1997.

95   *Miracles*, 34.

96   David Michael Levin, *The Opening of Vision: Nihilism and the Postmodern Situation*. New York: Routledge, 1988, 440.

97   Iris Murdoch, *The Sovereignty of Good*. London: Routledge, 1970, 91. For the application of this point, see Alister E. McGrath, "The Cultivation of Theological Vision: Theological Attentiveness and the Practice of Ministry." In *Perspectives on Ecclesiology and Ethnography*, edited by Pete Ward, 107–23. Grand Rapids, MI: Eerdmans, 2011.

98   For important discussions of the ultimate grounding of such metaphors, see Hans Blumenberg, *Paradigmen zu einer Metaphorologie*. Frankfurt am Main: Suhrkamp, 1997; Bernhard H. F. Taureck, *Metaphern und Gleichnisse in der Philosophie. Versuch einer kritischen Ikonologie der Philosophie*. Frankfurt am Main: Suhrkamp 2004.

99   *Miracles*, 34.

100 "Shelley, Dryden, and Mr. Eliot"; *Selected Literary Essays*, 207.

101 Lewis uses this phrase in his essay "High and Low Brows"; *Selected Literary Essays*, 269.

102 "Bluspels and Flalansferes"; *Selected Literary Essays*, 265. It is instructive to compare these ideas with the approach set out in Owen Barfield, *Saving the Appearances*. London: Faber & Faber, 1957.

5

Arrows of Joy: Lewis's Argument from Desire

"If I find in myself a desire which no experience in this world can satisfy, the most probable explanation is that I was made for another world."[1] One of the most striking and memorable themes to emerge from Lewis's apologetic writings is his "Argument from Desire."[2] In one sense, of course, this is not an "argument," in the strict sense of that term. It is better understood as reflection on the best explanation of a resonance of intuitive plausibilies; an affirmation of the intellectual capaciousness of the Christian faith to explain what we observe in the world around us and what we experience within us, rather than a "proof" of the existence of God. Especially in *Mere Christianity*, Lewis is mainly concerned to estab- lish the reasonableness of faith rather than to establish faith itself.

While some have misunderstood Lewis's approach as a deductive argu- ment for the existence of God,[3] it is clearly an abductive or inferential argument, primarily for the existence of Heaven or "another world," and only secondarily for the existence of God. Lewis's own account of his conversion merits consideration at this point:[4]

> I had hoped that the heart of reality might be of such a kind that we can best symbolise it as a place; instead, I found it to be a Person. For all I knew, the total rejection of what I called Joy might be one of the demands, might be the very first demand He would make upon me.

Two points emerge from this: first, that Lewis initially thought of "Joy" as pointing to a place, rather than a person; and second, that Lewis initially saw no necessary connection between "Joy" and "God." Indeed,

---

The Intellectual World of C. S. Lewis, First Edition. Alister E. McGrath.
© 2014 John Wiley & Sons, Ltd. Published 2014 by John Wiley & Sons, Ltd.

at one point he suggests that his conversion involved no "kind of desire" at all.[5] This raises the question of precisely how Lewis understood desire to be an indicator of divine presence or agency – an issue to which we shall return later in this essay.

It is clear that Lewis's "argument from desire" (we shall continue to use this inadequate designation, given its widespread use, while noting its obvious shortcomings) needs careful analysis, exploring its development and place within Lewis's intellectual development, and particularly the manner in which he locates it within his apologetic method. Lewis's detailed engagement with the western literary tradition inevitably means that his exploration of this theme is shaped and catalyzed by multiple influences, which need careful disentangling.

Lewis's Approach in its Theological Context

Lewis's musings on the deeper meaning of human yearning need to be set against a context of theological and philosophical reflection on the origins and significance of human desire, and especially its expressions in western European literature during the Middle Ages and Renaissance. Lewis's reflections on desire focus on two themes, both with a long pedigree within western culture: a general sense of longing for something that presents itself as both undefinable and unattainable; and a Christian affirmation that God alone is the heart's true desire, the origin and goal of human longings.

The "wistful, soft, tearful longing" (Matthew Arnold)[6] that German Romantic writers called *Sehnsucht* was well known to Lewis, both as a personal experience and as a major theme in western literature. A deep yearning for seemingly unreachable states of life or poignant desire for something agonizingly elusive can be documented from all ages, and is not limited to individuals who might be deemed to be "religious" or "spiritual,"[7] or to a German cultural context.[8]

Two examples of this may be noted, both taken from the writings of prominent English atheists in the early twentieth century. The modernist novelist Virginia Woolf (1882–1941) was convinced there was no God. Nevertheless, in an autobiographical essay of 1938, Woolf recounted how she experienced privileged "moments of being," which seemed to her to be "a token of some real thing behind appearances."[9] Such "moments" convinced her that hidden webs of meaning and connectedness were to be discerned behind the apparent realities of the phenomenal world.

The second example is taken from the writings of Bertrand Russell (1872–1970), one of the most articulate and influential British atheist

writers of the twentieth century. Russell both experienced and went on
to express this sense of longing poignantly, identifying its deep existential
significance.[10]

> The centre of me is always and eternally a terrible pain...a searching
> for something beyond what the world contains, something transfigured
> and infinite – the beatific vision, God – I do not find it, I do not think it is
> to be found – but the love of it is my life...it is the actual spring of life
> within me.

This longing cannot really be defined; at best, it can only be described.
Lewis's "argument from desire" takes as its starting point this "searching
for something beyond what the world contains." How is this to be
accounted for? And, perhaps more importantly, what does it mean?
Where does it take us?

The importance of the theme of spiritual longing has long been recognized within Christian thought, both at the level of theological reflection
and spiritual practice. The soul's intrinsic – if unrecognized and veiled –
desire for God plays a major role in the thought of Augustine of Hippo.[11]
Humanity has been created in order to relate to God; until and unless
this happens, we experience a sense of emptiness and dissatisfaction.
As Augustine framed this point in his famous prayer: "You have made
us for yourself, and our heart is restless until it finds its rest in you."[12]
Similar themes are found in other leading patristic writers, such as
Gregory of Nyssa,[13] as well as leading theologians of the Middle Ages.[14]
What is striking about such accounts, especially that of Augustine, is how
experience is interpreted through a theological framework[15] – that of a
transcendent *res*, which brings stability to an otherwise changeable and
transient world.

Although theologically important, the theme of desiring God has
perhaps found its most distinctive application in the field of Christian
spirituality, especially during the Middle Ages.[16] Anselm of Canterbury is
one of many to argue that God is both the origin of our longings, and
their ultimate goal.[17]

> Lord, give me what you have made me want. I praise and thank you for
> the desire that you have inspired. Perfect what you have begun, and grant
> me what you have made me long for.

Bernard of Clairvaux, interpreting the Song of Songs, saw this as an
allegorical reflection on God's love for the believer, and the believer's love
for God.[18] The "Shewings" of Julian of Norwich depict God as both the

origin and ultimate goal of desire: "I am who makes you to love, I am who makes you to long, I it am, the endless fulfilling of all true desires."[19]

Yet none of these writers present such an innate human desire for God as a formal proof for the existence of God. Indeed, such "proofs" are a relatively recent invention. When read in its original eleventh-century context, Anselm of Canterbury's "ontological proof" is neither *ontological* nor a *proof*, in the technical sense of those terms. Anselm makes it clear that he is setting out an *argumentum*, not a *demonstratio*.[20] It is only with René Descartes in the seventeenth century that a properly "ontological" argument emerges.[21] Some would suggest Anselm offers an essentially spiritual reflection on the nature of God and of the implications of the human apprehension of God, which later writers have interpreted or reformulated as a "proof" in the strict sense of the term.[22] The rise of the Enlightenment in the eighteenth century generated new pressure for a demonstration of the veracity of the Christian faith, created a new intellectual context within which "proofs" for God's existence assumed an important cultural and apologetic role.[23] In contrast, most pre-modern writers regarded the human experience of desire as something that could be integrated satisfactorily within a Christian framework affirming the rationality of faith in a prudential rather than an epistemic sense.[24]

Lewis's literary engagement with the phenomenon of desire tends to focus on works which either date from before the Enlightenment, or which – like Romanticism – can be considered to represent a conscious reaction against the Enlightenment.[25] His thinking has clearly been shaped by the poetics of desire of seventeenth-century writers such as George Herbert and Thomas Traherne,[26] and the Romantic notion of *Sehnsucht*. Lewis tells us that he has long been a self-confessed "votary of the Blue Flower"[27] – a motif in German Romanticism which first makes its appearance in Novalis's posthumously published fragment of a novel *Heinrich von Ofterdingen* (1802), and came to symbolize a longing for the elusive reconciliation of reason and imagination, the observed world outside the mind and the subjective world within it. Lewis's thinking on the apologetic role of "desire" emerges within this literary context, and at points appears to have been shaped by it.

Lewis sets out versions of an "argument from desire" at several points in his writings. It is, for example, clearly formulated in the "Chronicles of Narnia," which often explore a "longing for Narnia" and a "longing for Aslan" – two themes which, though clearly inter-related, are nevertheless to be seen as distinct. Hints of it can also be seen in the late work *Till We Have Faces*.[28] The most important statements of the argument, however, are to be found at the following points.

1. *The Pilgrim's Regress* (1933), in which Lewis sets out an allegorical account of his own conversion, in which the theme of desire plays a leading role.
2. The sermon "The Weight of Glory," delivered in Oxford in 1941. This is the most elegant statement of the argument, framed primarily in terms of the human quest for beauty.
3. The talk "Hope," given during the third series of Broadcast Talks for the British Broadcasting Corporation during the Second World War, and subsequently included as a chapter in *Mere Christianity*. This is widely regarded as Lewis's most influential statement of the argument.
4. The autobiographical work *Surprised by Joy*, which explores the basic elements of the argument from desire, set out as a series of "moves" made by God against Lewis, eventually leading to his "checkmate."

We shall begin our analysis of this argument by considering Lewis's autobiography, *Surprised by Joy*, whose complexities were noted earlier (7–29). Lewis here sketches his basic understanding and experience of "Joy," which plays such a significant role in his intellectual development and underlies his "argument from desire."

Lewis's Concept of Desire

When confronted with the need to express or refer to something new or significant, we can do one of two things. We can invent a new word, allowing us to freight this with the nuances and associations of our discovery or development. Or we can take an existing word, and use it idiosyncratically,[29] perhaps distinguishing it from the normal use of the term by capitalizing it. Lewis's use of the term "Joy" (note the use of the initial capital letter), falls into this second category. While Lewis later used the term "Joy" to refer to this experience in *Surprised by Joy*, it is referred to in other ways elsewhere in his writings. In *The Pilgrim's Regress* (1933), Lewis uses the phrase "sweet desire," and in *Mere Christianity* "desire," to refer to essentially the same experience. So what does he mean by this everyday word "Joy," which he clearly understands to have a special significance?[30]

In *Surprised by Joy*, Lewis described his childhood experiences of intense longing for something unknown and elusive, triggered by a range of stimuli – the fragrance of a flowering currant bush in the garden at Little Lea, or reading works such as Beatrix Potter's *Squirrel Nutkin* or Henry Wadsworth Longfellow's translation of some lines from the Swedish poet

Esaias Tegnér.[31] The quality of this experience is best judged from Lewis's prose, than from any attempt to formalize or analyze it:[32]

> It is difficult to find words strong enough for the sensation which came over me . . . It was a sensation, of course, of desire; but desire for what? . . . And before I knew what I desired, the desire itself was gone, the whole glimpse withdrawn, the world turned commonplace again, or only stirred by a longing for the longing that had just ceased.

This sense of yearning was so powerful and so desirable that Lewis returned again and again to what he thought were its sources. Yet "Joy" proved resistant to his attempts at control; the more he actively sought to secure it, the less he managed to grasp it. It lay beyond his control.

Though Lewis does not mention this, there are clear parallels between his experience of "Joy" and what the Harvard psychologist William James referred to as "mystical experiences." In his celebrated study *The Varieties of Religious Experience* (1902), William James drew extensively on a wide range of published works and personal testimonies, engaging with religious experience on its own terms, and taking accounts of such experiences at face value. James suggested that these "privileged moments" carry an "enormous sense of inner authority and illumination," transfiguring the understanding of those who experience them, often evoking a deep sense "of being revelations of new depths of truth."[33]

James's phenomenological analysis of "mystical experiences" led him to suggest that they possessed four distinctive characteristics:[34]

1. *Ineffability*. This kind of experience "defies expression"; it cannot be described adequately in words. "Its quality must be directly experienced; it cannot be imparted or transferred to others."[35]
2. *Noetic quality*. Such an experience is seen to possess luminosity and authority, allowing access to some deeper truth. These "states of insight into depths of truth unplumbed by the discursive intellect" are understood to be "illuminations, revelations, full of significance and importance, all inarticulate though they remain."
3. *Transiency*. Such "mystical states cannot be sustained for long." Usually they last from a few seconds to minutes and their quality cannot be accurately remembered, though the experience is recognized if it recurs. "When faded, their quality can but imperfectly be reproduced in memory."
4. *Passivity*. Such mystical experiences cannot be actively produced on demand; they are passively experienced as and when they (unpredictably) happen. Someone undergoing such mystical experiences

believes that they lie beyond his or her control, as if he or she "were grasped and held by a superior power."

Considered at the phenomenological level, Lewis's experience of "Joy" clearly belongs to what James describes as "mystical experience." This observation, it must be emphasized, neither invalidates nor verifies Lewis's experience; it simply helps us set it against a deeper context of a scholarly discussion of transcendent experiences,[36] which makes it clear that such experiences are not unique to Lewis. Lewis's characteristic insight that literature in general, and poetry in particular, represents an attempt to engage common human experience is given added significance by James's analysis, especially of the relation of mundane and epiphanic elements in human experience. "Epiphanic" moments carry with them a "sense of clarification, which seems to allow us to understand things in their true nature." Such epiphanies are like "bolts of lightning on a dark night that brilliantly illuminate everything in a single, instantaneous flash."[37] Lewis's epiphany of "Joy" baptized and bathed his everyday world of experience with beauty and wonder.

One of the most credible poetic accounts of such moments of illumination is found in William Wordsworth. These flashes of insight were "gleams like the flashing of a shield,"[38] rather than a steady source of light. Yet even such mental flashes of lightening were enough to disclose deeper truths, breaking into settled mundane habits of thought:[39]

> And I have felt
> A presence that disturbs me with the joy
> Of elevated thoughts; a sense sublime
> Of something far more deeply interfused.

Lewis fits this pattern in many ways. For example, Lewis clearly understands that reading literature can be "epiphanic," triggering off such moments of insight, illumination, and transformation. It is worth remembering here that two of the greatest modern novels – James Joyce's *Ulysses* (1918–20) and Marcel Proust's *À la recherche du temps perdu* (1913–27) – both feature "library scenes" in which their protagonists undergo decisive literary conversions. Yet the importance of this broader pattern is best seen at those points at which Lewis reflects on how his experiences of "Joy" seemed to illuminate the landscape of reality, and allow him to perceive the deeper unity of reality that needs to be accounted for in any theoretical account of its structures.

The "epiphanic" aspect of "Joy" is most clearly stated toward the end of *Surprised by Joy*, as Lewis explains how he began to realize its significance for his philosophical Idealism. Lewis represented his intellectual pilgrim-age from atheism to Christianity as proceeding through a series of stages: "from 'popular realism' to Philosophical Idealism; from Idealism to Pantheism; from Pantheism to Theism; and from Theism to Christianity."[40] About half-way through this process, Lewis described an "*éclaircissement* about Joy," and attempted to unpack the substance of the resulting illumination that it brings.

Joy disclosed that Lewis was really searching for "something other, outside." Lewis initially thought that Joy was the true object of his desire; however, he came to realize that Joy was a signpost, not a goal. This point is developed in *The Pilgrim's Regress* in which the pilgrim is told that "what you desire is no state of yourself at all, but something, for that very reason, Other and Outer."[41] Lewis was now able to see how Joy could "fit in" to his broader philosophical vision. Our experience of Joy arises because we have "a root in the Absolute":[42]

> That is why we experience Joy: we yearn, rightly, for that unity which we can never reach except by ceasing to be the separate phenomenal beings called "we." Joy was not a deception. Its visitations were rather the moments of clearest consciousness we had, when we became aware of our fragmentary and phantasmal nature and ached for that impossible reunion which would annihilate us or that self-contradictory waking which would reveal, not that we had had, but that we *were*, a dream.

What Lewis struggles to describe here is the epiphanic dimension of Joy, in which its transient "visitations," like flashes of lightning, allow us to see a greater vision of reality, and thus to grasp, however fleetingly, our true place within it.

Lewis does not at this stage see Joy as evidence for the existence or activity of God. In fact, as the passage just cited indicates, his initial instinct is to interpret this philosophically in pantheist terms. We experience Joy because we are in fact isolated elements of divinity, isolated or estranged from the Absolute Spirit, awaiting our "impossible reunion" with the Absolute. This idea, so easily adapted in terms of the Gnostic redeemer myth,[43] clearly stands at some distance from Lewis's earlier atheism. But it is neither theistic nor Christian; and Lewis's account of his subsequent development suggests that "Joy" did not play a significant role in the final stages of his journey.

Reflections on his experiences of Joy led Lewis from his early rationalistic atheism to a growing belief in another world (105–6). The "visitations" of Joy pointed to a transcendental reality from which humanity came and to which, in some sense, it belonged. Yet Lewis interpreted this primarily as a *place*. If Joy intimated anything, it was not so much that there was a God, but that there was a transcendent realm beyond us – in other words, a heaven. The very existence of such a heaven was enough for Lewis at this point in his reflections; he concluded that "it matters more that Heaven should exist than that we should ever get there."[44] Why so? Because heaven would function as a transcendent ground of our existence, providing coherence to our experiences. The fundamental unity of reality was thus maintained.

This, however, proved to be a temporary and unstable resting place. Lewis found his way, initially to theism, and subsequently to Christianity. His views on the significance of Joy changed, reflecting his realization that God was not to be thought of as a passive *archē*, but as an active questing personal agent. Lewis now began to speak of God as the "source from which those arrows of Joy had been shot at me ever since childhood."[45] Yet Lewis's narratives of his conversion do not indicate Joy playing a pivotal role in these final stages of his intellectual pilgrimage. Reflection on "the inherent dialectic of desire"[46] led Lewis to realize that this experience of recurring desire and inconsolable yearning pointed to heaven as the true home of humanity. After coming to faith in God, he was able to expand his understanding of the nature of joy in the light of this faith – a retrodictive interpretation of the experience of Joy as something which originated from God.

A close reading of *Surprised by Joy* thus leads to a conclusion which might, at first sight, seem puzzling, given the importance of the "argument from desire" in Lewis's apologetics. The experience of desire does not appear to have played any significant role in his initial transition from pantheism to theism (which I suggest took place in 1930) nor in his later transition from theism to Christianity (which is probably to be dated from September 1931).[47] Lewis makes it clear that he had not the "slightest hint" that there ever had been or ever would be any connection between God and Joy.[48] "No kind of desire was present at all," either in his initial conversion to theism, or his subsequent embrace of Christianity.[49]

Are we therefore to conclude that Lewis's "argument from desire" played no part in his own conversion? That Lewis later deployed an apologetic argument that he did not himself find persuasive? Though not without some foundation, this suggestion is to be regarded as something of an overstatement. The experience of "Joy" raised Lewis's suspicions that there was more to life than a "glib and shallow rationalism" allowed; it hinted at a wholesome resolution of philosophical anomalies and existential anxieties. In short: "Joy" was of fundamental importance in Lewis's extended process of intellectual reorientation, even though it was not implicated in its final stages. But without those "arrows of Joy," Lewis might never have taken the steps which led away from his early "New Look" toward their source in God.

Nature: A Barrier and Pathway to God

A core theme of Lewis's "argument from desire" is that nature cannot, and is not meant to, satisfy our deepest desires. Nature is a sign of something beyond itself, not a self-signifying and self-referential closed system. Things within nature – what we see outside ourselves or experience within ourselves – point beyond themselves to "that indescribable something of which they become for a moment the messengers."[50]

Lewis's semiology of inexpressibility hints at the liminality of such experiences, while at the same time emphasizes the risks of confusing the sign with the thing that is signified.[51] Like Augustine before him, Lewis holds that we must know the thing that is signified before we can understand the significance of the sign itself.[52] Signs prove nothing. They do not – and cannot – function as the premises of a deductive argument. The realization of the resonance between *signum* and *significatum* rests on a prior knowledge of the *significatum*, and the retrospective realization of the semiotic congruence with the *signum*. Lewis's argument, considered from a semiotic standpoint, thus cannot be deductive; it can only be inferential or abductive – a point we shall consider in more detail later in this essay. The love of nature, when rightly understood, is thus a pathway to God; when wrongly understood, it is an impediment to the discovery of God. "Nature cannot satisfy the desires she arouses nor answer theological questions nor sanctify us."[53]

One of Lewis's most memorable images relating to desire is that of a bumblebee, trapped inside a room, constantly battering against a glass windowpane, believing that this offers an escape from its entrapment, and a route to the pollen-laden flowers that lie beyond it.[54] The image resonates with Lewis's language in "The Weight of Glory," especially his suggestion that an experience of desire is like "the scent of a flower we have not found."[55] Desire can become a semiotic barrier to the discovery of God, if we try to follow it, assuming it is the true object of longing, when it is merely a sign of a more distant goal. The true ground of such desires and yearnings "was not *in* them; it only came *through* them."[56]

Yet two issues remain unclear, and require further attention. First, is the "argument from desire" to be seen as suggestive of belief in *God* – or belief in *heaven*? And second, what sort of "argument" is this anyway? We have already hinted that Lewis's semiotics of desire suggests that this approach cannot function deductively. So how does Lewis's argument work? How does he understand the experience of desire to affirm the rationality of faith?

We may begin to reflect on the first question by focusing on Lewis's exploration of the "inherent dialectic of desire" in *The Pilgrim's Regress*, "The Weight of Glory," and *Mere Christianity*.

Desire for God? Or Desire for Heaven?

Arguments from desire generally focus on the "transcendent" as explaining the origins and marking the ultimate resolution of human longing.[57] This "desire" is sometimes experienced as overwhelming, evoking awe as much as it demands explanation and interpretation.[58] Yet such appeals to a transcendent reality leave open the question of what this might be. Is it a place? Is it a power? Is it a person? Lewis's own intellectual pilgrimage clearly involved the recognition of a "naked other." But what form did this take? Perhaps surprisingly, a close reading of Lewis's works suggests that Lewis's "argument from desire" is primarily about the intuition of "another world" – Heaven – rather than God.[59]

The first exploration of the significance of desire is found in *The Pilgrim's Regress* (1933). This work, written in a mere two weeks in Belfast in August 1932,[60] represents an allegorical exploration of the various false turns and continual misidentifications of the significance of longing that Lewis experienced, as he sought to make sense of his elusive experiences of "Joy." Despite the work's title, it is better seen as a reworking of George MacDonald's *Phantastes* than John Bunyan's *Pilgrim's Progress*.[61] Where Bunyan's classic springs from fear of sharing the fate of the "City of Destruction," Lewis's work arises from a sense of haunting desire, an experience of "intense longing" the object of which he gradually realizes to be a mysterious distant island.[62]

> There came to him from beyond the wood a sweetness and a pang so piercing... It seemed to him that a mist which hung at the far end of the wood had parted for a moment, and through the rift he had seen a calm sea, and in the sea an island, where the smooth turf sloped down unbroken to the bays.

Although "the Landlord" – God – features prominently in this religious allegory, it is quite clear that the sense of longing experienced by John, the pilgrim, concerns this island. Desire is not associated primarily with finding the Landlord; it is the island that John seeks, believing it to be the source of his heart's desire.[63] So he decided to "set his face to the West to seek for the Island."

Yet a closer reading of the text suggests that the sense of longing for this island needs to be set against a deeper context. In the important discussion entitled "History's Words,"[64] Lewis makes it clear that God is the origin of this feeling of desire – a feeling which is but one of the "pictures" that God uses to draw people back to faith. Not all people have this "vision of an Island." It is one of a number of means by which God speaks to people. This "sweet desire," John is told, "comes from the Landlord. We know this by its results. It has brought you to where you now are: and nothing leads back to him which did not at first proceed from him."[65]

Lewis explained his approach further in a "preface" added to the third edition of *The Pilgrim's Regress* in 1943. Perhaps realizing that the text was unduly impenetrable, Lewis offered an overview of its central themes. The work focuses on "moments of desiring," and the resulting question of their true objects. Everything that we might suppose to be the object of this desire "is inadequate to it."[66] As a result, we are forced to realize that nothing in this world is the true object of this desire, and consequently that nothing in this world can satisfy this longing.[67]

> If a man diligently followed this desire, pursuing the false objects until their falsity appeared and then resolutely abandoning them, he must come out at last into the clear knowledge that the human soul was made to enjoy some object that is never fully given – nay, cannot even be imagined as given – in our present mode of subjective and spatio-temporal experience.

A similar line of argument is developed in "The Weight of Glory," a sermon preached in Oxford in 1941. Lewis here argues that we possess an instinct of transcendence, stimulated by beauty – "a desire for our own far-off country, which we find in ourselves even now."[68] For Lewis, our experience of beauty evokes an ideal that seems to be more real than anything we encounter in this transitory world, evoking a sense of longing for a half-remembered realm from which we are presently exiled. It is a desire "for something that has never actually appeared in our experience," yet which is constantly suggested and intimated by what we do experience. This desire, he suggests, is what we call "beauty."

Yet the "quest for beauty," Lewis argues, eventually turns out to be a search for the *source* of that beauty, which is mediated through the things of this world, but not contained within them.[69] "The books of the music in which we thought the beauty was located will betray us if we trust to them: it was not *in* them, it only came *through* them, and what came through them was longing."[70] For Lewis, the desire, the sense of longing, remains with us, "still wandering and uncertain of its object."[71] This desire is to be understood as "a longing to be reunited with something in the universe from which we now feel cut off, to be on the inside of some door which we have always seen from the inside."[72] It is a summons "to pass in and through Nature, beyond her, into that splendour which she fitfully reflects."[73]

Lewis leaves his readers in no doubt that God is the true source of this desire. Yet its object is not *directly* God; it is the "far-off land," which Lewis has no hesitation in identifying as "Heaven."[74] Heaven is our true destiny, the place of glory, which is disclosed through nature, even though it lies beyond nature. "Nature is only the image, the symbol; but it is the symbol Scripture invites me to use. We are summoned to pass in through Nature, beyond her, into that splendour which she fitfully reflects."[75]

Finally, we turn to consider Lewis's appeal to desire in *Mere Christianity*. Once more, Lewis argues that the true object of human desire is heaven, rather than God. Lewis's line of reasoning proceeds as follows. People long for something, only to find their hopes dashed and frustrated when they attain it. "There was something we grasped at, in that first moment of longing, which just fades away in the reality."[76] Some suggest that this frustration arises from looking for its true object in the wrong places; others that, since further searching will only result in repeated disappointment, there is simply no point trying to find something better than the present world.

Lewis suggests that there is a third approach, which recognizes that these earthly longings are "only a kind of copy, or echo, or mirage" of our true homeland.[77] Since this overwhelming desire cannot be fulfilled through anything in the present world, this suggests that its ultimate object lies beyond the present world. "If I find in myself a desire which no experience in this world can satisfy, the most probable explanation is that I was made for another world."[78] Lewis clearly assumes that "heaven" entails God, so that an argument for the existence of heaven is an indirect argument for the existence of God. Yet the primary focus of the approach remains focused on a place, rather than a person.

We have already begun to explore the question of how the experience of desire relates to the rationality of faith. Such is the importance of this point that we must consider it in more detail. In what follows, we shall consider the structure of the "argument from desire," as this is set out in *Mere Christianity*.

Desire and the Rationality of the Christian Faith

Lewis often emphasized that his own conversion was essentially "intellectual" or "philosophical," stressing the capacity of Christianity to make rational and imaginative sense of reality. Lewis tells us that, on reading G. K. Chesterton's *Everlasting Man* (1925), he first began to appreciate how a Christian view of history made a lot of sense. After his conversion, Lewis took great satisfaction in noting the ability of Christianity to "fit in" science, art, morality, and non-Christian religions.[79] In his 1945 paper "Is Theology Poetry?," originally read to the Socratic Club at Oxford, Lewis argues that the Christian vision of God is both an *evidenced* and an *evidencing* explanation of reality. Its capacity to make sense of things is to be regarded as a measure of its truth. "I believe in Christianity as I believe that the Sun has risen, not only because I see it but because by it I see everything else."[80]

One of Lewis's core arguments in *Mere Christianity* is that Christianity can "fit in" our complex experience of the world – such as our sense of moral obligation, and our desire for something of ultimate significance, which remains frustratingly elusive. As we noted earlier, Lewis tends to explore such a notion of intellectual coherence primarily through an appeal to ocular analogies (83–104). Yet although Lewis generally seems reluctant to explore and apply musical analogies,[81] his approach could be described as enabling the believer to discern the harmonics of the cosmos, and realize that things fit together *aesthetically* – even if there are a few logical loose ends that still need to be sorted out. The musical notion of "harmony" thus has obvious potential in this respect,[82] as Lewis himself seemed to appreciate. The medieval vision of the universe, he suggested, was "overwhelming in its greatness but satisfying in its harmony."[83] This medieval emphasis on the "harmony" of the universe can be adapted to include the resonance of human intuitions with a deeper order of things.[84]

Lewis's "argument from desire" is subtle, and needs to be taken on its own terms, rather than forced into some Procrustean logical mould. It is most emphatically not a deductive argument. If it could be reduced to a single genre of argumentation, it is essentially *suppositional*. Suppose there were a God, such as that which Christianity proposes.[85] Does not this fit in well with what we actually experience of reality? And is not this resonance of supposal and observation indicative of the truth of the supposal?

Lewis initially deploys this approach in *Mere Christianity* when considering our sense of moral obligation. How are we to make sense of this? If there is a God – at this stage, Lewis is careful to speak generically, in terms of "a controlling power outside the universe" – this would both account for our moral intuitions, and place them on a firmer foundation.[86]

> If there was a controlling power outside the universe, it could not show itself to us as one of the facts inside the universe – no more than the architect of a house could actually be a wall or staircase or fireplace in that

house. The only way in which we could expect it to show itself would be inside ourselves as an influence or a command trying to get us to behave in a certain way. And that is just what we do find inside ourselves.

The structure of Lewis's argument is at least as important as its substance. Suppose *A* were true. Then we would expect to observe *B*. But we do observe *B*. This gives us reason to think that *A* might be right. Our observation of nature or our own experiences *proves* nothing. But it can suggest certain possibilities, and even intimate what they might mean.[87]

> A true philosophy may sometimes validate an experience of nature; an experience of nature cannot validate a philosophy. Nature will not verify any theological or metaphysical proposition (or not in the manner we are now considering); she will help to show what it means.

Though Lewis does not use their technical vocabulary, there are obvious parallels with two related modes of thinking developed within the philosophy of science to account for how science tries to work out how to make sense of things. The first of these, developed by the American philosopher Charles S. Peirce (1839–1914), is generally known as "abductive reasoning."[88] The basic form of this approach could be set out as follows.

Peirce, himself a scientist, argues that science begins by assembling a series of observations, then goes on to ask what framework of interpretation makes most sense of what is observed. It might be a theory borrowed from an earlier age, or a completely new way of thinking. The question that needs to be answered is: how good is the fit between theory and observation? What criteria should we use in assessing a theory? Peirce suggests that the following abductive process takes place:[89]

1. We observe phenomena *A* and *B*.
2. But if *C* were true, *A* and *B* would follow as a matter of course.
3. Hence, there is reason to suspect that *C* is true.

We can reframe this approach in terms of the lines of Lewis's main arguments in *Mere Christianity*:

1. We experience a sense of morality and a "desire which no experience in this world can satisfy."
2. Suppose that the Christian way of thinking is right; if this is so, these resonances or harmonies would be expected.
3. Therefore there is reason to suspect that Christianity is true.

Abduction is the process by which we observe certain things, and work out what intellectual framework might make sense of them. Sometimes, Peirce suggests, abduction "comes to us like a flash, as an 'act of insight.'" Sometimes, it comes about through slow, methodical reflection, as we try to generate every possibility that might make sense of what we observe. But the fundamental question concerns, not how the theory is generated,[90] but how well it explains what is observed. There are no good reasons for supposing that Lewis was familiar with Peirce's approach. Yet his own approach echoes its themes, especially in terms of the idea of a "supposal," and the role of the imagination in generating possible schemes of things within which experience and observation might be accommodated.

Desire, Faith, and Inference to the Best Explanation

Lewis's way of thinking also shows some similarity to a related approach, now generally known as "inference to the best explanation."[91] This approach recognizes that there are multiple explanations of observations, and suggests how criteria might be identified to determine which such explanation is to be considered as "the best." There is a clear verbal resonance with this approach in Lewis's statements in *Mere Christianity* about how "desire" is to be explained: "If I find in myself a desire which no experience in this world can satisfy, the most probable explanation is that I was made for another world."[92] This is not about "proving" anything; it is about trying to identify which, of several possible explanations, is the best. Lewis sets out three possible explanations of our experience of desire, and indicates which he considers to be the best.

For Lewis, experiences and intuitions – for example, concerning morality and desire – are meant to "arouse our suspicions" that there is indeed "Something which is directing the universe." Yet this process of reflection is not deductive. Lewis's phrasing suggests more that there is a resonance between intuition and reality. We come to see that our moral experience suggests a "real law which we did not invent, and which we know we ought to obey,"[93] and that our experience of desire is "a kind of copy, or echo, or mirage" of another place, which is our true homeland.[94] And as we track this suspicion, we begin to realize that it has considerable imaginative and explanatory potential. What was initially a dawning suspicion becomes solidified in a growing conviction.

Lewis's argument is best seen as the commendation of a "big picture," an overall way of seeing things which appears to position elements of reality in a plausible manner. It is not the individual components of this picture that provide explanatory persuasion, but the overall capaciousness of the intellectual web or net which results from their colligation. Austin Farrer, one of Lewis's more perceptive interpreters, noted the importance of this point. Lewis makes us "think we are listening to an argument," when in reality "we are presented with a vision, and it is the vision that carries conviction."[95] This helps us understand Lewis's reluctance to isolate doctrinal statements, or engage in detailed analysis of theories of the atonement. For Lewis, Christianity is seen at its best, not in its individual components, but in their combination in the Christian vision of reality. Where others look at the brush-strokes on a canvas, Lewis wants us to examine the picture they produce when they are combined. The "argument from desire" fits neatly into this overall approach.

More philosophically inclined critics of Lewis pay him the compliment of assuming that there is a fundamentally *philosophical* argument here, which is not quite as clearly stated as it ought to be. They helpfully clarify it (and hence actually *reformulate* it), generally as follows.[96]

> Major premise: Every natural or innate desire in us bespeaks a corresponding real object that can satisfy the desire.
>   Minor premise: There exists in us a desire which nothing in time, nothing on earth, no creature, can satisfy.
>   Conclusion: There exists something outside of time, earth, and creatures which can satisfy this desire.

This formalization of the "argument from desire" is illuminating in some ways, providing we do not assume that this is how Lewis himself understands it, states it, or uses it. The substance of Lewis's "argument," as it is presented in *Mere Christianity*, for example, is better stated as follows.

> Observation: I find in myself a desire which no experience in this world can satisfy.
>   Supposal: If I were made for another world, this is what I would expect.
>   Conclusion: The most probable explanation of this observation is that I was made for another world.

The appeal is not so much to cold logic, as to intuition and imagination – both of which Lewis held to be shaped and guided by a deeper order of things, including a resonance between the imaginative and real.[97] The logic of the argument may seem to be weak, in that it rests on an imaginative dynamic of discovery. Yet the "supposal" is not an invention, but a core element of Christian belief,[98] the reasonableness of which Lewis proposes to affirm by demonstrating its capacity to make sense of what is actually experienced.

As Lewis states this approach from desire, therefore, it is not really an argument; if anything, it is about affirming the fit between a theory and observation. It is like trying on a hat or shirt for size. How well does it fit? How many of our observations of the world can it accommodate, and how persuasively? Lewis clearly has his views on these matters, which he makes no attempt to conceal. His belief is that the "big picture" he discloses will win others over to his way of thinking.

Conclusion

This essay has argued that Lewis's formulation of this apologetic approach needs to be taken on its own terms, and not adapted or accommodated to other theistic arguments focusing on the theme of longing and desire. Lewis's formulation of the approach is literary and imaginative, rather than philosophical and logical. Yet it is quite clear that Lewis believes the approach is "rational," in his deeper understanding of this term – that is to say, something that is rationally adequate, and imaginatively satisfying.

In *Mere Christianity*, Lewis invites us, initially and provisionally, to trust him as he reflects on these questions, before transferring responsibility to his readers as they reflect on the answers he provides. He invites us to try on the set of spectacles that he has found so valuable in extending the range of his vision, and sharpening his focus. They work for him; might they also work for others?

Lewis clearly has his own "epistemic virtues," evident in the manner in which he handles experience and observation.[99] The rhetoric of *Mere Christianity* is clearly designed to engender trust in Lewis as a dialogue partner, as he opens up questions for our consideration. But in the end, Lewis invites his readers to judge these things for themselves, standing back to allow them space to reflect and muse. Perhaps this helps us understand the remarkable and continuing appeal of this work – including its celebrated "argument from desire."

Notes

1   *Mere Christianity*, 136–7.
2   For a useful overview, see Peter Kreeft, "C. S. Lewis's Argument from Desire." In *G. K. Chesterton and C. S. Lewis: The Riddle of Joy*, edited by Michael H. Mac-Donald and Andrew A. Tadie, 249–72. Grand Rapids, MI: Eerdmans, 1989.

3   See the somewhat misleading and superficial analysis of this approach in John Beversluis, *C. S. Lewis and the Search for Rational Religion*. Grand Rapids, MI: Eerdmans, 1985, 8–31.

4   *Surprised by Joy*, 267–8.

5   *Surprised by Joy*, 268.

6   Matthew Arnold, *On the Study of Celtic Literature*. New York: Macmillan, 1907, 117–18.

7   See, for example, Fergus Kerr, *Immortal Longings: Versions of Transcending Humanity*. London: SPCK, 1997. For an example of the literary exploration of this theme, see Stephen Gurney, "The 'Dialectic of Desire' in *Madame Bovary* and *Le Grand Meaulnes*." *Nineteenth-Century Contexts: An Interdisciplinary Journal* 7 (1983): 37–62.

8   See the important empirical study of Susanne Scheibe, Fredda Blanchard-Fields, Maja Wiest, and Alexandra M. Freund, "Is Longing only for Germans? A Cross-Cultural Comparison of *Sehnsucht* in Germany and the United States." *Developmental Psychology* 47, no. 3 (2011): 603–18.

9   Virginia Woolf, "A Sketch of the Past." In *Moments of Being*, edited by Jeanne Schulkind. 2nd edn. New York: Harcourt Brace & Company, 1985, 72.

10 Letter to Colette O'Niel, October 23, 1916; *The Selected Letters of Bertrand Russell: The Public Years 1914–1970*. London: Routledge, 2001, 85.

11 See Isabelle Bochet, *Saint Augustin et le désir de Dieu*. Paris: Études Augustiniennes, 1982, 107–10; Rowan Williams, "Language, Reality, and Desire in Augustine's *De Doctrina*." *Literature and Theology* 3 (1989): 138–50; Margaret Miles, *Desire and Delight: A New Reading of Augustine's Confessions*. New York: Crossroad, 1992.

12 Augustine of Hippo, *Confessions* 1.1.1.

13 Martin S. Laird, "The Fountain of His Lips: Desire and Divine Union in Gregory of Nyssa's *Homilies on the Song of Songs*." *Spiritus: A Journal of Christian Spirituality* 7, no. 1 (2007): 40–57.

14 Thomas Aquinas is perhaps the most important: see Lawrence Feingold, *The Natural Desire to See God According to St. Thomas and His Interpreters*. Rome: Apollinare Studi, 2001.

15 See especially Hans Geybels, "Experience Searching for Theology & Theology Interpreting Experience: Augustine's Hermeneutics of Religious Experience." In *Divinising Experience: Essays in the History of Religious Experience from Origen to Ricœur*, edited by Lieven Boeve and Laurence Paul Hemming, 33–57. Leuven: Peeters, 2004. See also the earlier study of Carol Harrison, "Augustine and Religious Experience." *Louvain Studies* 27, no. 2 (2002): 99–118.

16 See especially Jean Leclercq, *Love of Learning and the Desire for God: A Study of Monastic Culture*. New York: Fordham University Press, 1961.

17 *The Prayers and Meditations of St Anselm*, translated by Benedicta Ward. Harmondsworth: Penguin, 1973, 94–5.

18 Michael Casey, *A Thirst for God: Spiritual Desire in Bernard of Clairvaux's Sermons on the Song of Songs*. Kalamazoo, MI: Cistercian Publications, 1988.

19   Julian of Norwich, "Shewings" [longer text], 59. For a modern translation, see Julian of Norwich, *Showings*, translated by Edmund Colledge and James Walsh. New York: Paulist Press, 1978, 296.

20   On the medieval sense of *argumentum*, see Toivo Holopainen, *Dialectic and Theology in the Eleventh Century*. Leiden: Brill, 1996, 133–45. On *demonstratio*, see John L. Longeway, "Aegidius Romanus and Albertus Magnus vs. Thomas Aquinas on the Highest Sort of Demonstration (*Demonstratio Potissima*)." *Documenti e studi sulla tradizione filosofica medievale* 13 (2002): 373–434.

21   John Edward Abbruzzese, "The Structure of Descartes' Ontological Proof." *British Journal for the History of Philosophy* 15 (2007): 253–82. For the development of "ontological" arguments for the existence of God after Descartes, see Emanuela Scribano, *L'esistenza di Dio: Storia della prova ontologica da Descartes a Kant*. Bari: Laterza, 1994.

22   For some important discussions of Anselm's approach, see Marilyn McCord Adams, "Praying the *Proslogion*: Anselm's Theological Method." In *The Rationality of Belief and the Plurality of Faith*, edited by Thomas Senor, 15–39. Ithaca, NY: Cornell University Press, 1995; Eileen Sweeney, "Anselm's *Proslogion*: The Desire for the Word." *Saint Anselm Journal* 1 (2003): 17–31.

23   For an analysis of this important development in England during the "Augustan Age" (c. 1690–1745), see Alister E. McGrath, *Darwinism and the Divine: Evolutionary Thought and Natural Theology*. Oxford: Wiley-Blackwell, 2011, 49–84.

24   This applies also to Pascal's analysis of religious experience, which he holds to be confirmatory of the Christian faith. See Hélène Michon, *L'ordre du cœur: Philosophie, théologie et mystique dans les Pensées de Pascal*. Paris: Champion, 2007.

25   Although Romanticism can be seen in some respects as marking a break with the Enlightenment, there are far more continuities than such a simplistic narrative suggests: see the excellent recent study of Rüdiger Safranski, *Romantik: Eine deutsche Affäre*. Munich: Hanser Verlag, 2007. The relation between Romanticism and the Enlightenment is highly complex, partly because of the intrinsic diversity of both movements: see, for example, Isaiah Berlin, *Three Critics of the Enlightenment: Vico, Hamann, Herder*. Princeton, NJ: Princeton University Press, 2000; Zeev Sternhell, *The Anti-Enlightenment Tradition*. New Haven, CT: Yale University Press, 2010.

26   For the theme in Traherne, see Belden C. Lane, "Thomas Traherne and the Awakening of Want." *Anglican Theological Review* 81, no. 4 (1999): 651–64.

27   *Surprised by Joy*, 6.

28   See Peter J. Schakel, *Reason and Imagination in C. S. Lewis: A Study of Till We Have Faces*. Grand Rapids: Eerdmans, 1984, 27–34. The Augustinian legacy is clearly evident here. See especially Thomas R. Watson, "Enlarging Augustinian Systems: C. S. Lewis's *The Great Divorce* and *Till We Have Faces*." *Renascence* 46, no. 3 (1994): 163–74. There are some useful insights in the older study of Gisbert Kranz, "Amor und Psyche: Metamorphose eines Mythos bei C. S. Lewis." *Arcadia: Zeitschrift für vergleichende Literaturwissenschaft* 4 (1969): 285–99.

29 This is a significant theme in the later philosophy of Ludwig Wittgenstein, especially his *Philosophical Investigations*. See, for example, Duncan Richter, *Wittgenstein at His Word*. London: Continuum, 2004, 58–9; Michael N. Forster, *Wittgenstein on the Arbitrariness of Grammar*. Princeton, NJ: Princeton University Press, 2004, 129–44.

30 For an excellent study of this theme, see Corbin Scott Carnell, *Bright Shadow of Reality: Spiritual Longing in C. S. Lewis*. Grand Rapids, MI: Eerdmans, 1999.

31 *Surprised by Joy*, 16–18.

32 *Surprised by Joy*, 16.

33 William James, *The Varieties of Religious Experience*. London: Longmans, Green & Co., 1902, 379–429.

34 James, *The Varieties of Religious Experience*, 380–1.

35 This point is also emphasized by Rudolf Otto, who notes that such experiences are "inexpressible" or "ineffable." Rudolf Otto, *The Idea of the Holy*. London: Oxford University Press, 1977, 5.

36 For this notion, see Louis Roy, *Transcendent Experiences: Phenomenology and Critique*. Toronto: University of Toronto Press, 2001. For its relevance for natural theology, see Alister E. McGrath, *The Open Secret: A New Vision for Natural Theology*. Oxford: Blackwell, 2008, 23–79.

37 James Pawelski, *The Dynamic Individualism of William James*. Albany, NY: SUNY Press, 2007, 135–6.

38 Wordsworth, *Prelude* 1.614.

39 Wordsworth, *Tintern Abbey*, 93–6.

40 *The Pilgrim's Regress*, 5.

41 *The Pilgrim's Regress*, 129.

42 *Surprised by Joy*, 258.

43 John D. Turner, *Sethian Gnosticism and the Platonic Tradition*. Louvain: Peeters, 2001.

44 *Surprised by Joy*, 258.

45 *Surprised by Joy*, 267.

46 *Surprised by Joy*, 256.

47 McGrath, *C. S. Lewis – A Life*, 141–51.

48 *Surprised by Joy*, 267.

49 *Surprised by Joy*, 268.

50 "The Weight of Glory"; *Essay Collection*, 103.

51 There are interesting parallels with Charles Pierce at this point, too complex to be engaged here: see T. L. Short, *Peirce's Theory of Signs*. Cambridge: Cambridge University Press, 2007.

52 Augustine of Hippo, *On the teacher*, 33–6. See Phillip Cary, *Outward Signs: The Powerlessness of External Things in Augustine's Thought*. Oxford: Oxford University Press, 2008, 91–7.

53 *The Four Loves*, 26.

54 "Five Sonnets"; Sonnet 4; *Poems*, 127.

55 "The Weight of Glory"; *Essay Collection*, 98–9.

56 "The Weight of Glory"; *Essay Collection*, 98.

57   John Haldane, "Philosophy, the Restless Heart, and the Meaning of Theism." *Ratio* 19 (2006): 421–40.

58   This theme is found in the writings of Rudolf Otto, which play a significant role in Lewis's reflections on the nature of religion. On Otto, see Owen Ware, "Rudolf Otto's Ideal of the Holy: A Reappraisal." *Heythrop Journal* 48 (2007): 48–60. On Lewis's appeal to Otto, see *The Problem of Pain*, 5–13.

59   See the important discussion of the "eschatology of desire" in Sean Connolly, *Inklings of Heaven: C. S. Lewis and Eschatology*. London: Gracewing, 2007, 46–96.

60   McGrath, *C. S. Lewis – A Life*, 169–75.

61   Jeffrey Bilbro, "Phantastical Regress: The Return of Desire and Deed in *Phantastes* and *The Pilgrim's Regress*." *Mythlore* 28 (2010): 21–37. For the comparison with Bunyan, see U. Milo. Kaufmann, "*The Pilgrim's Progress* and *The Pilgrim's Regress*: John Bunyan and C. S. Lewis on the Shape of the Christian Quest." In *Bunyan in Our Time*, edited by Robert G. Collmer, 186–99. Kent, OH: Kent State University Press, 1989.

62   *The Pilgrim's Regress*, 24.

63   *The Pilgrim's Regress*, 32.

64   *The Pilgrim's Regress*, 151–6.

65   *The Pilgrim's Regress*, 152.

66   *The Pilgrim's Regress*, 9.

67   *The Pilgrim's Regress*, 10.

68   "The Weight of Glory"; *Essay Collection*, 97. There are some interesting parallels here with the ideas of the British philosopher C. E. M. Joad (1891–1953): for example, see his comments about the significance of a "fleeting glimpse of a distant country": C. E. M. Joad, "A Realist Philosophy of Life." In *Contemporary British Philosophy: Personal Statements*, edited by J. H. Muirhead, 157–90. London: Allen and Unwin, 1925. Quote at 188.

69   For the wider context in which Lewis's suggestion is to be explored, see John Dadosky, "Philosophy for a Theology of Beauty." *Philosophy and Theology* 19, no. 1 (2007): 7–35.

70   "The Weight of Glory"; *Essay Collection*, 98.

71   "The Weight of Glory"; *Essay Collection*, 99.

72   "The Weight of Glory"; *Essay Collection*, 106.

73   "The Weight of Glory"; *Essay Collection*, 108.

74   "The Weight of Glory"; *Essay Collection*, 100.

75   "The Weight of Glory"; *Essay Collection*, 104–5.

76   *Mere Christianity*, 135.

77   *Mere Christianity*, 135–6.

78   *Mere Christianity*, 136–7.

79   "Is Theology Poetry?" *Essay Collection*, 21.

80   "Is Theology Poetry?" *Essay Collection*, 21.

81   A rare example is his use of the "fugue" as an analogy for understanding medieval views of the universe: see *Studies in Medieval and Renaissance Literature*, 57. It is interesting to note how Aristotle's initial tendency to use

musical imagery gave way to more ocular metaphors: see P. Christopher Smith, "From Acoustics to Optics: The Rise of the Metaphysical and the Demise of the Melodic in Aristotle's *Poetics*." In *Sites of Vision: The Discursive Construction of Sight in the History of Philosophy*, edited by David Michael Levin, 69–92. Cambridge, MA: MIT Press, 1997.

82 For the relation of music and aesthetics in Augustine, of relevance to this discussion, see Carol Harrison, "Augustine and the Art of Music." In *Resonant Witness: Conversations between Music and Theology*, edited by Jeremy S. Begbie and Steven R. Guthrie, 27–45. Grand Rapids, MI: Eerdmans, 2011. For the symbolism of harmony in western culture as a whole, see the classic study of Leo Spitzer, "Classical and Christian Ideas of World Harmony." *Traditio* 2 (1944): 409–64; 3 (1945): 307–64.

83 *The Discarded Image*, 99.

84 John Hollander, *The Untuning of the Sky: Ideas of Music in English Poetry 1500–1700*. Princeton, NJ: Princeton University Press, 1961, 20–6, 37–43. This theme remains important in the poetry of the English Renaissance, such as John Dryden's *Song for St. Cecilia's Day, 1687*: see Clifford Ames, "Variations on a Theme: Baroque and Neoclassical Aesthetics in the St. Cecilia Day Odes of Dryden and Pope." *ELH* 65, no. 3 (1998): 617–35.

85 For this idea of a "supposal," see Lewis's letters to Mrs Hook, December 29, 1958; *Letters*, vol. 3, 1004–5; and to Sophia Storr, December 24, 1959; *Letters*, vol. 3, 1113–14. "Supposing there was a world like Narnia, and supposing, like ours, it needed redemption, let us imagine what sort of Incarnation and Redemption Christ would have there" (1113).

86 *Mere Christianity*, 24.

87 *The Four Loves*, 25.

88 See Lorenzo Magnani, *Abduction, Reason, and Science: Processes of Discovery and Explanation*. New York: Plenum Publishers, 2001; Sami Paavola, "Peircean Abduction: Instinct, or Inference?" *Semiotica* 153 (2005): 131–54. Pierce's analysis of what he terms the "fixation of belief" is relevant here: Christopher Hookway, *Truth, Rationality, and Pragmaticsm: Themes from Peirce*. Oxford: Clarendon Press, 2002, 21–43.

89 Charles S. Peirce, *Collected Papers*, edited by Charles Hartshorne and Paul Weiss. 8 vols. Cambridge, MA: Harvard University Press, 1960, vol. 5, 189.

90 Note the fundamental distinction implied between a "logic of discovery" and a "logic of justification." There are interesting parallels here with Michael Polanyi's idea of "tacit knowing": see Phil Mullins, "Peirce's Abduction and Polanyi's Tacit Knowing." *Journal of Speculative Philosophy* 16 (2002): 198–224.

91 For an excellent defense of the approach, see Peter Lipton, *Inference to the Best Explanation*. 2nd edn. London: Routledge, 2004. For its roots in the works of Gilbert Harman and N. R. Hanson, see Sami Paavola, "Hansonian and Harmanian Abduction as Models of Discovery." *International Studies in the Philosophy of Science* 20 (2006): 93–108.

92 *Mere Christianity*, 136–7.

93   *Mere Christianity*, 21.

94   *Mere Christianity*, 135–6.

95   Austin Farrer, "The Christian Apologist." In *Light on C.S. Lewis*, edited by Jocelyn Gibb, 23–43. London: Geoffrey Bles, 1965. Quote at 37. Although Farrer has *The Problem of Pain* (1940) in mind, it is clear that the same approach is found elsewhere in Lewis's apologetic writings.

96   I here follow Kreeft, "C. S. Lewis's Argument from Desire," 250.

97   See "Shelley, Dryden, and Mr. Eliot"; *Selected Literary Essays, 207; Surprised by Joy*, 193–4.

98   *Surprised by Joy*, 193: "I do not think the resemblance between the Christian and the merely imaginative experience is accidental."

99   For the debate about such virtues, see Linda Zagzebski, *Virtues of the Mind*. Cambridge: Cambridge University Press, 1996; Ernest Sosa, *A Virtue Epistemology: Apt Belief and Reflective Knowledge*. Oxford: Oxford University Press, 2007. Lewis scholarship has much to gain by reflecting on whether Lewis's apologetic approach discloses him to be a "virtuously reliable person" (Zagzebski, *Virtues of the Mind*, 244–5).

6

Reason, Experience, and Imagination: Lewis's Apologetic Method

By the end of the Second World War, C. S. Lewis was firmly established as Britain's best-known and most winsome Christian apologist. While his *Problem of Pain* (1940) was widely praised for both its style and substance, Lewis's reputation within Great Britain as an apologist rested largely on his "wartime broadcasts" for the British Broadcasting Corporation. Lewis was invited to deliver these talks on the basis of the clarity of his discussion of religious questions in *The Problem of Pain*. Subsequent microphone tests made it clear that his rich, assured speaking voice would be ideal for the medium of radio.[1] Lewis's four series of "Broadcast Talks" formed the basis of what is widely regarded as his most important apologetic work – *Mere Christianity* (1952), which is regularly cited as one of the most influential religious books of the twentieth century.[2]

Apologetics is best thought of as a principled attempt to defend and commend the Christian faith, both meeting objections that might be raised against it, and attempting to explore and explain its potential attraction to those who have yet to discover it.[3] Apologetics has been part of the church's ministry throughout Christian history,[4] and includes such masterpieces as Justin Martyr's defense of Christianity against its Platonist critics in the second century,[5] Thomas Aquinas's affirmation of the rationality of the Christian faith in the thirteenth century,[6] and Blaise Pascal's defense of the reasonableness of belief in God in the seventeenth century.[7]

Lewis's public apologetic ministry began in 1940, with the publication of his first explicitly apologetic book, *The Problem of Pain*. Under Lewis's leadership, the Oxford University Socratic Club – which met for the first

The Intellectual World of C. S. Lewis, First Edition. Alister E. McGrath.
© 2014 John Wiley & Sons, Ltd. Published 2014 by John Wiley & Sons, Ltd.

time in January 1942 – became the focus of the intellectual defense and commendation of the Christian faith at one of England's leading universities.[8] The later publication of *Mere Christianity* (1952) solidified still further his reputation as one of the finest apologists of his age.

If we could speak of Lewis having a "Golden Age" as a public apologist, it would be between the years 1940 and 1955. Lewis's apologetic zenith is bracketed by the publication of the *Problem of Pain* at one end, and of *Surprised by Joy* on the other. During this period, Lewis produced his best-known apologetic books, along with a remarkable output of lectures and addresses on apologetic themes.

Yet Lewis's move to the University of Cambridge in January 1955 seems to have marked a change in his attitude to apologetics. Lewis was formally appointed to a newly established chair of Medieval and Renaissance English in May 1954, although he delayed moving to Cambridge until early the following year. There are good reasons for supposing that Lewis saw his move from Oxford as marking the end of his explicit apologetic role. Apologetics was what Lewis did at Oxford; at Cambridge, things would be different.

Surprised by Joy – which can in several respects be regarded as an apologetic writing – was completed after a long period of gestation in March 1955, and published in September of that year. In that same month, the American evangelical leader Carl F. H. Henry (1913–2003) invited Lewis to write some apologetic pieces for an American audience. Lewis politely declined. While he had been engaged in the past on "frontal attacks" on unbelief, he was now "quite sure those days are over."[9]

It is interesting to note that Lewis's popular writings dating from his Cambridge period – such as *Reflections on the Psalms* (1958) and *The Four Loves* (1960) – are about *exploring an assumed faith*, rather than *defending a challenged faith*. As the opening pages of *Reflections on the Psalms* suggest, Lewis's focus shifted from persuading those outside the church of the truth of the Christian faith to exploring and appreciating the depths of the Christian faith for the benefit of those who believed, or were close to believing.[10]

> This is not what is called an "apologetic" work. I am nowhere trying to convince unbelievers that Christianity is true. I address those who already believe it, or those who are ready, while reading, to "suspend their disbelief." A man can't always be defending the truth; there must be a time to feed on it.

This is not to say that Lewis ceased to regard the rational and imaginative affirmation of faith as significant. It is not difficult to find reflections on these themes in some of his essays of his Cambridge period; nevertheless, such essays were generally not high-profile public engagements with apologetic issues.[11] Lewis seems to have shifted his focus from the public defense of the Christian faith to exploration of its spiritual and imaginative dimensions.

This change in focus helps us understand Lewis's continuing appeal to a substantial Christian readership. Not only does Lewis offer his readers apologetic approaches which both reassure them concerning the credibility of their faith and enable them to engage the concerns of others; he provides them with explorations of the spiritual richness and imaginative depths of their faith, potentially allowing them to gain an enhanced level of understanding and appreciation.

Yet our concern in this essay is specifically with Lewis's apologetic method. Lewis's approach to apologetics is best considered not so much as a coherent system, but as a series of loosely coordinated and shifting strategies. Over a period of years, Lewis came to develop a connected series of approaches to apologetics, often in response to specific requests or needs. In what follows, we shall examine some of the core themes of Lewis's approach in more detail.

Language: The Translation of Faith

Lewis's remarkable ability to engage a wider audience appears to have been partly innate, and partly acquired. Although his letters of the 1920s often show him to have a deft ability to express himself succinctly and memorably, this took some time to find its way into his published writings. *The Pilgrim's Regress* (1933) makes considerable demands of its readers, its flashes of brilliance being inadequate to sustain most of its readers' commitment. Lewis was clearly aware of this, and worked on his style, aiming to make it more accessible and interesting.

In deliberating choosing to develop his role as a popular apologist, Lewis found himself facing the question of theological translation. How could he express academic theological notions in plain language? How could an academic such as himself talk to ordinary people without talking down to them?[12] How could he avoid creating an alienating impression of condescension? How could he use ordinary English as a medium for often quite complex theological ideas, such as the rationality of the incarnation? How could he reach into the rich Christian past without suggesting faith was outdated? To use T. S. Eliot's words from "Little Gidding," Lewis was obliged to find words that were "exact without vulgarity," yet "precise but not pedantic."[13]

It seems clear that Lewis gradually learned how to adapt his style and vocabulary to meet the needs and concerns of an audience he had never encountered before. This was stimulated to no small extent by his experience in speaking to aircrews at Royal Air Force bases in England during the Second World War, which obliged him to restate his ideas in much more accessible ways. Lewis summarized what he learned from these experiences in a post-war lecture of 1945 entitled "Christian Apologetics." The two points that Lewis emphasized were the empirical necessity of discovering how ordinary people speak *through observation and encounter*, followed by reflection on how religious ideas might best be translated into language that was within their experience and comfort zones.[14]

> We must learn the language of our audience. And let me say at the outset that it is no use at all laying down *a priori* what the "plain man" does or does not understand. You have to find out by experience.

Lewis's discussion and debate with hard-nosed, no-nonsense, tough-talking aircrew doubtless helped him realize that his academic style did not connect with them. Lewis was clear what needed to be done about it.[15]

> You must translate every bit of your Theology into the vernacular. This is very troublesome, and it means that you can say very little in half an hour, but it is essential. It is also of the greatest service to your own thought. I have come to the conviction that if you cannot translate your thoughts into uneducated language, then your thoughts were confused. Power to translate is the test of having really understood one's own meaning.

Lewis's notion of "translation," however, cannot be reduced to that of a transaction between two languages – the academic or technical, and the everyday or popular. Long before the more general realization of this point in the 1980s,[16] Lewis appreciated that words are culturally embedded, having developed meanings which echo their cultural contexts. What is required is a "cultural translation,"[17] which attempts to express ideas from one language, embedded in its social context, to another language, embedded in a different social context. Translation is a cultural, not simply a linguistic, matter. As Lewis discovered, it was one thing to talk about Christianity to Oxford undergraduates, and quite another to talk about it to aircraft mechanics.

Yet Lewis's genius lay only partly in his acquired capacity to translate theological idioms into the cultural vernacular; it lay also in his intrinsic ability to transpose such idioms into other literary genres – above all, images and narratives. Where *Mere Christianity* is a rational exploration of the themes of the Christian faith, the "Chronicles of Narnia" are its imaginative counterpart.[18] Lewis did not content himself with translating words into other words; he proved adept at interweaving and transposing words, images, and narratives.

Few have shown Lewis's capacity to tell a story that illustrates and embodies Christian ideas, allowing us to "feel" what it is like to believe and trust them. Austin Farrer perhaps captured Lewis's achievement best when he spoke of his "imaginative realizations of doctrine."[19] Lewis's explorations of eschatology, so intriguingly re-presented in *The Last Battle*,[20] are perhaps one of the finest examples of his apologetic transpositions of Christian beliefs.

Lewis's approach to apologetics is multi-layered, expressing itself in different ways. *Miracles* offers an essentially rational apologetic; *Mere Christianity* mingles reasoned argument with a much more subjective appeal to the longings of the human heart; while the "Chronicles of Narnia" set out to captivate the imagination of its readers. It is therefore important to try to disentangle and appreciate the characteristics of these three quite different apologetic gateways deployed by Lewis: reason, longing, and the imagination. Having mastered the art of popular communication, Lewis now had to consider what approaches he might adopt to defend the Christian faith against its critics, and commend it to skeptics.

The rational approach is the perhaps the easiest to grasp. We therefore begin by considering Lewis's defense and commendation of the reasonableness of faith.

The Appeal to Reason

Lewis developed argumentative approaches to apologetics during the 1940s and early 1950s, offering accessible accounts of various traditional theistic arguments, such as the "argument from morality." His fundamental theme in *Miracles* and *Mere Christianity* is that the Christian faith makes more sense of things than its religious or secular alternatives. Lewis, however, was quite clear that reason was unable to *prove* the fundamental beliefs of the Christian faith. Especially in *Mere Christianity*, his concern was to explore what could be worked out about God "on our own steam," instead of "taking anything from the Bible or the Churches."[21]

It is important to pause here, and note that Lewis assumes no biblical or ecclesiastical knowledge on the part of his audience. His concern is not to enable the churched to reconnect with their faith, but with the unchurched, who need to have their eyes opened to the rational and imaginative potential of faith. Lewis's approach is to show how intelligent reflection on the experiences of life strongly *suggests* – but does not *prove* – that there is a God.

Why was this important? If reason cannot prove the basic themes of faith, what point is there in appealing to it? The Oxford theologian and New Testament scholar Austin Farrer (1904–68) argued that Lewis's demonstration of the reasonableness of faith was of fundamental importance in helping to secure its cultural acceptance.[22]

> Though argument does not create conviction, the lack of it destroys belief. What seems to be proved may not be embraced; but what no one shows the ability to defend is quickly abandoned. Rational argument does not create belief, but it maintains a climate in which belief may flourish.

Farrer rightly recognized that Lewis's affirmation of the reasonableness of faith maintained the cultural plausibility of Christian life and thought – an integral aspect of any approach to apologetics.

To demonstrate the reasonableness of faith does not mean proving every article of Christian belief. Rather, it means showing that there are good grounds for believing that these beliefs are trustworthy and reliable. For Lewis, the Christian faith makes sense of what we observe and experience, even if it cannot offer unassailable and incorrigible proof of its truths. In the years immediately preceding his conversion in 1930, Lewis became increasingly aware of the imaginative and existential deficiencies of most Enlightenment notions of rationality – "a glib and shallow rationalism"[23] – which in effect imprison humanity within a cold logical cage, and deny the imagination and emotions any role in reasoning. In 1926, while moving away from his "New Look" (31–54), Lewis informed his Oxford friend Cecil Harwood that he was increasingly convinced that reason was "utterly inadequate to the richness and spirituality of real things."[24]

We find this point echoed and developed throughout Lewis's later writings. Lewis's criticism of pure reason does not reflect a descent into irrationality, but reflects an increased awareness of the austerity and bleakness of a rationalist outlook.[25] In *Surprised by Joy*, Lewis was severely critical of the "shallow rationalism" that he espoused as a young man: "Nearly all that I loved I believed to be imaginary; nearly all that I believed to be real I thought grim and meaningless."[26] A deeper understanding of rationality was required, if his deepest intuitions were to be accommodated within a coherent worldview. Lewis's "reconciliation" of imagination and reason, which appears to have taken place in the late 1920s, allowed him to maintain a "reasonable" approach to faith, while at the same time doing justice to its emotional and imaginative dimensions. One of the most important outcomes of Lewis's apologetic method has been to secure cultural traction for Christianity after the slow death of modernity, in that its richer concept of reason allows it to resonate with some core themes of postmodern culture.

Lewis's remarks on the "glib and shallow rationalism" he once himself espoused fits in well with more recent discussions of human reason, which often draw a distinction between "thick" and "thin" notions of rationality.[27] "Thin" accounts of human reason treat it as ahistorical and culturally disembodied, in effect reducing reason to the austere domains of logic and mathematics. "Thick" accounts of rationality are alert to the "bounded" nature of human reasoning, which is partly shaped by socially constructed cultural norms on the one hand, and significantly influenced by history, imagination, and story on the other.[28] Inevitably, this means that decisions about what counts as "rational" are shaped by historical, cultural, and imaginative factors which often make the criterion of "rationality" difficult to apply – as, for example, in political and economic theory.[29] Yet it remains culturally significant to affirm that human beings act in a reasonable manner, including in their reflections about belief in God.

There is another point to consider here. During the 1930s, Lewis became aware that reasoned argument on its own lacked existential force; it required rhetorical embellishment to secure both acceptance and transformation. In his *Preface to Paradise Lost*, Lewis argued that the "proper use" of rhetoric that shapes the human emotions was both[30]

> . . . lawful and necessary because, as Aristotle points out, intellect of itself "moves nothing": the transition from thinking to doing, in nearly all men at nearly all moments, needs to be assisted by appropriate states of feeling.

The deployment of rhetoric is necessary to shape – and, above all, to *change* – a person's "vision of concrete reality."[31]

Lewis's use of reason is sometimes characterized as deductive, proving the existence of God from first principles. This is not strictly correct, as we noted when considering his celebrated "argument from desire" (105–28). Lewis's argument here, as elsewhere, is fundamentally *inductive*, aiming to show how the Christian faith can "fit in" our experiences of life. Lewis himself was drawn to Chesterton's *Everlasting Man* because of the scope of its intellectual and imaginative vision. This principle is perhaps most clearly stated in his celebrated declaration: "I believe in Christianity as I believe that the Sun has risen, not only because I see it but because by it I see everything else."[32] Lewis tends to treat Christianity as a "big picture," whose ability to embrace or position our observations of the external world and our internal experience of longings is itself to be seen as an indication of its truth.

This is clearly seen from his famous popular statement of the "argument from morality" in the opening pages of *Mere Christianity*.[33] Lewis here invites us to reflect on two people having an argument. Any attempt to determine who is right and who is wrong depends on acknowledging some norm or standard which stands over and above both parties to the dispute, and which both implicitly recognize as binding and authoritative. Lewis suggests that everyone has some sense of there being something "higher" than us – an objective norm to which people appeal, and which they expect others to observe; a "real law which we did not invent, and which we know we ought to obey."[34]

Lewis is not arguing here that such reflections on the foundations of a viable morality *prove* that there is a God; he is rather pointing out how such reflections both subvert non-theistic accounts of morality, while at the same time emphasizing how Christianity is able to accommodate these issues in an intellectually and aesthetically satisfying manner.[35] Right and wrong are treated as "clues to the meaning of the universe." They "arouse our suspicions."[36] Clues, taken by themselves, prove nothing; their importance lies rather in their cumulative and contextual force. In other words, the greater the number of clues that can be satisfactorily accommodated by a given view of reality, the more reliable that view of reality.

Although Lewis does not use this language, his approach is very similar to the notion of "inference to the best explanation," now widely regarded as the dominant philosophy of the natural sciences.[37] What "big picture" makes the most sense of observation (120–2)? What metanarrative offers the best map of reality, positioning observations in the most comprehensive and plausible manner? This is far removed from a "glib and shallow rationalism" which holds that the great truths about the purpose and value of human existence can be solved by unaided human reason.[38] For Lewis, the kind of "sense-making" offered by the Christian vision of reality is about discerning a resonance between its theory and the way the world seems to be. Its theoretical spectacles seem to bring reality into sharp focus,[39] just as a false theory prevents us from seeing what is really there.[40]

As we noted earlier (83–104), Lewis sees God as an intellectual sun that lights up the landscape of reality, allowing us to see things *as they really are*. Such imagery, which can be traced back to Plato and Augustine of Hippo, suggests that the ability of a worldview or metanarrative to illuminate reality is an important measure of its reliability, and an indicator of its truth.

Mere Christianity presents Christianity as an eminently reasonable account of life, using accessible language and imagery that secured its wide acceptance within western culture. Indeed, the work is widely cited as one of the most influential Christian books of the twentieth century. Yet it is not a work of "rational" apologetics, deriving its appeal from a modernist worldview that privileges rational demonstration over and against existential adequacy. Even its core notion of reason is shaped by imaginative concerns,[41] reflecting Lewis's realization of the inadequacy of the cold rationalism he once embraced himself.

This naturally leads us to consider how Lewis integrates reason and feelings in his apologetic method.

The Appeal to Human Longing

At several points in his works, Lewis develops an "argument from desire" that builds on earlier approaches (such as those of Augustine and Aquinas), while at the same time giving it a distinct literary identity and focus. We considered this argument in more detail in an earlier essay, to which the reader is referred for a fuller discussion (105–28). Here, we shall simply outline the general trajectory of Lewis's argument, and note how it fits into Lewis's apologetic method as a whole.

The essential point to appreciate is that Lewis's approach to apologetics allows the integration of an appeal to human longing – for example, based on the beauty of the world, or memories of one's childhood – within a thick "rational" approach to the Christian faith. Lewis's argument is that the Christian "map" of reality adequately accommodates such longings, offering an explanation of their origins, accounting for their significance, and indicating how they may be fulfilled.

An early statement of this approach is found in *The Pilgrim's Regress* (1933), in which Lewis reflects on the significance of human yearning and a desire for justice. These, he suggests, are signposts of transcendence, disclosing the true situation of humanity. Human desire is initially understood as a yearning for something tangible within the world. However, when we realize that nothing within the world is able to satisfy this desire, we begin to consider other explanations and proposed goals for this sense of yearning. This exploration of conceptual possibilities gradually leads to the conclusion that desire cannot be anchored to, or fulfilled by, anything transient or finite. Its true significance lies in pointing to its transcendent origins and goal, which is "never fully given" in this world.[42]

Although Lewis developed this approach more thoroughly in his University Sermon "The Weight of Glory," preached at Oxford in June 1941, it is best known in the form in which it is stated in *Mere Christianity*. We all, Lewis suggests, long for something of ultimate significance, only to find our hopes dashed and frustrated when we actually achieve or attain it. "There was something we grasped at, in that first moment of longing, which just fades away in the reality."[43] So how is this common human experience to be interpreted? What is the best explanation of this sense of yearning?

Lewis suggests that there are three possible ways of dealing with this sense of longing, and proceeds to argue that only one is ultimately persuasive, intellectually or existentially. Human frustration at failing to identify or secure the ultimate goal of our longings might come about because we are looking in the wrong places. Or we might conclude that further searching will only result in repeated disappointment, so that there is no point in bothering to try and find something better than the world. Yet there is, Lewis argues, a third approach – to recognize that these earthly longings are "only a kind of copy, or echo, or mirage" of our true homeland.[44] "If I find in myself a desire which no experience in this world can satisfy, the most probable explanation is that I was made for another world."[45]

So how does such an argument fit into his overall apologetic approach? Lewis does not argue that this deep human sense of "yearning" proves anything. It is, to use his own language, a "clue" – something which required to be explained by being set within an explanatory context. Lewis argues that the explanatory framework offered by the Christian faith makes sense of this experience. It is able to "fit it in." Once more, Lewis's approach turns out to be inductive, rather than deductive. It is about intuiting the best explanation, not securing logical proof. Yet for Lewis, it is simply impossible to secure such a "proof" in relation to the great questions of life, which simply transcend reason's capacity to grasp the full depth of a complex picture.

Lewis was also alert to the evidential power of beauty, and was able to draw on a rich vein of Christian reflection on the theological and apologetic significance of aesthetic experience.[46] Both Lewis's sermon "The Weight of Glory" and *Till We Have Faces* explore the nature of beauty, and the question of its ultimate signification.[47] For Lewis, there is a fundamental resonance between the beauty of the created order and human aesthetic sensitivities, which transcends the limits of reason.

This is one of the reasons why Lewis appealed to the imagination – not to retreat into irrationality, but to escape the austerity of a purely rational view of reality, which could only offer a partial and inadequate account of things. In view of the importance of this aspect of Lewis's approach to apologetics, we shall consider it further.

The Appeal to the Human Imagination

One of the reasons why Lewis abandoned his earlier "glib and shallow rationalism" was his growing awareness of its existential deficiencies. Access to what was logically true did not resolve the greater questions of life, which focused on identity, meaning, and value. Lewis's youthful experiences of "joy" played an important role in exposing the limitations of a "thin" rationalist account of reality. Each such experience, he later recalled, "left the common world momentarily a desert."[48]

The real apologetic issue was about the meaning of life, not the propositional truth of creedal statements. The statement "I believe in God," if interpreted purely rationally, is "in a sense alien to religion, crippling, omitting nearly all that really matters."[49] Lewis was emphatic that only a fraction of human experience could be communicated using "Scientific language" or "precise and literal language."[50] Conveying the quality of religious experience to someone who has yet to discover it requires an appeal to the imagination. "The very essence of our life as conscious beings, all day and every day, consists of something which cannot be communicated except by hints, similes, metaphors, and the use of emotions (themselves not very important) which are pointers to it."[51]

For Lewis, it was necessary to make a clear distinction (without implying a separation) between human reason and imagination: reason was the "organ of truth," but imagination was the "organ of meaning."[52] Lewis, it must be emphasized, was not retreating into an invented imaginary world, seeing the imagination as the creator of false consolations. The "imaginary," Lewis insists, is to be distinguished from the "imaginative."[53] The former fabricates reality in an attempt to escape from the crushing burdens of life; the latter is a gateway to other and better worlds. Lewis first articulated this insight on the apologetic role of the imagination in *The Pilgrim's Regress*: "For this end I made your senses, and for this end your imagination, that you might see My face and live."[54]

So how does Lewis appeal to the imagination in apologetics? Austin Farrer had little doubt about the distinctive feature of Lewis's apologetic approach, especially in *The Problem of Pain*: "We think we are listening to an argument; in fact, we are presented with a vision, and it is the vision that carries conviction."[55] Lewis projected "the force of Christian ideas, morally, imaginatively, and rationally," enabling the imaginative power of the Christian myth – using this term in its proper, technical sense (55–81) – to be seen at its best. Above all, this "myth" allows the fundamental interconnectedness of all things to be grasped, and hence appreciated.

Where some apologists offer a defense of individual Christian ideas – such as the existence of God, the incarnation, or the Trinity – and then argue for the truth of the Christian faith *as a whole*, Lewis inverts this procedure. The fundamental appeal of the Christian faith is imaginative, and is grasped through an apprehension of the panorama of reality that it offers. Where some look at snapshots, defended by reason, then paste them together to yield the "big picture," Lewis argues that Christianity sets out a bold and brilliant illumination of the intellectual landscape, grasped through the imagination, which leads to reflection on its individual components.[56]

For Lewis, the internal unity and coherence of the "big picture" of reality offered by Christian faith is better apprehended by an imaginative leap than by rational dissection. Reason allows the individual components of that vision to be identified and correlated; the imagination, however, is the means by which its coherence and depth is grasped and valued. (There are obvious echoes here of Samuel Taylor Coleridge's notion of the primary imagination as the faculty by which human beings shape their experience of the world into meaningful perception.[57])

The imaginative "vision" that Lewis offers, which allows us to see things as interconnected rather than disjointed, is best expressed through narratives and images, rather than in the formal statements of the creeds. Unsurprisingly, such an approach to apologetics is seen at its best in Lewis's novels, such as the "Science Fiction" trilogy, and the seven volumes of the "Chronicles of Narnia." Lewis here uses a compelling narrative to "steal past" the "watchful dragons" of a childhood familiarity with religious imagery and his rationalist suspicion of religious ideas.[58] Lewis here allowed his "supposals" to be given imaginative depth. Suppose God became incarnate in a place like Narnia?[59] What would it be like?

Yet such theological explorations are arguably secondary to Lewis's apologetic intentions. Lewis is primarily concerned to enable his readers' "imaginative embrace"[60] of the deeper meaning of the Christian faith. This demanded its expression in a mythical form – in other words, in the form of a special kind of narrative. Lewis's apologetic method involves remythologizing the Christian faith, allowing it to "steal past" the "watchful dragons" of a hypervigilant rationalism or disdain for religious sentimentalism.[61]

Lewis's use of the imagination in apologetics is complex, and goes beyond a general attempt to construct a reworked "myth," capable of captivating the imagination of an age. Lewis regularly uses counterintuitive imaginative strategies to subvert some of the more familiar modern criticisms of core religious beliefs – such as rationalist criticism of the Christian faith as a folk legend, or the view of the German Hegelian philosopher Ludwig Feuerbach (1804–72), who asserted that God was simply an imaginary enlargement or "projection" of human desires.[62] As we noted earlier (73), Lewis's apologetic method involved the out-narration of secularism, by providing a "grand narrative" that provided a more plausible, engaging, and enticing account of what we see around us and experience within us.

Lewis's later approach to many apologetic questions often takes the form of an imaginative transposition – a suggestion that we try seeing them in a new way, using an unfamiliar perspective to see old issues in a fresh and revealing light. For example, in reassuring his readers of the ultimate rationality of the idea of the Trinity, Lewis provides them with a new way of seeing the concept. He does not use logical argument, but rather asserts iconic similarity. Why do so many people have difficulty in understanding the doctrine of the Trinity? In his 1943 essay "The Poison of Subjectivism," Lewis suggests that the problem arises because we are "Flatlanders," two-dimensional people trying to visualize three-dimensional objects.[63]

> Flatlanders attempting to imagine a cube, would either imagine the six squares coinciding, and thus destroy their distinctness, or else imagine them set out side by side, and thus destroy the unity. Our difficulties about the Trinity are of much the same kind.

What Lewis is offering his readers here is not a theological defense of the doctrine of the Trinity, but a new way of looking at it that enables us to appreciate that our difficulties arise from a failure to see it properly. There is, he suggests, a parallel between one situation and another – a situation that we all know, or can easily imagine, and one that Lewis believes that we need to grasp. "Try seeing it this way." We are not given fresh evidence for a belief, but a visual framework that enables us to appreciate its intrinsic reasonableness – an angle of gaze which allows us to see things in a new way, or realize that our previous difficulties arose from seeing things from a limited and limiting perspective.

Lewis also used such an approach to subvert the logic of a classic argument against religious belief, which emerged in the 1830s – namely, that God is merely a projection of human longing and experience. This position is especially associated with Feuerbach, who argued that the human idea of "God" is fundamentally a projection of human needs and aspirations onto an imaginary transcendental plane. God is copied from our experience in this world, in a process by which we "project" or "objectify" our human feelings, and by doing so, create God in our own image. A series of "projectionist" theories of religion, including those of Sigmund

Freud and Karl Marx, have their intellectual roots in this analysis of the notion of God.

This critique of religious belief can be challenged at many points, most notably its logical coherence.[64] Lewis, however, chose to engage it at the *imaginative* level, reframing the argument in a way that allowed it to be seen in a new light, which subverted its plausibility. In *The Silver Chair*, two children (Eustace Scrubb and Jill Pole) find themselves trapped with a Narnian prince in an underground kingdom. They have no direct knowledge of the world above the ground, save their memories. They are confronted with a witch, one of whose chief aims is to convince the children that there is no outside world. It is a delusion, an invention based on what they see around them. When the witch hears them speak of the "sun," she pounces, seeing an opportunity for a Feuerbachian critique of their beliefs.[65]

> "What is this *sun* you speak of? Do you mean anything by the word?"... asked the Witch...
>
>   "Please it, your grace," said the Prince, very coldly and politely. "You see that lamp. It is round and yellow and gives light to the whole room; and hangeth moreover from the roof. Now that thing which we call the sun is like the lamp, only far greater and brighter. It giveth light to the whole Overworld and hangeth in the sky."
>
>   "Hangeth from what, my Lord?", asked the Witch; and then, while they were all still thinking how to answer her, she added, with another of her soft, silver laughs: "You see? When you try to think out clearly what this *sun* must be, you cannot tell me. You can only tell me that it is like the lamp. Your *sun* is a dream; and there is nothing in that dream that was not copied from the lamp. The lamp is the real thing; the *sun* is but a tale, a children's story."

By setting Feuerbach's argument in a narrative context, Lewis relies on his readers seeing its vulnerability. Once more, Lewis *shows*; he does not *argue*. The "thin" rationality of the witch's argument is countered by a "thick" rationality which is suffused with a prior experience of the overworld and its sun. The narrative transposes what seems to be a sophisticated argument into a demonstration of ignorance of a greater vision of reality. The flaw in the argument is exposed, not through relentless philosophical demolition of the Hegelian notion of "objectification," but through a simple and subtle appeal to the world of common experience. We see the objection in a new light; and when seen in this light, its apparent persuasiveness crumbles. An imagined world provides a laboratory in which such criticisms of faith can be seen in another context – and their seemingly incontrovertible rationality deconstructed.[66]

Conclusion

Lewis's apologetic method weaves together a thread of approaches. The critical reader is often left wondering whether these are best seen as separate arrows in a quiver, rather than as different aspects of a coherent overall strategy. Are these approaches coherently integrated, or merely conveniently colligated? Perhaps the best answer is that they represent a coherent whole in Lewis's mind, held together within a grander personal view of things not always shared by his readers.

Lewis's apologetic palette has a rich range of vibrant colors not often found elsewhere, especially those locked into the rigidities of certain "schools of apologetics." As a result, Lewis has been embraced by both modernist and post-modernist apologists; by those commending the rational defense of faith, and those advocating its imaginative exploration; by those focusing on argument, and those preferring narrative; by those who privilege rationality, and those who long for imaginative stimulation. Lewis is able to engage apologetic issues at multiple levels, transcending the limits and dullness of traditional rational defenses of the Christian faith. Rarely has an apologist secured – and retained – such a wide and varied readership.

Notes

1   For a useful account of these talks, see Justin Phillips, *C. S. Lewis at the BBC.* London: HarperCollins, 2003.

2   Mark A. Noll, "C. S. Lewis's 'Mere Christianity' (the Book and the Ideal) at the Start of the Twenty-First Century." *Seven: An Anglo-American Literary Review* 19 (2002): 31–44.

3   For an introduction, see Alister E. McGrath, *Mere Apologetics.* Grand Rapids, MI: Baker Academic, 2012.

4   The best study is Avery Dulles, *A History of Apologetics.* 2nd edn. San Francisco, CA: Ignatius Press, 2005. For Dulles's assessment of Lewis, see *A History of Apologetics*, 318–19.

5   Ragner Holte, "*Logos Spermatikos*: Christianity and Ancient Philosophy According to St. Justin's Apologies." *Studia Theologica* 12 (1958): 109–68; Mark J. Edwards, "Justin's *Logos* and the Word of God." *Journal of Early Christian Studies* 3 (1995): 261–80.

6   Especially in his *Summa contra Gentiles*, which seems to anticipate a Jewish and Muslim readership at points: Norman Kretzmann, *The Metaphysics of Creation: Aquinas's Natural Theology in Summa Contra Gentiles II.* Oxford: Clarendon Press, 1999.

7   James R. Peters, *The Logic of the Heart: Augustine, Pascal, and the Rationality of Faith*. Grand Rapids, MI: Baker Academic, 2009, 161–95.

8   McGrath, *C. S. Lewis – A Life*, 250–2.

9   Letter to Carl F. H. Henry, September 28, 1955; *Letters*, vol. 3, 651.

10   *Reflections on the Psalms*, 7.

11   For example, consider the 1960 paper "The Language of Religion," which explicitly explores apologetic issues during the course of its analysis: *Essay Collection*, 255–66, especially 261–3.

12   This specific issue is addressed by G. K. Chesterton, especially in his early study of the poet Robert Browning: G. K. Chesterton, *Robert Browning*. London: Macmillan & Co., 1903.

13   T. S. Eliot, Quartet No. 4, *Little Gidding* (1942), part 5.

14   "Christian Apologetics"; in *Essay Collection*, 153.

15   "Christian Apologetics"; in *Essay Collection*, 155.

16   For the emergence of this awareness at that time, see Susan Bassnett and André Lefevere, *Translation, History, and Culture*. London: Pinter Publishers, 1990.

17   Talal Asad, "The Concept of Cultural Translation in British Social Anthropology." In *Writing Culture: The Poetics and Politics of Ethnography*, edited by James Clifford and George E. Marcus, 141–84. Berkeley, CA: University of California Press, 1986.

18   Gilbert Meilander, "Theology in Stories: C. S. Lewis and the Narrative Quality of Experience." *Word and World* 1, no. 3 (1981): 222–30; Ralph C. Wood, "The Baptized Imagination: C. S. Lewis's Fictional Apologetics." *Christian Century* 112, no. 25 (1995): 812–15.

19   Austin Farrer, "The Christian Apologist." In *Light on C. S. Lewis*, edited by Jocelyn Gibb, 23–43. London: Geoffrey Bles, 1965. Quote at 31.

20   Sean Connolly, *Inklings of Heaven: C. S. Lewis and Eschatology*. Leominster: Gracewing, 2007, 87–91.

21   *Mere Christianity*, 29.

22   Farrer, "The Christian Apologist," 26. For comment on this assessment of Lewis, see John T. Stahl, "Austin Farrer on C. S. Lewis as 'The Christian Apologist.'" *Christian Scholars' Review* 4 (1975): 231–7.

23   *Surprised by Joy*, 197.

24   Letter to Cecil Harwood, October 28, 1926; *Letters*, vol. 1, 670.

25   See the analysis in David C. Downing, *Into the Region of Awe: Mysticism in C. S. Lewis*. Downers Grove, IL: InterVarsity Press, 2005.

26   *Surprised by Joy*, 197.

27   For this distinction, see Jon Elster, *Sour Grapes: Studies in the Subversion of Rationality*. Cambridge: Cambridge University Press, 2–26; Jon Elster, *Explaining Technical Change: A Case Study in the Philosophy of Science*. Cambridge: Cambridge University Press, 69–88.

28   For the political implications of such notions, see Albert S. Yee, "Thick Rationality and the Missing 'Brute Fact': The Limits of Rationalist Incorporations of Norms and Ideas." *Journal of Politics* 59, no. 4 (1997): 1001–39.

29 See the points made in Donald P. Green, and Ian Shapiro, *Pathologies of Rational Choice Theory: A Critique of Applications in Political Science*. New Haven, CT: Yale University Press, 1994.

30 *Preface to Paradise Lost*, 52. Lewis clearly has Aristotle in mind here: see Nicomachean Ethics, VI.ii.5.

31 *Preface to Paradise Lost*, 53. See further Gary L. Tandy, *The Rhetoric of Certitude: C. S. Lewis's Nonfiction Prose*. Kent, OH: Kent State University Press, 2009.

32 "Is Theology Poetry?" In *C. S. Lewis: Essay Collection*. London: Collins, 2000, 1–21; quote at 21.

33 *Mere Christianity*, 3–32.

34 *Mere Christianity*, 21.

35 A point emphasized in David Baggett and Jerry L. Walls, *Good God: The Theistic Foundations of Morality*. New York: Oxford University Press, 2011, 9–11.

36 *Mere Christianity*, 25.

37 The best recent study is Peter Lipton, *Inference to the Best Explanation*. 2nd edn. London: Routledge, 2004.

38 For a popular apologetic application of this approach, echoing Lewis's approach, see Alister E. McGrath, *Surprised by Meaning: Science, Faith, and How We Make Sense of Things*. Louisville, KY: Westminster John Knox Press, 2010.

39 For the image of "theoretical spectacles," see N. R. Hanson, *Patterns of Discovery: An Inquiry into the Conceptual Foundations of Science*. Cambridge: Cambridge University Press, 1961, 23.

40 See the analysis in Ian Shaw and Amanda Compton, "Theory, Like Mist on Spectacles, Obscures Vision." *Evaluation* 9, no. 2 (2003): 192–204.

41 See the discussion in Michael Ward, "The Good Serves the Better and Both the Best: C. S. Lewis on Imagination and Reason in Apologetics." In *Imaginative Apologetics: Theology, Philosophy, and the Catholic Tradition*, edited by Andrew Davison, 59–78. London: SCM Press, 2011.

42 *The Pilgrim's Regress*, 10.

43 *Mere Christianity*, 135.

44 *Mere Christianity*, 135–6.

45 *Mere Christianity*, 136–7.

46 See, for example, Thomas Dubay, *The Evidential Power of Beauty: Science and Theology Meet*. San Francisco: Ignatius Press, 1999; Anne-Marie Miller Blaise, "'Sweetnesse Readie Penn'd': Herbert's Theology of Beauty." *George Herbert Journal* 27 (2003): 1–21; Marianne Djuth, "Veiled and Unveiled Beauty: The Role of the Imagination in Augustine's Esthetics." *Theological Studies* 68 (2007): 77–91.

47 Carla A. Arnell, "On Beauty, Justice and the Sublime in C. S. Lewis's *Till We Have Faces*." *Christianity and Literature* 52 (2002): 23–34.

48 *Surprised by Joy*, 209.

49 "The Language of Religion"; *Essay Collection*, 262.

50 "The Language of Religion"; *Essay Collection*, 263.

51 "The Language of Religion"; *Essay Collection*, 265.

52 "Bluspels and Flalansferes"; *Selected Literary Essays*, 265.

53 Letter to Eliza Butler, September 25, 1940; *Letters*, vol. 2, 445.

54 *The Pilgrim's Regress*, 171.

55 Farrer, *"The Christian Apologist,"* 37.

56 This is reflected in Lewis's high view of myths, which are apprehended through an "imaginative embrace"; "Myth Became Fact"; *Essay Collection*, 141.

57 See further J. Robert Barth, *The Symbolic Imagination: Coleridge and the Romantic Tradition*. 2nd edn. New York: Fordham University Press, 2001.

58 "Sometimes Fairy Stories may say best what's to be said"; *Essay Collection*, 527–8.

59 Letter to Mrs. Hook, December 29, 1959; *Letters*, vol. 3, 1004–5.

60 For the phrase, see "Myth Became Fact"; *Essay Collection*, 141.

61 "Sometimes Fairy Stories may say best what's to be said"; *Essay Collection*, 528.

62 For a good account of this position, see Heinrich Fries, "Ludwig Feuerbach." In *Religionskritik von der Aufklärung bis zur Gegenwart*, edited by Karl-Heinz Weger, 78–93. Freiburg im Breisgau: Herder, 1979. Feuerbach himself used the German term *Vergegenständlichung*, which George Eliot (1819–80) translated as "projection." This English term has since come to be used extensively in Feuerbach reception, often with misleading outcomes: see the points made by Thilo Holzmüller, "Projektion – ein fragwürdiger Begriff in der Feuerbach-Rezeption?" *Neue Zeitschrift für Systematische Theologie und Religionsphilosophie* 28 (1986): 77–100.

63 "The Poison of Subjectivism"; *Essay Collection*, 664. This image is developed further in *Mere Christianity*, 162.

64 See, for example, Hans Küng, *Existiert Gott? Antwort auf die Gottesfrage der Neuzeit*. Munich: Piper, 2001.

65 *The Silver Chair*, 141–2.

66 There are obvious parallels with the literary device of "defamiliarization" – seeing something familiar in a unfamiliar context or light, thus forcing its re-examination and re-assessment. See Lawrence Crawford, "Viktor Shklovskij: *Différance* in Defamiliarization." *Comparative Literature* 36 (1984): 209–19; Carlo Ginzburg, "Making Things Strange: The Prehistory of a Literary Device." *Representations* 56 (1996): 8–28.

7

A "Mere Christian": Anglicanism and Lewis's Religious Identity

"I am a very ordinary layman of the Church of England."[1] Lewis's statement in *Mere Christianity* is characteristically modest, avoiding any claims to ecclesial privilege either on Lewis's own part, or on the part of his own religious denomination. Lewis does not write as one who is authorized to speak on behalf of any Christian body; his authority is vested simply in his shared consensual vision of the Christian faith and his proven ability to communicate its themes by the written and spoken word. Nor does Lewis see the Church of England as having unique or special insights into the nature of the Christian faith. Its authority, for Lewis, lies in its embodiment of a generous theological orthodoxy, unadulterated by any claims to ecclesial imperialism.

So what is Lewis's relation to Anglicanism – the term used by many to refer to the worldwide communion of churches which trace their origins, directly or indirectly, to the Church of England?[2] Lewis is one of the best-known Anglican writers in history; yet most of those who read him are totally unaware of his association with the Church of England. In part, this is because Lewis chose not to draw attention to this fact, preferring to be seen as a representative of something less specific and correspondingly more important – what he came to term "mere Christianity."

Lewis's Suspicions of Denominationalism

Lewis is best seen as a religious writer and apologist who happened to be a member of the Church of England, not someone who intentionally saw

The Intellectual World of C. S. Lewis, First Edition. Alister E. McGrath.
© 2014 John Wiley & Sons, Ltd. Published 2014 by John Wiley & Sons, Ltd.

himself – or presented himself – as a specifically *Anglican* religious writer and apologist. Indeed, Lewis would regard the defense of any Christian denomination with suspicion, seeing this as prioritizing or privileging a specific implementation of Christianity over the Christian faith itself. "You will not learn from me whether you ought to become an Anglican, a Methodist, a Presbyterian, or a Roman Catholic."[3]

Lewis directs a "hermeneutic of suspicion" against inflationary visions of Anglican identity, perhaps most succinctly expressed in his evaluation of Richard Hooker (1554–1600), regarded by many Anglican apologists as embodying the key ecclesial and theological virtues of their tradition: Hooker, Lewis declares, "had never heard of a religion called Anglicanism."[4] For Lewis, the Church of England represents a distinctly English vision of Christianity, adjusted to the social and cultural realities of this specific region, in much the same way as recent scholarship has emphasized how the Enlightenment – once thought of as a universal movement – is known to have adapted to the specifics of local contexts.[5]

Furthermore, Lewis's own writings suggest a downplaying of any denominational distinctiveness or privilege on his part. He does not write for a specifically Anglican audience, and does not cite from writers regarded as canonical by Anglican apologists – save when these have established their claim to prominence on account of their literary excellence, rather than their positions of ecclesial privilege or authority.[6] It is well known that Lewis was invited by the British Broadcasting Corporation to deliver his famous "wartime talks" because he was an articulate layman who could be relied upon to rise above denominational disputes. And this is precisely what Lewis provided: a consensual, non-clerical, trans-denominational vision of the Christian faith, which we now know as "mere Christianity."

Lewis's notion of "mere Christianity" probably began to emerge in the early 1940s, even if his use of this specific term dates from slightly later. His suspicions of any forms of denominational triumphalism or claims to theological privilege were unquestionably given added urgency by the wartime context. Particularly during 1940 and 1941, the "total war" against Nazi Germany had led to denominational disputes and rivalries within Great Britain being seen as of little significance, in the light of the greater conflict which threatened to overwhelm the nation. The lay Anglican writer Dorothy L. Sayers (1893–1957) was one of many to press for greater ecumenical understanding and collaboration during these difficult times.[7] She was not the first to note that a credible common enemy allowed mutual differences to be seen in a helpful and corrective perspective.

Lewis developed such ideas further around this time, noting the need to focus on shared beliefs rather than divisive differences. The wartime situation demanded a recalibration of denominational sensitivities and agendas, which was best served by the reaffirmation of a consensual form of Christian belief – an idea that the Puritan writer Richard Baxter (1615–91) expressed in the phrase "mere Christianity." Writing in 1944, Lewis argued for a "standard of plain, central Christianity ("mere Christianity" as Baxter called it) which puts the controversies of the moment in their proper perspective."[8]

Baxter came to believe that the religious controversies and violence of his age – including the English Civil War and the execution of Charles I – distorted and damaged the Christian faith, causing matters of penultimate importance to be treated as if they were essential to the faith. Protesting against the divisiveness of religious controversy, Baxter declared that he believed in "meer Christianity, Creed, and Scripture."[9] The word "mere" could bear the sense of "pure" or "unadulterated," suggesting a form of Christianity that is ecclesiologically "unadorned." Elsewhere, however, Baxter uses the word "mere" in the sense of "simply," or "nothing more than."

What was for Baxter a counsel of despair was for Lewis a counsel of wisdom. Although the wartime situation appears to have increased Lewis's interest in Baxter's vision of a non-denominational core Christianity, his belief in its importance did not wane with the end of the war. Indeed, his deliberate decision to use the phrase "mere Christianity" in 1952 as the title of what is now his best-known religious book points to the abiding importance of this idea.

Lewis was not advocating the abolition of individual Christian denominations, such as his own Church of England. Nor was he suggesting that the Christian life was to be seen as individualist, without any sense of attachment to or involvement in a Christian community. His point was rather that while denominations played an important role in living out the Christian faith, each such denomination was to be seen as a distinct embodiment or manifestation of something more fundamental – "mere Christianity."[10]

[Mere Christianity is] like a hall out of which doors open into several rooms. If I can bring anyone into that hall I shall have done what I attempted. But it is in the rooms, not in the hall, that there are fires and chairs and meals. The hall is a place to wait in, a place from which to try the various doors, not a place to live in.

It is instructive to compare this passage with its counterpart in the writings of Richard Baxter:[11]

> For one sect then to say, ours is the true Church, and another to say, nay, but ours is the true Church, is as mad as to dispute, whether your hall, or kitchen, or parlour, or coal-house is your house.

The notion of "Mere Christianity" might take conceptual primacy over individual denominations; yet those denominations are essential to the business of Christian living. Lewis did not advocate "mere Christianity" as an idealized abstraction, nor did he suggest that the Christian life could be divorced from ecclesial or denominational commitment. His argument is rather that this basic form of Christianity underlies and nourishes all authentic forms of Christian belief and life, and allows these specific embodiments to be seen in a helpful context.

Lewis thus does not hesitate to affirm the ecclesial distinctiveness and spiritual necessity of denominations for Christian living – while at the same time insisting that these be seen in their proper perspective, avoiding any divisive and destructive "denominational triumphalism." While Lewis might himself have chosen to become a communicant member of the Church of England, he avoided any suggestion that this amounted to anything more than his personal preference.[12]

Lewis's sense of calling to be an apologist for the Christian faith made him wary of being associated with the public defense of any specific Christian institution. Lewis was more than willing to defend God; he was not, however, prepared to defend the Church of England. He was not alone in this. Dorothy L. Sayers, widely regarded as Lewis's counterpart as an apologist and lay theologian during the 1940s, was quite clear that any sense of an institutional affiliation was apologetically counterproductive. "Any good I can do in the way of presenting the Christian faith to the common people is bound to be hampered and impeded the moment I carry any sort of ecclesiastical label."[13]

Lewis occasionally registers concerns about developments in Anglicanism as a whole, particularly when he believes that these will cause unnecessary tensions with other denominations. One such development was the decision of the Anglican Church in Hong Kong to ordain a woman as priest in the 1940s.[14] Lewis believed this would cut Anglicanism "off from the rest of Christendom," and asked Dorothy L. Sayers to criticize this development publicly.[15] Sayers agreed that this would indeed lead to a "new and totally unnecessary barrier between us and the rest of Christendom."[16] However, she could see no "logical or strictly theological reason" against the ordination of women to the priesthood.

Lewis's concern about this issue, however, is to be seen primarily as an expression of his commitment to "mere Christianity," and only secondarily as reflecting concerns about Anglican theological identity or ecclesial practice. Lewis's point is that the communion of churches to which he belongs was creating difficulties for other Christians. Anglicanism was unwittingly damaging the coherence of "mere Christianity" – something which Lewis clearly regarded as unacceptable.

Anglicanism and Lewis's Reconversion

Following the death of his mother in August 1908, Lewis was sent to English boarding schools, where he was obliged to follow the religious observances of the Church of England. On December 6, 1914, shortly after his sixteenth birthday, Lewis was confirmed at St. Mark's, Dundela. Yet Lewis submitted to this with the greatest reluctance, and then only for reasons of family loyalty. For by this stage, Lewis had become an atheist, dismissive of religion in general as an outmoded belief system.

So did Anglicanism contribute to the emergence of Lewis's strident atheism? The most important source for understanding the origins and nature of Lewis's atheism is his extended correspondence with Arthur Greeves, which began in 1914, and continued until Lewis's death in 1963. Two major themes can be discerned in Lewis's rejection of belief in God during the late 1910s:

1. Religion is simply a primitive human instinct, a response to forces within the natural world which would now be explained scientifically rather than supernaturally. Religion was a natural development, "a kind of endemic nonsense into which humanity tended to blunder,"[17] from which the wise extricated themselves as soon as they could.
2. God is silent and uncaring in the face of human suffering and misery. This theme is developed with particular intensity in some of Lewis's works written on the battlefields of France in late 1917 and early 1918, such as the "Ode for New Year's Day," written when under fire near Arras in January 1918.

Neither of these concerns are to be seen as a specific response to anything Anglican; indeed, they are not even concerns that are specific to Christianity. It is difficult to attribute the onset of Lewis's atheism to anything directly related to his Anglican context.

But what of his rediscovery of Christianity? Is there any way in which Anglicanism can be implicated in Lewis's initial "reconversion"[18] to theism (traditionally dated to 1929, but which the evidence suggests took place in 1930), or subsequently to Christianity (which is traditionally dated to September 1931)?

At first sight, Anglicanism seems to have played little part in this process. Lewis's correspondence indicates that two individuals were of particular significance in this process: Owen Barfield and J. R. R. Tolkien. Barfield's challenge to "chronological snobbery" and his critique of what Lewis terms the "New Look" did not in themselves bring Lewis to faith; they nevertheless removed significant obstacles to that development. Tolkien's 1931 conversation with Lewis about the nature and power of myth proved decisive in enabling Lewis to grasp the appeal – the *meaning* – of the gospel. Yet neither were Anglican. Tolkien was a Catholic;[19] at this stage, Barfield was a theosophist. Anglicans – such as Neville Coghill – certainly played a part in Lewis's theological reflections. Yet the main influences and catalysts for his conversion came from outside Anglicanism.

Yet what of other influences? Lewis, we must recall, was a student of literature, who read voraciously. More than that: Lewis attributed at least some part of his conversion to books which raised fundamental questions, and planted the seeds of doubt in his mind. "A young man who wishes to remain a sound Atheist cannot be too careful of his reading. There are traps everywhere."[20] There is little doubt about the identity of two works which Lewis came to see as being pivotal in his thoughts about God: George MacDonald's *Phantastes* (1858), and G. K. Chesterton's *Everlasting Man* (1925).[21] Neither of these writers was an Anglican. MacDonald was a somewhat idiosyncratic Scottish Congregationalist; Chesterton had converted to Catholicism in 1922, shortly before writing *The Everlasting Man*.

Yet Lewis notes other influences – specifically, John Donne (1572–1661), Thomas Browne (1605–82), and above all George Herbert (1593–1633).[22] These three Anglican writers all contributed to Lewis's growing realization that what he termed the "Christian mythology" provided an immensely satisfying lens through which the world could be seen – and understood. Perhaps this is to be seen as a reinforcement of a growing conviction, triggered by others. Nevertheless, these and other Anglican writings – such as Thomas Traherne's *Centuries of Meditations*, which Lewis regarded as containing some of the most sublime prose writing he had ever read – played an important role in Lewis's development in the mid-1920s.

But what sort of Anglicanism did they represent? Lewis notes no Anglican writer of the nineteenth or twentieth century as having played a significant role in his conversion. It is the Anglicanism of the "classical Age," which Lewis studied for professional purposes in preparing for his teaching at Oxford University. This form of Anglicanism was, as Lewis often noted, an essentially English adaptation of Christianity, accommodated to its context, which was innocent of the ecclesial imperialism that crept into its later history.

Anglicanism as a Local Enactment of Faith

Having rediscovered the Christian faith, Lewis was faced with the issue of how to put it into practice. He started attending Magdalen College chapel on weekdays, and Holy Trinity parish church in Headington Quarry on Sundays. Lewis first records this change in his routine in a letter to his close friend Arthur Greeves, dated October 29, 1930.[23] Both Magdalen College Chapel and Holy Trinity were Anglican institutions. If Lewis wished to express his faith in God institutionally at his college, he would have had no alternative: under the college foundation, the chapel services followed the order of the Church of England, just as there was a statutory requirement that the college chaplain – referred to as the "Dean of Divinity" at Magdalen – would be an ordained member of the Church of England.

Lewis's decision to attend Holy Trinity was a more explicit affirmation of an Anglican commitment, in that there were churches of other denominations within easy reach of The Kilns, the property that Lewis purchased in July 1930. It remains unclear whether this was an inherited ecclesial habit from his Belfast childhood, or a principled decision about his future course of life. Lewis clearly considered Holy Trinity as his local parish church, and regarded it as part of his Christian commitment to attend public worship there.

Lewis's writings suggest that he saw the English parochial system as a reflection of a deeper "order of place," which involved attending a local church, irrespective of one's own liturgical predilections and theological commitments.[24] This sense of an "order of place" reflects Lewis's emphasis – echoed in medieval and Renaissance writings – upon a fundamental cosmic ordering, which is to be acknowledged and acted upon by wise human beings.[25] Yet the existence of such an order did not reduce the universe to an impersonal mechanism – a tendency many scholars suggest emerged in the Newtonian natural philosophy of the late seventeenth and early eighteenth centuries.[26] For Lewis, such an ordered universe was "tingling with anthropomorphic life, dancing, ceremonial, a festival not a machine."[27] Lewis's sense of the importance of a local church fits into this overall pattern. While the church is "spread out through all time and space and rooted in eternity,"[28] it is nevertheless focused on certain points.

Yet if Lewis's commitment to a parochial system is as firmly grounded in a deeper vision of reality, as his comments suggest, it is impossible to overlook their implications for his adoption of Anglicanism. The parochial system is ultimately a reflection of political establishment, in which each locality is allocated its own parish church.[29] The Church of England maintained this system as an expression of its identity as the national church.

A close reading of Lewis's works suggests that his commitment to the Church of England might ultimately reflect its identity as the established church of the English people, rather than its theological beliefs or liturgical practices. So what if Lewis had become a Christian in Scotland? Would his commitment to an "order of place" have led him to attend his local Church of Scotland parish,[30] thus adopting Presbyterianism rather than Anglicanism? We cannot answer this question, for obvious reasons. Yet it is a question which, once posed, sets his commitment to the Church of England in its proper context.

The Absence of an Anglican Ecclesiology

Having sorted out his religious beliefs and ecclesial commitments, Lewis would now think of himself as a "layman of the Church of England." Yet as we have seen, he regarded this as his personal enactment of his Christian faith, and had no inclination to impose his own understanding of Christian beliefs or practices on anyone, to the extent that these were shaped by Anglican specifics. In developing his series of "Broadcast Talks" for the BBC during late 1941, Lewis thus entered into dialogue with four clergy colleagues, to ensure that he spoke for Christianity as a whole. The clergy were Eric Fenn (Presbyterian); Dom Bede Griffiths (Roman Catholic); Joseph Dowell (Methodist); and an unknown clergyman of the Church of England (generally believed to have been Austin Farrer, then chaplain of Trinity College, Oxford). Interestingly, Lewis does not seem to have considered himself sufficiently competent in the ways of Anglican theology (or sufficiently committed to them) to make his own judgments on these matters.

Yet even at this stage, it is clear that Lewis's conception of the Christian faith in these broadcast talks is such that he has little to say about the *institution* of the church. The comparison with Lewis's Anglican colleague Farrer is particularly striking at this point. Farrer was both an ordained clergyman of the Church of England, and an intentional apologist for its ideas and practices.[31] For Lewis, it is Christianity itself that gives us a lens through which we can see things as they really are; for Farrer, it is the church. As Farrer remarks in his important essay "On Being an Anglican," we "see through the Church of Christ as a man sees through the telescope to the stars."[32] For Lewis, it is not the institution of the church, but its underlying ideas and narratives, that enable us to see things clearly.

This relative lack of interest in the institution of the church is reasonably easily accommodated within the broad spectrum of opinion on matters of ecclesiology within the Church of England. Lewis may not be representative of that church as a whole in this respect; he nevertheless fits well into a more "low church" mentality.[33] Although Lewis made it clear that he was neither "low" nor "high" in his churchmanship,[34] there are certainly individual aspects of his thought and practice which might reasonably be designated in either manner. He was not consistently "low" or "high," and tended in any case to regard such matters as being of little consequence. Indeed, a study of his fictional writings suggests that he did not hold either the institution of the church or its clergy in particularly high regard.[35]

Yet although Lewis is somewhat critical of the church as an institution, he has no doubts of the importance of the communal dimensions of the Christian faith. Christianity generates a community of faith, which is indispensable to spiritual growth and theological reflection. "The one really adequate instrument for learning about God is the Christian community, waiting for Him together."[36] Lewis studiously avoids the institutional and cultural overtones of "church" in Britain during the 1940s and early 1950s; the image of the "community" allows him to affirm that he believes needs to be said. It is within such a community of people "united together in a body, loving one another, helping one another, showing [God] to one another" that the life of faith takes root and develops.[37] Considered at the purely functional level, all Christian churches are communities;[38] the theological interpretation of the purpose, place, and status of those communities is clearly something that Lewis regards as a denominational issue, not a distinguishing characteristic of "mere Christianity."

Lewis and Anglican Theological Method

Some might suggest that Lewis's identity as an Anglican is to be found in his attitude to theological sources – to the classical Anglican "threefold cord" of Scripture, reason, and tradition, espoused by writers such as Richard Hooker.[39] Such an appeal must be used with some caution, in that writers from most ecclesial traditions – including Catholicism, Lutheranism, and Calvinism – have all seen their theology as grounded on these three sources.[40] To appeal to such a "threefold cord" may be typical of

Anglicanism; it is most certainly not a defining characteristic of Anglicanism, by which it may be distinguished from other denominational approaches to theology. One of the most elementary ecclesiological insights is that a *characteristic* feature of a church is not necessarily a *distinguishing* feature. There is no doubt that writers of the classical age of Anglican theology integrated these three sources of theology; but so did many others in other Christian traditions. Indeed, it might be argued to be a characteristic feature of "mere Christianity," and thence of its specific denominational embodiments.

In any case, it soon becomes clear that an appeal to such a "threefold cord" does not necessarily lead to the conclusion that Lewis is a representative Anglican writer. As we noted earlier, there is no doubt that Lewis makes a powerful appeal to reason, especially in his apologetic writings. Yet Lewis understands "reason" in his own distinct way, which is deeply influenced by imaginative elements. It is equally clear that Lewis regards tradition as vital to good theology. His essay "On the Reading of Old Books" is perhaps one of his finest defenses of the positive and productive use of tradition in engaging with both religious and literary questions, allowing "the clean sea breeze of the centuries blowing through our minds."[41] It is not unreasonable to see hints of Vincent of Lérin's fifth-century appeal to tradition here, allowing the wisdom of the past to nourish the present, without imprisoning it.[42] But what about the Bible?

Lewis's attitude to the Bible does not fit easily into a classical Anglican template. Lewis offers a literary explanation of the observed centrality of the Bible to the Christian faith, not a theological defense of its right to occupy that place.[43] The Bible is seen by Lewis as something that is woven into the fabric of faith by generations of interpreters, and is best studied as it is incorporated into the Christian tradition, rather than in isolation. "The basis of our Faith is not the Bible taken by itself but the agreed affirmation of all Christendom."[44] Lewis thus tends to read the Bible indirectly, through the interpretative lens of the Christian tradition, often drawing primarily on its *imagery* and secondarily on its *ideas*.[45] This approach to Scripture allows Lewis to read it through the lens of Christian literature. The Bible, as Lewis remarked, needs to be "read in the right spirit and with the guidance of good teachers."[46]

On the relatively few occasions when Lewis does engage directly with the Bible – as in *Reflections on the Psalms* – he tends to problematize the text, and offer interpretative strategies to minimize the difficulties experienced in reading it. In contrast, Lewis had little hesitation in commenting on the failures of modern biblical scholarship. Yet such criticisms often rested primarily on his belief that such scholarship failed to do justice to the New Testament *as literature*, or that it was inattentive to the literary genre of myth (55–81) and its importance as a vehicle for evangelical articulation.[47]

Lewis does not fit into popular Anglican theological templates of identity, above all the simplistic model of the "threefold cord." This is not to deny that Lewis was an Anglican. The point being made is that Lewis was neither a typical nor a paradigmatic Anglican, who can be accommodated easily to traditional definitions of the essence of Anglicanism. Lewis had his own distinct understanding of the nature of Christianity, and was content to worship in his college chapel and local parish church – as we have seen, not necessarily because of a sense of shared theological identity, but because of a sense of obligation to become part of his local Christian communities, as a specific embodiment of his broader vision of "mere Christianity."

Lewis and the *Via Media*

Finally, it might be argued that Anglicanism is characterized by its *via media* – its principled attempt to avoid extremes, and hold together what is good from divergent Christian spiritual traditions, without necessarily achieving an ultimate resolution of the theological differences that underlie them.[48] There is no doubt that such an approach can be seen throughout Lewis's writings, which often attempt to "hold together in dynamic tension principles of truth that are apparently opposed but really complementary."[49] This principle is clearly evident in Lewis's earliest published work, *The Pilgrim's Regress*, which uses the image of a "Main Road" to denote the soul's journey toward God. To its north lie approaches that place an emphasis upon reason and objectivity; to its south, those that stress emotion and subjectivity.[50] It is by remaining on the "Main Road" – a phrase that hints of the classical notion of the *via media* – that the pilgrim remains theologically sound and spiritually sane.

In this sense of the term, Lewis could indeed be viewed as a classical Anglican. This *via media* approach to Anglican identity is best seen in the later sixteenth and seventeenth centuries, in the writings of theologians such as Bishop John Jewel (1522–71) and Richard Hooker, or poets such as George Herbert, and expressed in the literary forms of the King James Bible (1611) and the Book of Common Prayer (1662). This is the form of Anglicanism to which Lewis approximates the most closely, and for which he clearly felt the greatest affinity.

Yet once more, questions must be raised. Lewis appears to have conceived his personal *via media* primarily in theological or philosophical terms – that is, as avoiding the excesses of an arid rationalism or a florid subjectivism. This polarity can, however, be found within internal debates of all denominations, and is not specific to Anglicanism. It is certainly true that Lewis construes the *via media* in a more specifically ecclesiological manner at certain points – namely, as avoiding certain extremes of religious practice or belief. Yet this reflects his fundamental commitment to "mere Christianity," not to Anglicanism. It seems entirely probable that Lewis was comfortable with his personal implementation of "mere Christianity" within the Church of England. Yet Anglicanism seems to have provided the vehicle, rather than the substance, for Lewis's personal religious ideas and practices.

Conclusion

So is Lewis to be seen as an Anglican writer? It is impossible to answer this question in the negative. Lewis chose to self-identify as a member of the Church of England, both in his public declarations and his patterns of church attendance. Furthermore, Lewis shows a clear literary and theological resonance with Anglican writers of the late 1500s and early 1600s. Lewis may not be a "typical Anglican writer" (a deeply problematic notion, by the way). Yet the historical study of Anglicanism reveals such complex and shifting patterns of Anglican identity that Lewis can easily be accommodated within its broad spectrum.

Yet from about the year 2000, when internal debates over the future directions of Anglicanism as a family of churches began to raise awkward questions about any notion of a shared Anglican identity, the question of Lewis's Anglican credentials is increasingly being framed in new ways. Many younger Anglicans, anxious to affirm both theological orthodoxy and their denominational commitment, are coming to regard Lewis as a benchmark of Anglican identity. For them, Lewis embodies – and, for some, even *defines* – what Anglicanism ought to be: a theologically orthodox, culturally literate, imaginatively engaged, and historically rooted vision of the Christian faith.

The recent failure of professional Anglican theologians and church leaders to captivate the imaginations and enlighten the minds of a rising generation within global Anglicanism has created a vacuum – which Lewis is increasingly coming to fill. Lewis embodies a liturgically and ecclesiologically unfussy Anglicanism that is rooted in the "Golden Age" of its divinity, rather than being shaped by more recent controversies; that is lay rather than ordained; that speaks in eloquent and imaginatively satisfying ways, rather than in the less accessible jargon of academic theology, which so often seems disconnected from personal faith; and which has no desire to dominate or belittle other denominations. Paradoxically, the question that a future generation might ask is not "Is Lewis really Anglican?" but "Why isn't Anglicanism more like Lewis?"

Notes

1 *Mere Christianity*, viii.
2 For an earlier study, see Lee W. Gibbs, "C. S. Lewis and the Anglican *Via Media*." *Restoration Quarterly* 32, no. 2 (1990): 105–19. For general introductions to Anglicanism, including reflections on problems of definition, see William M. Jacob, *The Making of the Anglican Church Worldwide*. London: SPCK, 1997; Mark Chapman, *Anglicanism: A Very Short Introduction*. Oxford: Oxford University Press, 2006.
3 *Mere Christianity*, viii. Lewis's later writings suggest a degree of impatience with post-war theological trends within the Church of England – such as the explicit theological revisionism advocated in the early 1960s by John Robinson, the Anglican bishop of Woolwich, in his *Honest to God* (1963): see "Must our Image of God Go?"; *Essay Collection*, 66–7.
4 *English Literature in the Sixteenth Century*, 454.
5 Brian W. Young, *Religion and Enlightenment in Eighteenth-Century England: Theological Debate from Locke to Burke*. Oxford: Clarendon Press, 1998; John G. A. Pocock, *Barbarism and Religion*. 2 vols. Cambridge: Cambridge University Press, 1999. The comparison with the link between Enlightenment and religion in the German situation, especially in Berlin and Halle, is of interest: Martin Gierl, *Pietismus und Aufklärung: Theologische Polemik und die Kommunikationsreform der Wissenschaft am Ende des 17. Jahrhunderts:* Göttingen: Vandenhoeck und Ruprecht, 1997.
6 Thus John Donne is cited on account of his poetic brilliance, not because he was Dean of St. Paul's Cathedral, London.
7 Giles Watson, "Dorothy L. Sayers and the Oecumenical Penguin." *Seven* 14 (1997): 17–32.
8 "On the Reading of Old Books"; *Essay Collection*, 439. For Lewis's dependence on Baxter at this point, see N. H. Keeble, "C. S. Lewis, Richard Baxter, and 'Mere Christianity.'" *Christianity and Literature* 30, no. 3 (1981): 27–44. See also Lewis's letter to the editor of the *Church Times*, published on February 8, 1952: *Letters*, vol. 3, 164.
9 Richard Baxter, *The Church History of the Government by Bishops*. London: Thomas Simmons, 1681, folio b. For Baxter in his historical context, see N. H. Keeble, *Richard Baxter, Puritan Man of Letters*. Oxford: Clarendon Press, 1982.
10 *Mere Christianity*, 11–12.
11 Baxter, *Christian Ethics ii,2; The Practical Works of Richard Baxter*. 4 vols. London: George Virtue, 1838, vol. 1, 53. Note the references to a "mere catholic Christian" in his *Christian Directory* iv, 6; *The Practical Works of Richard Baxter*, vol. 1, 796. Baxter here seems to use the word "sect" simply to designate a

"faction"; it is important not to read the modern associations of this term within the sociology of religion into its seventeenth-century use.

12   Lewis was, however, committed to certain "specifically Protestant beliefs," which he was content to defend to his Catholic correspondents, such as Dom Bede Griffiths. See Lewis's letter to Dom Bede Griffiths, February 20, 1936; *Letters*, vol. 2, 178.

13   Dorothy L. Sayers to William Temple, September 24, 1943; *The Letters of Dorothy L. Sayers*, vol. 2, edited by Barbara Reynolds. Cambridge: Dorothy L. Sayers Society, 1996, 431.

14   Lewis's views on this matter were set out in the 1948 essay "Notes on the Way," subsequently (and somewhat provocatively) retitled "Priestesses in the Church?": *Essay Collection*, 398–402. It is not Lewis's best-argued piece.

15   Lewis to Sayers, July 13, 1948; *Letters*, vol. 2, 860–1.

16   Sayers to Lewis, July 19, 1948; *The Letters of Dorothy L. Sayers*, vol. 3, edited by Barbara Reynolds. Cambridge: Dorothy L. Sayers Society, 1998, 387–8.

17   *Surprised by Joy*, 71.

18   For Lewis's use of the language of "reconversion," see *Surprised by Joy*, 135. More generally, see Michael Ward, "Escape to Wallaby Wood: Lewis's Depictions of Conversion." In *C. S. Lewis: Lightbearer in the Shadowlands*, edited by A. J. L. Menuge, 143–67. Wheaton, IL: Crossway, 1997.

19   For a careful study of the tensions within the Inklings between Catholics and Anglicans, see Joseph Pearce, *C. S. Lewis and the Catholic Church*. San Francisco: Ignatius Press, 2003, 58–77.

20   *Surprised by Joy*, 221–2.

21   *Surprised by Joy*, 207–9, 221, 248, 260.

22   *Surprised by Joy*, 249.

23   Letter to Arthur Greeves, October 29, 1930; *Letters*, vol. 1, 942.

24   This point is clearly stated in the 16th "Screwtape Letter": see *The Screwtape Letters*, 81–5. The deeper vision of cosmic ordering that this letter suggests is best studied from *The Discarded Image*.

25   For Lewis's discussion of this theme in Milton, see *A Preface to Paradise Lost*, 72–80.

26   For contemporary concerns about this understanding of the universe, see Margaret J. Osler, *Divine Will and the Mechanical Philosophy: Gassendi and Descartes on Contingency and Necessity in the Created World*. Cambridge: Cambridge University Press, 2004.

27   *English Literature in the Sixteenth Century*, 4. The best exploration of this point from Lewis's pen is the 1952 essay "The Empty Universe"; *Essay Collection*, 633–7.

28   *The Screwtape Letters*, 12–13.

29   See N. J. G. Pounds, *A History of the English Parish: The Culture of Religion from Augustine to Victoria*. Cambridge: Cambridge University Press, 2000, 3–40.

30   See the older, but still valuable, study of Janet G. Macgregor, *The Scottish Presbyterian Polity: A Study of its Origins in the Sixteenth Century*. Edinburgh: Oliver and Boyd, 1926.

31 See Robert MacSwain, "Above, Beside, Within: The Anglican Theology of Austin Farrer." *Journal of Anglican Studies* 4 (2006): 33–57. There is also some useful material in David Hein and Edward Hugh Henderson, eds., *Captured by the Crucified: The Practical Theology of Austin Farrer*. London: T & T Clark International, 2004.

32 Austin Farrer, "On Being an Anglican." In *The End of Man*. London: SPCK, 1973, 48–52; quote at 52.

33 For the development of this notion, see William Gibson, *The Church of England, 1688–1832: Unity and Accord*. London: Routledge, 2001, 55–7.

34 *Mere Christianity*, viii.

35 Lewis's somewhat negative views of the institution of the Church are explored by Michael Ward, "The Church in C. S. Lewis's Fiction." In *C. S. Lewis and the Church: Essays in Honour of Walter Hooper*, edited by Judith Wolfe and B. N. Wolfe, 67–89. London: T. & T. Clark, 2011.

36 *Mere Christianity*, 165.

37 *Mere Christianity*, 165.

38 See the sociological analysis of Abby Day, *Believing in Belonging: Belief and Social Identity in the Modern World*. Oxford: Oxford University Press, 2011.

39 Rowan Williams, "Hooker the Theologian." *Journal of Anglican Studies* 1 (2003): 104–16.

40 For example, consider their integration in the theology of the great Calvinist writer Theodore Beza (1519–1605): Jeffrey Mallinson, *Faith, Reason, and Revelation in Theodore Beza, 1519–1605*. Oxford: Oxford University Press, 2003. For the best evaluation of Hooker's views on scripture, see A. J. Joyce, *Richard Hooker and Anglican Moral Theology*. Oxford: Oxford University Press, 2012, 103–47.

41 "On the Reading of Old Books"; *Essay Collection*, 440.

42 Vincent of Lerins, *Commonitorium* xxiii.1–12. See further Thomas G. Guarino, "Tradition and Doctrinal Development: Can Vincent of Lérins Still Teach the Church?" *Theological Studies* 67 (2006): 34–72.

43 See Michael J. Christensen, *C. S. Lewis on Scripture*. London: Hodder & Stoughton, 1980.

44 Letter to Janet Wise, October 5, 1955; *Letters*, vol. 3, 653.

45 There are parallels here with seventeenth-century English poets: see, for example, Donald R. Dickson, *The Fountain of Living Waters: The Typology of the Waters of Life in Herbert, Vaughan, and Traherne*. Columbia, MO: University of Missouri Press, 1987.

46 Letter to Mrs Johnson, November 1, 1952; *Letters*, vol. 3, 246.

47 "Fern-Seed and Elephants" (originally entitled "Modern Theology and Biblical Criticism"); *Essay Collection*, 242–54.

48 William J. Abraham, *Canon and Criterion in Christian Theology*. Oxford: Clarendon Press, 1998, 188–214.

49 Gibbs, "C. S. Lewis and the Anglican *Via Media*," 119.

50 For an analysis, see Andrew Wheat, "The Road before Him: Allegory, Reason, and Romanticism in C. S. Lewis' *The Pilgrim's Regress*." *Renascence: Essays on Values in Literature* 51, no. 1 (1998): 21–39.

8

Outside the "Inner Ring": Lewis as a Theologian

On June 28, 1946, the ancient Scottish University of St. Andrews conferred the honorary degree of Doctor of Divinity upon C. S. Lewis. At the ceremony, Professor Donald M. Baillie (1887–1954), Dean of the Faculty of Divinity, explained the reason for the faculty's decision to honor Lewis in this way. Lewis, he declared, had "succeeded in capturing the attention of many who will not readily listen to professional theologians," and had "arranged a new kind of marriage between theological reflection and poetic imagination."

It was then, to put it mildly, somewhat unusual for an ancient Scottish university with a distinguished history of association with the Church of Scotland[1] to bestow such an honor on a layman of the Church of England with no formal theological qualifications, who wrote about religious matters primarily for a popular audience, and eschewed engagement with the more traditional topics then associated with academic theology. Furthermore, Baillie's assessment of Lewis's theological significance was made at a comparatively early stage in Lewis's career, before the publication of much of what is now regarded as his most important work. Yet many would say that history has vindicated Baillie's words and his faculty's judgment, not simply in recognizing Lewis's eminence, but in honoring him as a *theologian* of distinction.

It is now clear that other senior theological minds had come to a similar conclusion around that same time. By the early 1940s, many were suggesting that the most significant public voices for Christian theology in the United Kingdom were Lewis and the novelist Dorothy L. Sayers

---

The Intellectual World of C. S. Lewis, First Edition. Alister E. McGrath.
© 2014 John Wiley & Sons, Ltd. Published 2014 by John Wiley & Sons, Ltd.

(1893–1957). In July 1943, Oliver Chase Quick (1885–1944), Regius Professor of Divinity at Oxford University, wrote privately to William Temple (1881–1944), archbishop of Canterbury, expressing his view that Lewis ought to be awarded an honorary Oxford Doctorate of Divinity.[2] However, he made it clear that the matter lay beyond his remit, as he was not a member of the university committee responsible for such nominations.

Quick's comment, as Oxford University's senior professor of theology at that time, is an important witness to the perception that Lewis was indeed a theologian – a distinct kind of theologian, to be sure, but one who was to be recognized and honored as such. Other weighty voices have urged a similar evaluation of Lewis. Rowan Williams – writing when archbishop of Canterbury, a former Lady Margaret Professor of Theology at Oxford University, and the President-elect of Magdalene College, Cambridge – recently remarked that he found himself "being repeatedly humbled and reconverted by Lewis in a way that is true of few other modern Christian writers."[3]

My own memories might be of interest and relevance here. I began to study theology in Lewis's Oxford in the mid-1970s, when I read for the Final Honor School of Theology, at the same time as completing my doctoral research in molecular biophysics. It soon became clear to me that one of the required initiation rites into the Oxford theological fraternity house was to rubbish Lewis as "outdated," "populist," and "theologically naive."

For a while I went along with this. Going with the flow is, after all, invariably intellectually undemanding and occasionally professionally rewarding. Yet as I read Lewis in private (for Lewis formed no part of Oxford's theological curriculum, even at the level of optional or elective papers), I gradually came to the conclusion that his writings offered a powerful intellectual, moral, and imaginative vision of the Christian faith that I simply found lacking in many of the lesser writers I was obliged to read.

As a young theologian, I was taught to despise Lewis; as a thinking person, I found him refreshing and energizing. As I listened to then-fashionable but now-forgotten voices faulting and dismissing him, I heard a deeper dissenting voice within me. All this may be true, I thought, but Lewis seems to have seen and grasped something that you have missed. That's why people still read him. Of course, they need to go *beyond* him. But as I have discovered in countless conversations since then, Lewis is the point of access for a large number of people to the serious study of theology. It seemed to me that, without him, there would be many who wouldn't be studying theology at all.

Lewis the Amateur Theologian

Professional theologians have long had an uneasy relationship with Lewis. The real issue is not Lewis's popularity and literary winsomeness, although these doubtless come into the picture at some point. It is a suspicion that Lewis offers simplistic answers to complex questions, and fails to engage with recent theological writers in his discussions. These are both fair concerns, and cannot be overlooked. Perhaps the most obvious case of theological oversimplification is found in the "trilemma" in *Mere Christianity*. Although Lewis's approach here can be defended,[4] it is vulnerable in the form in which he there states it, which could be argued to verge on naivete at points. And while *The Problem of Pain* had its admirers, some of the Inklings had their doubts about its core arguments. Lewis's brother Warren found it a curiously superficial and unpersuasive response to the issue of suffering.

Lewis always emphasized that he was an "amateur theologian," who addressed theological themes because professionals generally did not write with the needs of a wider audience in mind, thus creating space for his own efforts. Yet this does not really help us understand Lewis's general failure to engage theologians of the nineteenth or twentieth centuries. The religious writer of the nineteenth century valued most by Lewis appears to have been George MacDonald (1824–1905). Yet MacDonald is perhaps better considered a literary rather than a theological writer. We see no hint of any serious intellectual engagement with writers such as John Henry Newman (1801–90), now regarded by many as the greatest English-language theologian of the Victorian age.

While Lewis feels completely at home engaging Christian theologians of earlier generations – such as Augustine, Aquinas, or the sixteenth-century writer Richard Hooker, who "hardly ever wrote an obscure sentence"[5] – he had no time for more recent theological writers, such as the Protestant Karl Barth (1886–1968) or the Catholic Jacques Maritain (1882–1973).[6] Why not? In part, because Lewis is resistant to the notion of "chronological snobbery," and believes that classic expositions of religious or literary themes that have stood the test of time are generally to be preferred. Yet by failing to engage with more recent theological analyses or modern biblical scholarship, Lewis in effect disconnected himself from contemporary theological debate.

Supporters of Lewis could easily defend him at this point, noting, for example, that many of the best developments in the theology of the late twentieth century and early twenty-first centuries are "theologies of reappropriation" – in other words, taking older writers (such as Augustine of Hippo, Athanasius of Alexandria, or Thomas Aquinas), and putting them to contemporary use. Yet this does not entirely meet the point of criticism. The works of Jacques Maritain, for example, represented a major and constructive attempt to relate the ideas of Aquinas to modern culture[7] – the sort of thing that Lewis might be expected to endorse, or at least deem worthy of further exploration and discussion.[8] Yet Lewis makes no attempt to engage either the general principles of Maritain's work, or the specific outcomes that result from his approach.

So is Lewis to be considered a theologian? The answer, as might be expected, is determined entirely by how one defines "a theologian." In its broadest, and perhaps least meaningful sense, a "theologian" is someone who speaks about God, reflecting on the grounds and themes of the Christian faith. It is a defensible yet perhaps over-generous description of the theologian, which certainly includes Lewis, just as it includes most reflective Christian believers (and, arguably, critics of theism). The generality of the definition makes any conclusions reached on its basis of questionable significance. If Lewis is a theologian in this sense of the term, so is just about everyone else of theistic convictions and a reflective nature.

Yet this might prove to be a hasty judgment. During the period April 10–12, 1934, Karl Barth (1886–1968) delivered three lectures on the nature of theology to the Free Protestant Theological Faculty at Paris. In bringing a powerful affirmation of the scope and vision of Christian theology to its close, Barth turns to consider who is called to be a theologian. Barth's words might give us food for thought as we consider Lewis's credentials in this matter.[9]

> Theology is not a private subject for theologians only. Nor is it a private subject for professors. Fortunately, there have always been pastors who have understood more about theology than most professors. Nor is theology a private subject of study for pastors. Fortunately, there have repeatedly been congregation members, and often whole congregations, who have pursued theology energetically while their pastors were theological infants or barbarians. Theology is a matter for the Church.

Barth here affirms and refocuses Martin Luther's theme of the "priesthood of all believers."[10] Luther argued that all Christian believers were priests by virtue of their baptism – in doing so, not abolishing a professional "priesthood," but setting it in an interpretative context which affirmed both its distinctiveness and utility, yet negated any notion of spiritual privilege.[11] The professional clergy were to be seen as the servants, not the masters, of the people of God. In a similar manner, Barth sets the calling of the professional theologian within a theological frame-

work which affirms its validity and distinctiveness, without any suggestion that reflective believers outside the professional "theological guild"
forfeit any right to be deemed theologians.

There is a fundamental question here concerning who makes the rules
determining who is a "theologian." Lewis clearly did not regard himself –
and was certainly not regarded – as a "professional" theologian. His understandings of theological authority, method, and argument were not those
of the professional guild. Nor did he routinely reference recent members
of that guild in his writings. Lewis's frequent description of himself as an
"amateur" theologian is not to be interpreted as an admission of theological
ignorance or incompetence, but a principled assertion that he stood outside
the professional guild of theologians. He was, so to speak, an *independent*
theological voice, uninhibited by the conventions and loyalties of the theological academy.

There is a further point that needs to be considered here. In the recent
past, the English-language theological tradition has been dominated by
the core assumption that the "German-language tradition of academic
theology," as this developed in the nineteenth and twentieth centuries,
is "the best single tradition through which to be introduced to what it
means to do Christian theology in intelligent engagement with other
disciplines."[12] As a pedagogical judgment, this has some merit. This specific tradition of theology possesses a coherence and intellectual resilience
which makes for a good university lecture course in "trends in modern
theology," as I myself can attest.[13] But the pedagogy of historical theology
is one thing; engaging with the question of God in contemporary Anglo-
American culture is quite another matter.

Since about 1990, the hegemony of German-language theology has
collapsed.[14] This is evident in many ways, not least the growing numbers
of universities and theological seminaries in western Europe turning to
English-language theological resources, but also in the slackening interest
in recent German-language theology within the British and American
theological academies. The works of Karl Barth (1885–1968), Hans Urs
von Balthasar (1905–88), Jürgen Moltmann (born 1926), Wolfhart Pan-
nenberg (born 1928), Karl Rahner (1904–84), and a handful of others
remain highly regarded and equally highly studied; more recent German-
language writers, however, have generally failed to secure traction in the
United States and elsewhere, as a new generation of English-speaking
theologians gain the cultural ascendency.

Lewis represents a decidedly English approach to theology, which
assumes and explores the interconnectedness of religious experience,
thought, writing, and life. It is no accident that Lewis's conversion to

Christianity came about on account of his literary interests. As the Yale theologian Paul Holmer observed in his perceptive account of Lewis's thought, Lewis did not construct, or ever operate within, what could reasonably be termed a theological "system." Lewis "seems not to have been converted to a theological scheme at all, and he refused all of his life to think that an understanding of Christianity would necessitate that he adopt an elaborate theology."[15] Lewis's approach to theology would hold little interest for theological system-builders; he had little time for the view that "we must think and understand with a second-order scheme."[16] The rise of postmodernity has given a new cultural plausibility to Lewis's more theologically modest approach, which seeks to avoid the ambition of new scholasticisms, and focus instead on the role of language, culture, and story in the mediation and expression of divine truths.[17]

In particular, Lewis's dislike for a preoccupation with second-order "theories" – evident in his discussion of "theories of the atonement" in *Mere Christianity* – resonates with a cultural mood which is suspicious of theological over-precision, metaphysical inflation, and excessive conceptual elaboration. His emphasis upon the "baptized imagination" has resonated strongly with many who are uneasy about what they consider to be an aesthetically attenuated rationalism implicit within certain approaches to "systematic theology." Like Samuel Taylor Coleridge (1772–1834),[18] Lewis was a lay theologian whose fundamental intuitions have proved to be religiously stimulating and productive in the longer term.

The Problem of Professionalization

One of the issues attending any discussion of the nature of theology is fundamentally sociological in character – namely, the professionalization of theology as an academic discipline, with an accompanying shift in its methods and norms. To illustrate this point, let us consider the emergence of academic sociology itself. The origins of this academic discipline lay in non-professional geniuses of the nineteenth century such as Alexis de Tocqueville (1805–59) and Karl Marx (1818–83). The systematic exploration, modification, development, and application of their insights eventually led to the crystallization of a research methodology that is embodied – and enforced – by institutions. We could say that an academic field has become professionalized when it has developed the institutions and norms that serve to guide, constrain, and regulate the academic activities of its practitioners.[19]

By the middle of the twentieth century, sociology had become "professionalized" in this manner. The professional focus and boundaries of the discipline were affirmed and enforced through a complex fusion of journals and their editorial boards, annual conferences, professional associations, university departments of sociology, and tenure processes and their associated standards. Professional acceptance and advancement became partly dependent on conformity to the professional norms embodied in these associations and institutions, even though there are significant fault-lines within the discipline over fundamentally methodological questions.[20]

With this perspective in mind, let us consider this question: was Alexis de Toqueville a sociologist? In terms of the field of specialization and his academic competency, de Toqueville showed himself to be an innovative and rigorous thinker in trying to make sense of the social world around him. He was clearly a sociologist in this sense of the term. Yet he was clearly not a *professional* sociologist for several reasons. His reflections about society and history were based on his own intuitions about inference and explanation, rather than a community-based set of norms. Nor was he situated within a communal evaluative framework in the context of which his scientific work was to be assessed.

The situation is slightly more complex in the case of Emile Durkheim (1858–1917), a highly original thinker with his own intuitions about the nature of society and how it was to be investigated.[21] Although Durkheim was embedded within a tradition of thought that could reasonably be considered to be an emerging discipline of sociology, he should still be considered as a *sui generis* amateur – a "founding genius," whose work both contributed to the definition and articulation of a discipline of sociology, while also falling within the scope of that discipline.

Christian theology has a somewhat more extended history than that of sociology. Though no stranger to some of the debates over methods and priorities that have made sociology such an interesting topic in recent decades, Christian theology has traditionally been embedded within, and held accountable by, a somewhat different evaluative community – the church. There is no way in which writers such as Athanasius of Alexandria or Augustine of Hippo could be described as "professional theologians"; they were theologians nevertheless.

Nor is membership of the professional guild of theology a requirement for a religious writer to be deemed a "theologian." Theological luminaries such as Coleridge, John Henry Newman, and Hans Urs von Balthasar (1905–88) never held professional academic appointments. Their reputation ultimately rests on their *reception* – that is to say, the emergence of a committed readership, which came to regard them as insightful, reliable, or prophetic voices.

An Ecclesial Context: Theology and the Church of England

We need at this point to take into account Lewis's specific ecclesial location within the specific form of Christianity that he espoused. As we noted earlier (147–8), Lewis took some pleasure in declaring that he was "a very ordinary layman of the Church of England."[22] Following his conversion, Lewis chose to self-identify with the Church of England – not with "Anglicanism" as a specific ecclesiology, but with the more general ethos of the English national church.

Academic theology at Oxford University during the period between the two world wars was a highly clericalized discipline – an "inner ring"[23] from which Lewis was excluded. Oxford's Faculty of Theology then had seven statutory professorships – the Regius Chair of Divinity, the Lady Margaret Chair of Divinity, the Regius Chair of Ecclesiastical History, the Regius Chair of Moral and Pastoral Theology, the Regius Chair of Hebrew, the Oriel Professor of the Interpretation of Holy Scripture, and Dean Ireland's Professor of the Exegesis of Holy Scripture were held by scholars of distinction. Yet throughout most of Lewis's time at Oxford, these positions were all occupied by clergy.[24] The first four were linked with canonries at Christ Church Cathedral, and could only be held by priests of the Church of England. College deans or chaplains – all of whom were required to be priests of the Church of England during Lewis's lifetime – would often act as a college's tutorial fellow in theology.[25]

Furthermore, many have suggested that, as a matter of historical observation, the Church of England has not encouraged the kind of systematic theological reflection that one finds in writers such as Karl Barth, Paul Tillich, or Karl Rahner,[26] nor seen this as spiritually or apologetically advantageous.

It is a simple historical fact that the Church of England has long preferred to talk about "Christian doctrines," rather than "systematic theology."[27] Works of Anglican theology were often shaped around the traditional formularies of the church's creeds.[28] Perhaps the most important of these known to Lewis was published in May 1938 by Oliver Chase Quick (1885–1944), who subsequently became Regius Professor of Divinity at Oxford University.[29] While Quick described his *Doctrines of the Creed* as an "essay in systematic theology,"[30] they are better seen as a systematic exploration of the doctrines of the church, similar to that found in John

Pearson's *Exposition of the Creed* (1659), widely cited as a model of classical Anglican divinity.

Lewis thus inhabited an ecclesial tradition which did not, on the one hand, attach particular value to certain philosophically driven models of theological exposition,[31] yet which on the other valued pedagogically illuminating, imaginative, and symbolic ways of exploring the landscape of faith – above all, the use of poetry as a medium of theological exploration and expression.[32]

Lewis had little enthusiasm for forms of theological exposition characterized by logical intricacy on the one hand, and an imaginative deficit on the other. It is no accident that Lewis attached such value to the poems of George Herbert (1593–1633), which could be argued to embody a distinctively Anglican mode of theologizing, appealing to the imagination and longings, as much as to reason.[33] Recent scholarship has noted how Herbert, though clearly possessing a good knowledge of the theological tradition of the Protestant Reformation, chose to express this theology using rhetorical forms capable of captivating the imagination,[34] rather than in the more formal logical categories of systematic theology.

Herbert's use of evocative figures of speech ("tropes") allowed theologically and apologetically significant links to be forged between the secular world of his age and the core themes of the Christian faith.[35] Herbert's genius was to offer a way of expressing the core themes of the Christian faith in a manner that was more powerful and imaginative than the learned biblical commentaries and dense tomes of systematic theology of his age. Herbert's poetry is thus theological in its foundations, while deriving its power from an understanding of how words can be used to bridge the gap between heaven and earth, between the believer and Christ.[36]

Herbert reflected on the dilemma of the theological communicator – whether preacher or poet – at several points, showing an acute awareness of the importance of the envisaged audience and the limits of human words as a means of communication.[37] For example, his poem "Windows" opens with a question addressed to God:

Lord, how can man preach thy eternal word?

This quickly develops into a discussion of the limits of purely verbal forms of preaching, which risk being "waterish, bleak, and thin." To be faithful and effective, preaching must marry and merge "doctrine and life, colours and light." Herbert's poetry itself can be seen as an attempt to enact the preacher's role to be a "window" for divine truth, which affects real life, not simply the understanding.[38] Herbert is arguing the case for an

emotionally and imaginatively engaging form of theology, which transcends the limits of theological textbooks.

The Anglican poets John Donne and George Herbert both demon-
strated the potential of the poetic genre to communicate theology through
an essentially imaginative engagement. Each proved that it was possible
to communicate – and commend – Protestant ideas through the poetic
medium. Herbert's poem *The Elixir* represents a powerful statement of
the transforming impact of Christ upon mundane human life,[39] especially
through the image of Christ as the fabled "philosopher's stone."[40] Similarly, Donne was able to use the same medium to set out the Augustinian
notion of the bondage of the will through sin, requiring God to "batter
down" human resistance to the transforming power of grace.[41]

Lewis's poems, which have never been well regarded, show a Herber-
tian concern to express theology through striking images.[42] Yet Lewis's
poetic skills are better realized in his prose,[43] which many came to see as
offering an approach to Christian ideas that was both elegant and accessible – not least on account of Lewis's ability to translate theology into
the cultural vernacular.

Lewis and the Art of Theological Translation

Herbert and Donne both point to an understanding of the theological
enterprise which they clearly considered to be an integral element of the
Church of England's intellectual heritage – the imaginative translation or
transposition of the classical themes of Christian theology.[44] Theological
notions were rendered as verbal images and tropes, enabling a deeper
level of engagement with the realities of faith than that which might be
expected to result from a purely logical dissection of ideas. Lewis shows
himself to be heir to this tradition of theological translation, offering an
imaginative and rhetorical rendering of some core themes of the Christian
faith that were superbly adapted to the cultural geography of his own age.

We have already noted Lewis's gifts as a theological translator (131–3),
which led to his rise to fame in Great Britain during the 1940s. Yet Lewis
was as adept at theological *transposition* as he was at theological *translation*.
By "transposition," I mean restating ideas in a different genre.[45] Lewis's
transposition of theological themes in the "Chronicles of Narnia" can be
seen as an imaginative restatement of the theological ideas he explored
in a more traditional manner in *Mere Christianity*. Lewis, as one of his
more perceptive interpreters has rightly noted, "is not *just* trying to 'translate' Christian doctrine; he is trying to evoke what it feels like to believe
in the God of Christian Revelation."[46] The "Chronicles of Narnia" are not

simply a verbal exploration of some theological notions; they represent an imaginative rendering of some of the core themes of the Christian faith in a narrative form, aimed at captivating our imagination more than informing our reason.

Yet perhaps Lewis is seen at his best as a theological transposer when developing metaphors as imaginative vehicles of theological analysis. The Oxford theologian Paul Fiddes (born 1947) points out how Lewis explores the image of the "divine dance" as a means of elucidating God's relation to the world, and particularly to human beings.[47] This rich image, which has been widely used by theologians since about 1980 to explore aspects of both extra-Trinitarian and intra-Trinitarian relationships, was originally formulated by Lewis as an imaginative gateway to aspects of the Christian doctrine of God.

Lewis's conversion experience had brought home to him that God was active, questing, and engaging – three classic motifs of a Trinitarian conception of God. Yet these convictions still needed to be expressed in a language and genre that Lewis believed would engage the imaginations, not merely satisfy the intellects, of his readers. So how might these themes be expressed imaginatively? Lewis found the image of a dance to be a potent means of expressing some characteristics of the Christian God vividly, faithfully, and memorably.[48]

> In Christianity God is not a static thing – not even a person – but a dynamic, pulsating activity, a life, almost a kind of drama. Almost, if you will not think me irreverent, a kind of dance.

The image is fertile and vibrant, both theologically and imaginatively, opening the way to an enhanced appreciation of this vision of God. It is interesting to recall here that, during his atheist phase, Lewis used this same image of a dance to express the *absence* of purpose in life. The universe was a "meaningless dance of atoms," exuding a "subjective phosphorescence" of beauty and purpose, which lacked any real substance.[49]

Lewis's growing commitment to a classic incarnational and Trinitarian theology in the early 1930s is evident from a letter written in the autumn of 1934 to the American philosopher Paul Elmer More (1864–1937).[50] Lewis had read More's new book, *The Sceptical Approach to Religion*, published earlier that year, and had found it helpful in clarifying his own thinking about God. While conceding that some Christians might reject Idealism, Lewis refused to "relinquish the Absolutist view of God." For him, this was the doorway through which he had himself entered Christianity. The concept of God which seemed to him to be most intellectually and spiritually satisfying – which he teasingly refers to as a "wish-belief" – would incorporate both the "eternal" and the "necessary," while at the same time "not wanting the immobile, the unanswering."

This, Lewis concedes, might seem to be the "flimsiest of self-indulgence" on his part – were it not for "the huge historic fact of the doctrine of the Trinity." With theological adroitness, Lewis points out how this classic Christian understanding of God allows Christians to affirm a doctrine of a God who is utterly transcendent on the one hand, yet is capable of action and engagement with the world on the other. Lewis then anchors this Trinitarian notion of God in an understanding of the incarnation.[51]

> Is the traditional Christian belief not precisely this; that the same being which is eternally perfect, *purus actus*, already at the End etc etc, yet also, in some incomprehensible way, is a purposing, feeling, and finally crucified Man in a particular place and time? So that somehow or other, we have it both ways?

Lewis clearly presents this line of thought as an existing belief, not a new development, making it clear that by the time of this letter, he has settled on a surprisingly traditional vision of the Christian faith – not on account of any incipient traditionalism on Lewis's part, but because he believed that the traditional formulations of Trinitarian and Christological beliefs were the best representations of his own developed spiritual intuitions.

Lewis also showed himself adept at a distinctive form of intellectual defense of the Christian faith – demonstrating the something seemingly rather complicated and difficult to grasp actually resonated with the fundamental intuitions of the religious believer. In the case of the doctrine of the Trinity, Lewis applies this approach by noting how it chimes in with familiarities of Christian practice:[52]

> An ordinary simple Christian kneels down to say his prayers. He is trying to get into touch with God. But if he is a Christian he knows what is prompting him to pray is also God: God, so to speak, inside him. But he also knows that all his real knowledge of God comes through Christ, the Man who was God – that Christ is standing beside him, helping him to pray, praying for him. You see what is happening. God is the thing to which he is praying – the goal he is trying to reach. God is also the thing inside him which is pushing him on – the motive power. God is also the road or bridge along which he is being pushed to that goal. So that the whole threefold life of the three-personal Being is actually going on in that ordinary little bedroom where an ordinary man is saying his prayers.

I have quoted this passage in full to allow the tone and voice, as well as the intellectual content, of Lewis's approach to be appreciated. Some will wish to raise concerns about its lack of theological sophistication, noting the lack of any engagement on his part with any leading exponents of Trinitarian theology, classic or modern,[53] and perhaps expressing concern about its implicit modalist tendencies. Yet we must try to understand what Lewis chose to do, not what others believe he ought to have done. What Lewis has offered is a transposition of the doctrine of the Trinity into the quotidian, anchoring a complex theological abstraction in the everyday life of the believer. His primary concern is not to explore the doctrine's theological profundities, but to reassure the believer of its intrinsic spiritual plausibility.

So does this make Lewis a theologian? After all, someone who translates theological ideas into the cultural vernacular is no more a theologian than the translator of poetry is to be deemed a poet *for that reason alone*. Yet perhaps the translator who is *also* a poet might offer a more powerful and satisfying translation of a poem than a mere verbal technocrat – witness, for example, the power of Seamus Heaney's translation of *Beowulf* (1999), informed both by his own poetic instincts and J. R. R. Tolkien's scholarly reflections on its significance.[54] Similarly, in interpreting theological notions – such as the incarnation – Lewis is not approaching them as a stranger, puzzled by their strange forms and distinct language; he inhabits their world, both rationally and imaginatively, sensitive to the difference they make to the way we see things.

Only a highly attenuated definition of "theology" can prevent us from speaking of Lewis as a theologian. We may choose to qualify this – for example, a case could easily be made for speaking of him as a "popular theologian." A refusal to allow Lewis any kind of status as a theologian now seems increasingly petulant, and out of touch with the influence Lewis now exerts on the global Christian community, particularly in the English-language world. Just as Nietzsche (1844–1900) was professionally a professor of philology who was popularly acclaimed as a philosophical luminary after his death,[55] so Lewis was professionally a professor of English literature who has been acclaimed as a popular theological writer.

Lewis as Theologian: A Gramscian Perspective

The real debate over Lewis's credentials as a theologian concerns the sociological identity of the community which is authorized to make this judgment. This theme is fundamental to the writings of the Italian political theorist Antonio Gramsci (1891–1937), especially his landmark works dealing with the cultural role of intellectuals.[56] Gramsci's fundamental point – which can be argued to represent an ideological reworking of

Luther's doctrine of the "priesthood of all believers" – is that, while all people are intellectuals, only some assume the *social function* of intellectuals.[57] For Gramsci, the intellectual is someone who shapes culture by establishing cohesion, either by creating or challenging an ideological hegemony.[58] Every social group "creates together with itself, organically, one or more strata of intellectuals which give it homogeneity."

Unsurprisingly, Gramsci's ideas have found a particularly receptive audience within Latin American liberation theology.[59] Yet his analysis of the cultural role of intellectuals offers a way of understanding how Lewis has come to assume the social role of a theologian within a significant section of western Christianity. For the simple fact is that Lewis has secured an extraordinarily large support base within early twenty-first century American Christianity, including both its large Catholic and evangelical constituencies. To use the sociological categories developed by Gramsci, Lewis has emerged as an "organic intellectual" who challenges and subverts the traditional power structures within religious and academic groupings.[60]

Traditionally, such intellectuals were professional theologians or bishops; increasingly, intellectual leadership within American Christianity and beyond seems to be passing to figures whose authority is not grounded professionally or institutionally, but rests on their acceptance within the community at large. As Gramsci points out, any group that is moving toward dominance finds itself in conflict with the "traditional" intellectuals.[61] The popular appeal of Lewis is grounded in more fundamental concerns within western Christian communities about the quality and commitment of traditional sources of authority, and the search for more satisfactory alternatives. The implications of this Gramscian analysis are far-reaching.

In the first place, Gramsci's framework allows us to see Lewis as an intellectual who challenges the theological hegemony of bishops and priests, offering an understanding of theology which resonates with laity across the denominational divisions. As survey after survey since 2000 demonstrates, Lewis is widely regarded as one of the most influential Christian writers of the twentieth century, with continuing relevance for the twenty-first. He is clearly what Gramsci describes as an "organic intellectual" – that is to say, one whose authority is not grounded in "traditional" credentials, such as his location within a religious hierarchy, but rests on his acceptance within the relatively large and significant "social group" who affirm Christian fundamentals and dislike denominational imperialism.

In the second, Gramsci's approach allows us to see the refusal of professional theologians to accept Lewis as one of their number as a reflection of the threat he is seen to pose for their influence within or upon communities of faith. On a Gramscian reading of matters, Lewis is excluded by the academic theological community partly because he is perceived as weakening their authority over the "social groups" that have embraced him as their intellectual guide. Lewis may not be rated as a theologian by professional theologians; that judgment, however, is not shared outside this "inner ring."

The debate over whether Lewis is a "theologian" maps neatly onto a broader cultural debate about cultural élites, which became particularly significant in the period between the First and Second World Wars. In his provocative and challenging study *The Intellectuals and the Masses*, John Carey suggested that professional academics found their status and prestige coming under threat from an increasingly educated and literate lay public. They responded by attempting to construct barriers to exclude such people, retaining their professional standing by means of a policy of exclusion.[62]

> Modernist literature and art can be seen as a hostile reaction to the unprecedentedly large reading public created by nineteenth century educational reforms. The purpose of modernist writing…was to exclude these newly educated (or "semi-educated") readers, and so to preserve the intellectual's seclusion from the "mass."

If Carey is right – and he is certainly provocative – then Lewis's ability to communicate with the "mass" excludes him from the guild of intellectual theology. "What is truly meritorious in art is seen as the prerogative of a minority, the intellectuals, and the significance of this minority is reckoned to be directly proportionate to its ability to outrage and puzzle the mass."[63]

Gramsci's deft analysis of the implicit intellectual power struggles within social groupings makes it clear that the issue of *influence* cannot be ignored. Gramsci's account of hegemony helps us understand why at least some academic theologians are rankled by Lewis's sales figures, and his obvious and substantial impact on popular Christian culture. Lewis has been *received* and *accepted* as a theologian,[64] despite allegedly *not* being a theologian. A large number of intelligent Christians have come to adopt Lewis as *their* theologian.

This fits neatly with Gramsci's analysis of how intellectuals emerge and gain cultural traction. As Gramsci rightly pointed out: "An independent class of intellectuals does not exist; rather every social group has its own intellectuals."[65] The debate is only partly about Lewis's theological virtues; it is about the communities or "social groups" which make such judgments in the first place. And a large such "social group" has chosen to regard Lewis as their theologian.

While there is more to this question than a Gramscian reading of things suggests, it alerts us to aspects of the debate over Lewis's credentials as a theologian which are too easily overlooked. Who decides who is a theologian: the guild, or the masses? The academy, the church, or the *consensus fidelium?* The debate over whether Lewis is a "real" theologian raises unsettling issues, which reflect a significant degree of unease within the theological academy over its influence upon churches and culture.[66] Whether we like it or not, issues of power and "hegemony" – Gramsci's key theme – hover, uninvited, over such discussions.

So are we to speak of Lewis as a theologian? As we have seen, Lewis insisted on his "amateur" status. After a creative and constructive engagement with the doctrine of the incarnation, Lewis felt it necessary to offer a disclaimer. "I walk *in mirabilibus super me* and submit all to the verdict of real theologians."[67] Lewis was not a professional theologian by the standards of the 1960s. Yet he has been recognized and trusted as a theological voice by a remarkably large number of people, who have chosen to regard him as a theologian, irrespective of the judgment of the professional guild. Such readers cannot be dismissed as "low-brow" or "semi-educated," simply because they are not academics;[68] they choose to read what they find helpful and useful, and often seem to prefer Lewis as a theological guide to the labyrinth of faith over his more academic alternatives.

Back in 1946, the University of St. Andrews recognized two of Lewis's most distinctive and brilliant theological characteristics: his ability to *translate* theology into the cultural vernacular, and his *weaving together* of "theological reflection and poetic imagination." It is those two same characteristics that cause so many to respect Lewis as a theologian, two generations later. Whether for good reasons or not, since about 2000 surveys of North American Christian readers regularly cite Lewis as one of the most influential theologians of the twentieth century. Perhaps, to use a musical simile, Lewis is better seen as an arranger than composer;[69] nevertheless, some of these theological arrangements and variations on themes seem to have captured the popular imagination, where the originals did not.

Fifty years after Lewis's death, he has *become* a theologian – not because Lewis himself has changed, but because attitudes toward him are shifting. Lewis is now "received" as a theologian by a large number of individuals, who find in Lewis certain intellectual and cultural virtues that they do not find elsewhere. The perception has become the reality. I would venture to suggest that it is only a matter of time before courses on "The

Theology of C. S. Lewis" make their appearance in leading seminaries and universities, especially in the United States. Indeed, I am tempted to develop one such course myself.

Notes

1   For the development of this link in the 1580s, see Ronald G. Cant, *The University of St Andrews: A Short History*. Edinburgh and London: Oliver & Boyd, 1946.

2   Oliver Quick to William Temple, July 24, 1943; Lambeth Palace Library, William Temple Papers, vol. 39, fol. 269. The letter also commended Sayers as an intelligent theological voice in the public sphere.

3   Rowan Williams, *The Lion's World: A Journey into the Heart of Narnia*. London: SPCK, 2012, xi.

4   For an analysis, see P. H. Brazier, "'God…Or a Bad, or Mad, Man': C. S. Lewis's Argument for Christ – A Systematic Theological, Historical and Philosophical Analysis of *Aut Deus Aut Malus Homo*." *Heythrop Journal* 51 (2010): 1–30.

5   *English Literature in the Sixteenth Century*, 453.

6   Lewis's reference to Barthianism as "a flattening out of all things into common insignificance before the inscrutable Creator" has won him few theological admirers: *English Literature in the Sixteenth Century*, 449; 453.

7   As noted by Gerald A. McCool, *From Unity to Pluralism: The Internal Evolution of Thomism*. New York: Fordham University Press, 1999, 114–60.

8   For Lewis's concerns about Maritain, see his letter to Dom Bede Griffiths, April 4, 1934; *Letters*, vol. 2, 134–5.

9   Karl Barth, "Theology," in *God in Action*. Edinburgh: T&T Clark, 1936, 39–57.

10   Karl Barth, *Church Dogmatics*. Edinburgh: T&T Clark, 2004, IV/2, 694. On Luther, see Norman E. Nagel, "Luther and the Priesthood of All Believers." *Concordia Theological Quarterly* 61 (1997): 277–98.

11   Alister E. McGrath, *Christianity's Dangerous Idea: The Protestant Revolution*. San Francisco: HarperOne, 2008, 35–6; 52–3; 57–8; 73.

12   David Ford and Rachel Muers, *The Modern Theologians: An Introduction to Christian Theology since 1918*. 3rd edn. Malden, MA: Blackwell, 2005, ix.

13   I used this approach myself at Oxford University in the mid-1980s, offering a lecture course on the development of modern German Christology from about 1770 to 1980.

14   The reasons for this are not fully understood, and are likely to be complex. One factor is the decline of Christianity in Germany itself: Jack D. Shand, "The Decline of Traditional Christian Beliefs in Germany." *Sociology of Religion* 59, no. 2 (1998): 179–84. Yet many believe the reason lies more fundamentally in the rise of English as the *lingua franca* of theology, and the emergence of a dissonance between Anglo-American and German-language approaches to theology.

15 Paul Holmer, *C. S. Lewis: The Shape of his Faith and Thought*. New York: Harper & Row, 1978, 100–1. Holmer (1916–2004) was Noah Porter Professor of Philosophical Theology at Yale Divinity School at the time of writing this short book, which remains one of the most theologically perceptive accounts of Lewis's ideas. The reference to doctrine as a "second-order" issue reflects "post-liberal" trends at Yale Divinity School, best seen in George Lindbeck, *The Nature of Doctrine*. London: SPCK, 1980. For criticism of this approach, see Alister E. McGrath, *The Genesis of Doctrine*. Oxford: Blackwell, 1990, 14–80.

16 Holmer, *C. S. Lewis: The Shape of his Faith and Thought*, 102.

17 See the points made in Alister E. McGrath, "Erzählung, Gemeinschaft und Dogma: Reflexionen über das Zeugnis der Kirche in der Postmoderne." *Theologische Beiträge* 41, no. 1 (2010): 25–38. The absence of reference to Lewis in Colin S. Gunton, ed., *The Cambridge Companion to Christian Doctrine*. Cambridge: Cambridge University Press, 1997, also reflects this restricted conception of the nature of theology.

18 For Coleridge's influence on the Victorian Church of England, see Stephen Prickett, *Romanticism and Religion*. Cambridge: Cambridge University Press, 1976, 9–89. For an account of his theology, see the classic study of J. Robert Barth, *Coleridge and Christian Doctrine*. Cambridge, MA: Harvard University Press, 1969.

19 Andrew Abbott, *The System of Professions: An Essay on the Division of Expert Labor*. Chicago: University of Chicago Press, 1988; Andrew Abbott, *Chaos of Disciplines*. Chicago: University of Chicago Press, 2001, 3–33.

20 See, for example, George Steinmetz, ed., *The Politics of Method in the Human Sciences: Positivism and Its Epistemological Others*. Durham, NC: Duke University Press, 2005.

21 The best study remains Steven Lukes, *Emile Durkheim, His Life and Work: A Historical and Critical Study*. Stanford, CA: Stanford University Press, 1985.

22 Lewis, *Mere Christianity*, viii.

23 I use this phrase deliberately, in the sense advocated by Lewis himself in his 1944 Memorial Lecture at King's College, London: "The Inner Ring"; *Essay Collection*, 721–8.

24 For the academic year 1925–6, see *Oxford University Calendar 1925*. Oxford: Oxford University Press, 68; for the academic year 1924–5, see *Oxford University Calendar 1925*. Oxford: Oxford University Press, 76.

25 During the academic year 1925–6, when Lewis took up his fellowship at Magdalen College, the Faculty of Theology had 44 members, 29 of whom were clergy: *Oxford University Calendar 1925*. Oxford: Oxford University Press, 8.

26 The classic exploration of this theme is Stephen W. Sykes, *The Integrity of Anglicanism*. London: Mowbray, 1978.

27 For this distinction, see Colin E. Gunton, "A Rose by Any Other Name? From 'Christian Doctrine' to 'Systematic Theology.'" *International Journal of Systematic Theology* 1, no. 1 (1999): 4–23.

28 A good example of the essentially creedal approach preferred by most Anglican theologians can be seen in W. H. Griffith-Thomas, *The Principles of Theology*. London: Longmans, Green & Co., 1930.

29 Quick engaged in a friendly correspondence with Lewis over some points arising from *The Problem of Pain* (1940). See Lewis's letter to Quick, dated January 18, 1941; *Letters*, vol. 2, 460–6.

30 Oliver Chase Quick, *Doctrines of the Creed: Their Basis in Scripture and Their Meaning To-day*. London: James Nisbet, 1938, ix.

31 For the emergence of such approaches in German theological faculties in the late nineteenth and early twentieth centuries, see Thomas A. Howard, *Protestant Theology and the Making of the Modern German University*. Oxford: Oxford University Press, 2009, 130–211.

32 Twentieth-century examples of Anglicanism's use of poetry as a means of theological exploration include Charles Williams and T. S. Eliot: see, for example, Glen Cavaliero, *Charles Williams: Poet of Theology*. Grand Rapids, MI: Eerdmans, 1983; Patrick Terrell Gray, "Eliot the Enigma: An Observation of the Development of T. S. Eliot's Thought and Poetry." *Anglican Theological Review* 85, no. 2 (2003): 309–40.

33 For some of the issues, see Ilona Bell, "'Setting Foot into Divinity': George Herbert and the English Reformation." *Modern Language Quarterly* 38 (1977): 219–41; Leah Sinanoglou Marcus, "George Herbert and the Anglican Plain Style." In *"Too Riche to Clothe the Sunne:" Essays on George Herbert*, edited by Claude J. Summers and Ted-Larry Pebworth, 179–93. Pittsburgh, PA: University of Pittsburgh Press, 1980.

34 Barbara Kiefer Lewalski, *Protestant Poetics and the Seventeenth-Century Religious Lyric*. Princeton, NJ: Princeton University Press, 1979; Elizabeth Clarke, *Theory and Theology in George Herbert's Poetry: "Divinitie and Poesy Met."* Oxford: Clarendon Press, 1997; R. V. Young, *Doctrine and Devotion in Seventeenth-Century Poetry: Studies in Donne, Herbert, Crashaw, and Vaughan*. Cambridge: Brewer, 2000; Daniel Doerksen, "George Herbert, Calvinism, and Reading 'Mattens.'" *Christianity and Literature* 59, no. 3 (2010): 437–51.

35 For example, see Richard Leonard Caulkins, *George Herbert's Art of Love: His Use of the Tropes of Eros in the Poetry of Agape*. New York: Lang, 1996.

36 See Heather A. R. Asals, *Equivocal Predication: George Herbert's Way to God*. Toronto: University of Toronto Press, 1981, especially 26–9. Note also Martin Elsky, *Authorizing Words: Speech, Writing, and Print in the English Renaissance*. Ithaca, NY: Cornell University Press, 1989, 147–83.

37 See Bruce A. Johnson, "The audience shift in George Herbert's poetry." *Studies in English Literature* 35 (1990): 89–103.

38 The use of "glass" in this poem may also take up some Pauline themes, most notably those found in 2 Corinthians 3:18: "But we all, with open face beholding as in a glass the glory of the Lord, are changed into the same image from glory to glory." See Ronald G. Shafer, "George Herbert's Poetic Adaptation of St. Paul's Image of the Glass." *Seventeenth-Century News* 35 (1977): 10–11.

39 Alister E. McGrath, "The Gospel and the Transformation of Reality: George Herbert's 'The Elixir.'" In Alister E. McGrath, *Mere Theology: Christian Faith and the Discipleship of the Mind*. London: SPCK, 2010, 39–50.

40 Helen Constance White, *The Metaphysical Poets: A Study in Religious Experience*. New York: Macmillan, 1936, 181–2; Clarence H. Miller, "Christ as the

Philosopher's Stone in George Herbert's 'The Elixir.'" *Notes and Queries* 45 (1998): 39–40; Yaakov Mascetti, "'This Is the Famous Stone': George Herbert's Poetic Alchemy in 'The Elixir.'" In *Mystical Metal of Gold: Essays on Alchemy and Renaissance Culture*, edited by Stanton J. Linden, 301–24. Brooklyn, NY: AMS Press, 2005.

41　Gillian R. Evans, "John Donne and the Augustinian Paradox of Sin." *Review of English Studies* 33 (1982): 1–22.

42　Don W. King, *C. S. Lewis: Poet*. Kent, OH: Kent State University Press, 2001, 203–23.

43　King, *C. S. Lewis: Poet*, 224–44.

44　Others could easily be added, including Thomas Traherne, who Lewis prized greatly: see Donald R. Dickson, *The Fountain of Living Waters: The Typology of the Waters of Life in Herbert, Vaughan, and Traherne*. Columbia, MO: University of Missouri Press, 1987; Denise Inge, "A Poet Comes Home: Thomas Traherne, Theologian in a New Century." *Anglican Theological Review* 86, no. 2 (2004): 335–48.

45　Lewis uses the term "transposition" in a somewhat more developed sense: see his paper "Transposition"; *Essay Collection*, 267–78.

46　Williams, *The Lion's World: A Journey into the Heart of Narnia*, 27.

47　Paul S. Fiddes, "On Theology." In *The Cambridge Companion to C. S. Lewis*, edited by Robert MacSwain and Michael Ward, 89–104. Cambridge: Cambridge University Press, 2010. For Fiddes's own reflections on the Trinitarian implications of this image, see Paul S. Fiddes, *Participating in God: A Pastoral Doctrine of the Trinity*. London: Darton, Longman, and Todd, 2000, 72–81.

48　*Mere Christianity*, 175.

49　*Surprised by Joy*, 200.

50　Letter to Paul Elmer More, October 25, 1934; *Letters*, vol. 2, 145–6.

51　Letter to Paul Elmer More, October 25, 1934; *Letters*, vol. 2, 146.

52　*Mere Christianity*, 163.

53　We must not, however, overlook Lewis's obvious attempts to restate some classic Trinitarian and Christological themes – for example, his remark (*Mere Christianity*, 173–4) that "we must think of the Son always, so to speak, streaming forth from the Father, like light from a lamp, or heat from a fire, or thoughts from a mind. He is the self-expression of the Father – what the Father has to say." This is clearly a reworking of some classical Athanasian themes.

54　Seamus Heaney, *Beowulf: A New Verse Translation*. New York: Farrar, Straus, and Giroux, 2000. For comment on this aspect of Heaney's excellent translation, see Felicia Jean Steele, "Dreaming of Dragons: Tolkien's Impact on Heaney's *Beowulf*." *Mythlore* 25, no. 1 (2006): 137–46.

55　For the dynamics of this process, see Steven E. Aschheim, *The Nietzsche Legacy in Germany, 1890–1990*. Berkeley, CA: University of California Press, 1992.

56　The best study in English of this theme is Peter D. Thomas, "Gramsci and the Intellectuals: Modern Prince vs Passive Revolution." In *Marxism, Intellectuals, and Politics*, edited by David Bates, 69–85. Basingstoke: Palgrave Macmillan, 2007.

57 Antonio Gramsci, *Gli intellettuali e l'organizzazione della cultura*. Cagliari: Davide Zedda Editore, 2007, 16: "Tutti gli uomini sono intellettuali, si potrebbe dire perciò; ma non tutti gli uomini hanno nella società la funzione di intellettuali."

58 For the critically important notion of "hegemony" in Gramsci, see Peter D. Thomas, *The Gramscian Moment: Philosophy, Hegemony and Marxism*. Leiden: Brill, 2009, 159–241. This displaces the older (though still valuable) study of Luciano Gruppi, *Il concetto di egemonia in Gramsci*. Rome: Edirori Riuniti, 1972. Notice particularly Gramsci's comments about "la conquista 'ideologica' degli intellettuali tradizionali": Gramsci, *Gli intellettuali e l'organizzazione della cultura*, 16.

59 See, for example, Atilio Borón, ed., *América Latina en los '90: Gramsci y la teología de la liberación*. Buenos Aires: Utopías del Sur, 1992.

60 See especially the section entitled "La formazione degli intellettuali" in Gramsci, *Gli intellettuali e l'organizzazione della cultura*, 13–16. Note how Gramsci sees *gli intellettuali "organici"* as challenging the special interests of traditional ecclesiastical power structures.

61 Gramsci, *Gli intellettuali e l'organizzazione della cultura*, 13–15.

62 John Carey, *The Intellectuals and the Masses: Pride and Prejudice among the Literary Intelligentsia, 1880–1939*. New York: St. Martin's Press, 1993, vii.

63 Carey, *The Intellectuals and the Masses*, 18.

64 For the (occasionally puzzling) factors that shape such "reception" processes, see Hans Robert Jauss, *Toward an Aesthetic of Reception*. Minneapolis: University of Minnesota Press, 1982.

65 Antonio Gramsci, *Il Risorgimento*. Turin: Einaudi, 1966, 71. Gramsci's interpretation of the *Risorgimento* is open to criticism – see, for example, Rosario Romeo, *Risorgimento e capitalismo*. Bari: Laterza, 1970. But the point that Gramsci makes about the social embeddedness of intellectuals remains significant.

66 For the three main audiences theology is required to engage – the church, the academy, and the general public – see David Tracy, *The Analogical Imagination: Christian Theology and the Culture of Pluralism*. New York: Crossroad Publishing Company, 14–24.

67 "Transposition"; *Essay Collection*, 277. The Latin tag means "in wonders which are beyond me."

68 A point made with particular force by Jonathan Rose, *The Intellectual Life of the British Working Classes*. New Haven, CT, Yale University Press, 2000. For the relation of intellectuals to popular culture in the later twentieth century, see Andrew Ross, *No Respect: Intellectuals & Popular Culture*. New York: Routledge, 1989.

69 For the use of musical performance as a metaphor for hermeneutical reflection and theological formulation, see Frances M. Young, *Virtuoso Theology: The Bible and Interpretation*. Cleveland, OH: Pilgrim Press, 1993, published in the United Kingdom as *The Art of Performance: Towards a Theology of Holy Scripture*. London: Darton, Longman and Todd, 1990.

Works by Lewis Cited

The Abolition of Man. New York: HarperCollins, 2001.
All My Road before Me: The Diary of C. S. Lewis, 1922–1927. Edited by Walter Hooper. San Diego: Harcourt Brace Jovanovich, 1991.
Collected Letters. Edited by Walter Hooper. 3 vols. San Francisco: HarperOne, 2004–6.
The Discarded Image. Cambridge: Cambridge University Press, 1994.
English Literature in the Sixteenth Century, Excluding Drama. Oxford: Clarendon Press, 1954.
Essay Collection and Other Short Pieces. London: HarperCollins, 2000.
An Experiment in Criticism. Cambridge: Cambridge University Press, 1992.
The Four Loves. London: HarperCollins, 2002.
The Great Divorce. London: HarperCollins, 2002.
Miracles. London: HarperCollins, 2002.
The Pilgrim's Regress. London: Geoffrey Bles, 1950.
Poems. Edited by Walter Hooper. Orlando, FL: Harcourt Brace Jovanovich, 1992.
A Preface to Paradise Lost. London: Oxford University Press, 1942.
The Problem of Pain. London: HarperCollins, 2002.
Reflections on the Psalms. London: Collins, 1974.
The Screwtape Letters. London: HarperCollins, 2002.
Spirits in Bondage: A Cycle of Lyrics. London: Heinemann, 1919. [Originally published under the pseudonym "Clive Hamilton."]
Studies in Medieval and Renaissance Literature. Cambridge: Cambridge University Press, 2007.
Surprised by Joy. London: HarperCollins, 2002.

The Intellectual World of C. S. Lewis, First Edition. Alister E. McGrath.
© 2014 John Wiley & Sons, Ltd. Published 2014 by John Wiley & Sons, Ltd.

Index

Abductive reasoning strategies in
    Lewis's apologetics, 120
Abolition of Man (1943), 41, 48
Adorno, Theodor, 72–3
Alexander, Samuel, 51 n. 33
Allegory of Love (1936), xi
Anglicanism, Lewis's relation to, 4,
    147–61
Anselm of Canterbury, 107, 108
Apologetics, Lewis's approach to, 4,
    57, 67, 68–9, 73–4, 105–22,
    129–46
Aquinas, Thomas, 129, 165, 166
Arendt, Hannah, 84
Argument from desire, 4, 105–28,
    137–8
Arnold, Matthew, 106
Aristotle, 13, 60, 89, 90, 135
ars memorativa, 13–14
ars oblivionalis, 13–14
Athanasius of Alexandria, 166, 169
Atheism, in Lewis's early thought, x,
    9–10, 32, 34–6, 57, 66, 90, 112,
    151, 173
Augustine of Hippo, 10–12, 25 n. 15,
    85, 89, 92, 93, 107, 114, 136,
    165, 169

Baker, Leo, 36
Baillie, Donald M., 163
Balthasar, Hans Urs von, 167, 169
Barfield, Owen, 18, 38, 42, 47–8, 62,
    152
Barth, Karl, 32, 85, 165, 166
Baxter, Richard, 148–50
Bentham, Jeremy, 86–7
Bergson, Henri, 41
Bernard of Clairvaux, 107
Bible, in Lewis's thought, 92–3, 133,
    156–7
Blake, William, 94
Bluebells, and dating of Lewis's
    conversion to Christianity, 20–1
"Blue Flower" motif, 21–2, 108
Blumenberg, Hans, 97 n. 7, 104 n. 98
Book of Common Prayer (1662), 157
da Brescia, Moretto, 22
British Broadcasting Corporation, xii,
    109, 129, 148
Browne, Thomas, 152
Bultmann, Rudolf, 66, 69–70
Bunyan, John, 9, 119

Calvin, John, 85
Cambridge Platonism, 39, 93

The Intellectual World of C. S. Lewis, First Edition. Alister E. McGrath.
© 2014 John Wiley & Sons, Ltd. Published 2014 by John Wiley & Sons, Ltd.

Carey, John, 177
Carritt, Edgar F., 33, 37, 49
Chesterton, G. K., 9, 118, 135, 152
Chodowiecki, Daniel, 94
Chronicles of Narnia, xii, 1, 2, 10, 85, 133, 140, 172
"chronological snobbery," 42–3, 152, 165
Church of England, 4, 147–54
Coghill, Neville, 152
Coleridge, Samuel Taylor, 140, 168
Conversion, Lewis's, xi, 12, 17–20, 61–5, 152
Cook Wilson, John, 37–8
Croce, Benedetto, 38

Dante Alighieri, 13, 60, 85, 88, 91
Davidman, Joy, xii, 10
Derrida, Jacques, 84
Descartes, René, 108
Desire, argument from, 4, 105–28, 137–8
Dewey, John, 90
Donne, John, 152, 172
Durkheim, Emile, 169
Dyson, Hugo, 12, 19–20, 62, 65

Eco, Umberto, 26 n. 31
Eliot, T. S., 32, 39–40, 131
Enlightenment, Lewis's relationship to, 35, 44–5, 56, 71–3, 94, 108, 134
Evolutionism, popular, 47

Farrer, Austin, 80 n. 90, 133, 134, 139, 154–5
Feuerbach, Ludwig, 141–2
Fiddes, Paul, 173
Foord–Kelcy, Edward, 21
Forgetting, Renaissance art of, 13–14
Foucault, Michel, 84, 87
The Four Loves (1960), 95, 130
Freud, Sigmund, 32, 43–5, 141–2
Frye, Northrop, 16

Goethe, Johann Wolfgang von, 28 n. 76, 83
Gramsci, Antonio, 175–8
Great War (1914–18), 3, 13, 31–3, 39–40, 57–9
Green, T. H., 36
Greeves, Arthur, 18–19, 42, 55, 62, 66
Gregory of Nyssa, 107
A Grief Observed (1961), xii, 10

Habermas, Jürgen, 72–3
Harwood, Cecil, 22, 134
Havard, Humphrey, 16
Heaney, Seamus, 175
Heidegger, Martin, 26 n. 31
Henry, Carl F. H., 130
Herbert, George, 60, 89, 108, 152, 157, 171–2
Holmer, Paul, 168
Holy Trinity Church, Headington Quarry, Oxford, xiii, 18, 153
Hooker, Richard, 148, 155, 157, 165
Horkheimer, Max, 72–3
Houseman, A. E., 20

Illumination, as metaphor for knowledge in Lewis's writings, 83–97
Incarnation, xii, 63, 67, 131, 140, 173, 174, 175, 178
Inference to the best explanation, 120–2
Inklings, The, 16, 165
"Is theology poetry?" [Socratic Club Address], 83, 118

James, William, 110–11
Jewel, John, 157
Joad, C. E. M., 126 n. 68
Joseph, H. W. B., 34, 37
"Joy," as technical term in Lewis's writings, 3, 44, 105–6, 109–13
Joyce, James, 32, 59, 71, 111
Julian of Norwich, 107

Jung, Carl Gustav, 80 n. 95
Justin Martyr, 67, 78 n. 64, 129

Keats, John, 56
Keble College, Oxford, 31
Kepler, Johann, 99 n. 30
King James Bible (1611), 78 n. 69,
    157
Kirkpatrick, William T., x

Lang, Andrew, 58
The Last Battle (1956), 88
Lewis, C. S.
    on Anglicanism, 4, 147–61
    on apologetics, 4, 57, 67, 68–9,
        73–4, 129–46
    on the argument from desire, 4,
        105–28, 137–8
    on the Bible, 92–3, 133, 156–7
    on "chronological snobbery," 42–3,
        152, 165
    conversion to Christianity, xi, 12,
        19–20, 62–5, 152
    conversion to theism, xi, 17–19,
        61–2
    early atheist views of, x, 9–10, 32,
        34–6, 57, 66, 90, 112, 151, 173
    early years at Oxford University,
        31–4
    on the importance of the
        imagination, 139–42
    his intellectual "New Look," x, 3,
        31–54, 114, 134, 152
    on interconnectedness of reality,
        91
    on "Joy," 3, 44, 105–6, 109–13
    and Jungian archetypes, 80 n. 95
    on memory, 9, 13–14, 17–18, 20,
        40, 56, 67
    on "mere Christianity," 148–55
    on myth, xi, 3–4, 12, 19–20, 42,
        55–81, 139–40, 152, 157
    "personal heresy" controversy,
        7–8
    poetic writings of, 34, 172

    on the purpose of poetry, 7–8
    on the rationality of faith, xii, 4, 9,
        56, 59, 72, 108, 115, 117–22,
        133–7
    as a theologian, 5, 163–83
    on translation, 131–3, 172–5
    on his "treaty with reality," 13,
        39–42
    use of ocular imagery, 4, 83–104
    on the *via media*, 157–8
Lewis, W. H. [Warnie], ix, 10, 15
Light, metaphors of in Lewis's
    thought, 83–97
The Lion, the Witch, and the Wardrobe
    (1950), xii, 2, 12
Literae Humaniores, x, 33, 60
logos spermatikos, 65
Lucretius, 35
Luther, Martin, 85, 166

MacDonald, George, 11, 57, 115, 152,
    165
Magdalen College, Oxford, xi, 17,
    18–19, 46, 58, 153
Malebranche, Nicolas, 84
Maritain, Jacques, 165, 166
Marx, Karl, 142, 168
Memory, Renaissance cultivation of
    faculty of, 13–14
"mere Christianity," as Lewis's version
    of a consensual faith, 148–55
Mere Christianity (1952), xii, 105,
    117–20, 129
Miller, Henry, 84
Moore, G. E., 36
Moral argument for the existence of
    God, 118–20, 133, 136
More, Henry, 39
More, Paul Elmer, 173
Müller, Max, 58
Murdoch, Iris, 102 n. 67
Myth, as theme in Lewis's thought,
    xi, 3–4, 12, 19–20, 42, 55–81,
    139–40, 152, 157
mythos spermatikos, 65

Narnia, Chronicles of, xii, 1, 2, 10, 85,
    133, 140, 172
Neo-Platonism, 12, 93
New College, Oxford, 31
"New Look," Lewis's, x, 3, 31–54,
    114, 134, 152
Newman, John Henry, 9, 165,
    169
Newton, Isaac, 86
Novalis, 22, 108
Nunn, Thomas Percy, 36

O'Neill, Eugene, 59
Ontological argument for the
    existence of God, 108
Otto, Rudolf, 126 n. 58
Oxford Realism, 36–9
Oxford University, x–xii, 3–4, 22–3,
    31–4, 36–9, 48–9, 57–9, 92, 118,
    129, 137, 152, 164, 170

Pascal, Blaise, 129
Pearson, John, 170–1
Peirce, Charles S., 119
The Pilgrim's Regress (1933), xi, 9,
    44–5, 63, 88, 109, 115–16,
    157
Plato, 17, 24, 60, 90, 93, 136
Potter, Beatrix, 109
Preface to Paradise Lost (1942), 135
Prichard, Harold Arthur, 37–8
The Problem of Pain (1940), xi, 67,
    129, 130, 139, 165
Proust, Marcel, 14, 111

Quick, Oliver Chase, 164, 170–1

Rackham, Arthur, 56
Reflections on the Psalms (1958), 130
Romanticism, 56, 71–2, 94–5, 108,
    124 n. 25
Rousseau, Jean–Jacques, 86–7
Ruskin, John, 91–2
Russell, Bertrand, 36, 46, 47,
    106–7

St. Mark's church, Dundela, Belfast,
    151
Sayer, George, 15–16
Sayers, Dorothy L., 148, 150,
    163
Schlegel, August Wilhelm, 56
The Screwtape Letters (1942), xi,
    160 n. 24
Seeing and sight, metaphors of in
    Lewis's thought, 83–97
Shakespeare, William, 28 n. 67
Shaw, George Bernard, 47, 60
Smith, John Alexander, 49
Socratic Club, Oxford, 83, 118,
    129–30
Somerset Light Infantry, x, 31
Spengler, Oswald, 32
Spirits in Bondage (1919), 34
Stapledon, Olaf, 47
Stout, G. F., 36
Sun, as epistemological metaphor in
    Lewis's thought, 83–97
Surprised by Joy (1955), 3, 7–29, 40,
    90–1, 109, 130
    and *ars memorativa,* 13–14
    Augustine of Hippo, as influence,
        10–12
    as autobiography, 7–10, 14–17
    historical reliability of, 17–21
    intended audience for, 21–3
    origins of work's title, 7–8
    as recollection of the past, 13–14
    as source for Lewis's conversion
        narrative, 17–21

Taylor, Charles, 89
Tegnér, Esaias, 110
Temple, William, 164
Till we have Faces (1956), 138
Tillyard, E. M. W., 7
Tolkien, J. R. R., xi, 12, 19–20, 58–9,
    62–3, 64–5, 66–7, 72, 78 n. 72,
    87, 152, 175
Tocqueville, Alexis de, 168
Traherne, Thomas, 108, 152

"Treaty with reality," Lewis's, 13, 39–42
Trinity, doctrine of, 91, 140, 141–2, 174–5

University College, Oxford, ix, 31, 59

via media, 157–8

Wagner, Richard, 28 n. 76, 56
Ward, Michael, 97 n. 3

Webb, Clement C. J., 58
"The Weight of Glory" [University Sermon], 109, 116–17, 137–8
Wells, H. G., 47, 60
Whipsnade Park Zoo, 20–1
Wilde, Oscar, 23–4
Williams, Rowan, 164
Woolf, Virginia, 106
Wordsworth, William, 7, 111

Yeats, W. B., 71